NEWPORT IN THE ROCKIES

BY MARSHALL SPRAGUE

The Business of Getting Well

Money Mountain

Massacre: The Tragedy at White River

Newport in the Rockies

The Great Gates:
The Story of the Rocky Mountain Passes

A Gallery of Dudes

The Mountain States

So Vast So Beautiful a Land
(Louisiana and the Purchase)

Colorado: A Bicentennial History

El Paso Club: A Century of Friendship

Newport

in the Rockies

The Life

and Good Times

of Colorado Springs

by Marshall Sprague

Revised for the 1990's

**SWALLOW PRESS/
OHIO UNIVERSITY PRESS**
Athens

This up-dated account is for my wife
Edna Jane Ailes
who needs no revision

Contents

Illustrations

Newport in the Rockies

Foreword

by

Stephen May

I am pleased to introduce this latest edition of *Newport in the Rockies*, because it gives me a chance to talk about Marshall Sprague and the city and region with which he is so closely identified. Almost everyone knows that Marshall came to Colorado in the 1940s to recuperate from the ravages of tuberculosis. He recovered and became an accomplished author, chronicling some of the West's most colorful and dramatic episodes from the Louisiana Purchase forward. But few people probably know that before coming west he had already established a solid reputation as a journalist for the New York Times, and had spent time in depression-lean Paris in the thirties with a knot of other correspondents intent on capturing the mood of the French scene between the wars. He even found time to travel in China as a correspondent. Today he is an authority on everything from Cripple Creek gold mines to jazz piano, and the latter he still plays with delight and tenacity.

But his real knowledge is saved for this place tucked between mountain and plain, bordered on the north by the pine-studded Palmer Ridge Divide and on the south by the copses of cottonwoods that dwindle into the dry yucca beds near Pueblo. As Marshall explains in the following pages, it first began as a treeless temperance colony, then emerged as a lavish watering hole during the 1920s, and today is home to the Olympic Training Center and is emerging as a growing center for the exploration of space. General William Jackson Palmer, the city's founder and Union commander in the Civil War, would have loved its near antebellum civility: not a smokestack mars the horizon and residents are bent on keeping it that way.

xiii

Peopling this landscape was a rich assortment of characters: the elegant Palmer; the enterprising and swaggering Spencer Penrose, who built the world-class Broadmoor Hotel; Helen Hunt Jackson, the coltish author of *Ramona*; Dr. William Bell, the Irish-born railroad chum of Palmer's, who stayed on to help form the burgeoning nucleus of the little colony; Count James M. Pourtales, a shady aristocrat, who came looking for cheap mortgages to buy up and eventually employed his keen German know-how in establishing a large dairy farm below Cheyenne Mountain; and Alice Bemis Taylor, who after falling in love with the art of the Southwest, put forward most of her inherited wealth to design a city museum in which to showcase it. Besides these stalwarts, there were the perennial visitors: Jack Dempsey, Charles Kingsley (British author of *Westward Ho!*), and a string of others ready to take the cure in the clean dry air and the bubbling springs of Manitou.

Ask Marshall Sprague about any of these figures and immediately some story bursts from his lips. He knows them all, even beneath their smooth jackets, cocked hats, polo shirts, and ball gowns. Any secrets they wished to preserve in their lifetimes I'm sure have been uncovered by Marshall at least once in his research. Whether he shall offer them to us is another matter, but we can always anticipate.

Many honors have come his way since he first settled into the cultural scene of Colorado Springs, including awards from the Colorado Authors League, and Benjamin McKie Rastall Award for "distinguished service to the cultural development of Colorado," and a Pulitzer Prize nomination in history. But Marshall is probably the last person who wishes to talk about them—not because he is indifferent, but because he has the humility of a great man. He lives in a large Cape Cod with wife E. J. and a bevy of cats. The cats take kindly to visitors, though they rule the house like indolent lions. E. J. possesses, among other things, two major talents: the ability to create a warm, genial atmosphere, and the skill to edit her husband's work with intelligence and care. Much of *Newport's* textual spruceness is the result of her heavy pencil. The house was built in 1896 when the Cripple Creek mining tycoons needed an area in town in which to erect their symbols of wealth. It is no mansion, however. It is just right for gracious, practical living.

When Marshall isn't poking around the house, he is usually out at some civic event or busy in his office. He is the recognized cultural ambassador of Colorado. And if he is a careful observer of its history, he is also a passionate spokesman about its future. He cares. He cares about its growth and despoiling industries, and he is quick to remind us that we must preserve as we progress. In essence, Marshall might be one of principal figures in *Newport in the Rockies*, a twentieth century answer to Palmer, Stratton, and all the other people who added their vision, courage and wisdom to this place.

If, after all these years, *Newport in the Rockies* retains its original vigor, the credit must go entirely to Sprague himself. He is a writer's writer, possessing several old-fashioned virtues that are still valid: talent, craft and discipline. But, I believe, it is discipline which has made Marshall Sprague the writer he is today and which provides the enduring zest found in *Newport*. "Talent is quite common," Kurt Vonnegut once wrote. "What is uncommon is the ability to endure the life of a writer." *This* writer has endured, and perhaps there is no better testament than this vital book.

Still a tireless worker, he rises early, leaves the big house and tramps out to his office in the backyard. Originally it was a horse stable in those glory days when the story of *Newport* was just unfolding. Now, amid commodious clutter, Marshall continues the business of being a writer. The manual Underwood, which has banged out such works as *Money Mountain, A Gallery of Dudes*, and *Newport in the Rockies*, sits conspicuously alone on the long table, ready for fingers.

Drawers and files are crammed with clippings, notes, and odds and ends; maps curl in layers, their tanned edges turned to the creeping sun, and lie as casually as the discarded work of a 17th century Dutch geographer. In a metal chair, between typewriter and table, sits Marshall Sprague, his blue eyes alive with the voices, and faces and doings of the past—Colorado Springs' unique past.

Here they are again in a brand new edition: Palmer, Stratton, Penrose, Taylor, Bell, and the rest. I find Marshall Sprague's handling of them irresistible. Read on, and see if you don't agree.

End

PREFACE
To the 1990s Edition

In 1871, General William Jackson Palmer, a Civil War cavalry hero, built on the sheltered warm side of Pikes Peak (alt. 14,110 feet) something brand new in the Rockies—a resort where sedate temperate people from back east could enjoy life in tranquil comfort. The General named his village Colorado Springs though the springs were in Manitou Springs five miles away.

The proper sort of people hurried west seeking repose or better health or romance or a touch of adventure in the untamed wilds of Colorado. They were drawn by the equable climate, the beauty of the setting and the elation that came to them with so much sunlight and the tonic effect of the high mountain air. Many of them were from England which was why the resort was nicknamed "Little London."

The town developed slowly in the beginning. But in 1900 occurred the first of four separate decades of explosive growth. The fast growth was caused by the unexpected discovery of gold worth half a billion dollars at Cripple Creek on the other side of Pikes Peak. Most of that treasure from the world's richest gold camp was dumped on the 30,000 residents of Colorado Springs. Many of them became filthy rich, including a swarm of polo players and their decorative wives in Broadmoor. They were not (by General Palmer's standards) notably sedate or temperate. Their style of living created an art of having a good time that has guided later generations at Pikes Peak.

The gold of Cripple Creek was exhausted before the start of World War I. For the next twenty years Colorado Springs endured a period of economic deflation. But the doldrums of those years were enlivened by the flamboyant activities of a Philadelphia multimillionaire named Spencer Penrose. After pushing an automobile highway to the top of Pikes Peak, Penrose built a sumptuous pink *palazzo* (1918) that he called the Broadmoor Hotel. Penrose had a gift for publicizing the Pikes Peak region. He made news everywhere when he rode his pet llama bareback down North Tejon Street during his one man campaign to end National Prohibition.

After the death of Penrose in 1939, his long-time associate, Charles L. Tutt, and other local boosters decided to lift their beloved city out of the hard times of the Thirties. Armed with a variety of enticements they descended on the Army brass of Washington like a plague of locusts. Perhaps to get rid of the infestation, in 1942 the boosters were awarded Camp Carson (Fort Carson today)—a $30,000,000 post for the 89th Division and the training of 30,000 soldiers. Thus Colorado Springs moved into its second decade of explosive growth during which the population increased by 1950 from 30,000 to 75,000.

The proximity of Fort Carson brought more military plums to Pikes Peak—Peterson Field in 1948, Ent Air Force Base, and in the 1950s the North American Air Defense Command and Combat Operations Center in its vast cave under Cheyenne Mountain. These plums should have satisfied the appetite of the town's boosters. But some of them had their hearts set on winning the biggest plum of all—the $200,000,000 U. S. Air Force Academy.

They were competing this time with hundreds of cities. But once again their presentation won the prize. On June 24, 1954, Harold Talbott, Secretary of the Air Force, announced that the Air Force Academy, as approved by Colonel Charles A. Lindbergh and the selection committee, would be built on 17,500 acres of land ten miles north of Colorado Springs. And so during the 1950s came more explosive growth with the population soaring from 75,000 to 150,000.

The last chapter, "Harvest Time", of this revision will describe the coming of the Consolidated Space Operations Center, the Olympic Training Center, the Olympic Hall of Fame, more high-tech factories and advances in cultural, educational and recreational facilities. The metro population passed 365,000 in the late 1980s with the possibility of reaching 500,000 by 1990.

As Colorado Springs—a 138 square mile city—spreads eastward far out into the prairie it bears no resemblance to General Palmer's village of 1871. And still the General's dream of a quality town in a quality environment has inspired all the leaders who followed him. In essence, Colorado Springs retains the General's ideals from the start.

MARSHALL SPRAGUE

ACKNOWLEDGMENTS

Much of the early history of this book was given to me years ago by the late Percy Hagerman, Mrs. Spencer Penrose, Mrs. A. E. Carlton, the painter Randall Davey, the historian John J. Lipsey, Willis Armstrong, Charles L. Tutt, Jr., H. Chase Stone and Harold Harmon.

I have had at my disposal for 35 years fine reference libraries and librarians, especially the magnificent Tutt Library at Colorado College (director John Sheridan succeeded by Col. George Fagan): also at Tutt, reference librarian, Susan Myers; Barbara Neilon (Colorado room), Judy Finley and Ellen Davis. Much of my material came from the Local History Collection at Penrose Public Library and the new East Library and Information Center.

Through the years old timers helped me immeasurably—Mrs. Edith Farnsworth (Mrs. M. R. Brann), Mrs. John W. Stewart (Marka Webb), Mrs. Madeline Gallagher, K. G. Freyschlag, Jasper Ackerman, Eugene McCleary, Robert Ormes and the late Juan Reid of Colorado College. To catch up with modern times I had the aid of Mrs. John Gaw Meem, Miss Alice Craig (granddaughter of Charles Craig), Mrs. Louisa Creed of York, England, and Mrs. Jane Kasmin of London, great grand daughters of General William J. Palmer; Douglass Cogswell, Ann Sanger of C.S. Water Divison; Mary Elizabeth Ruwell, archivist, Pioneers' Museum; Barbara Budd, the historian; Susan Watkins and Nancy Brisk, P.R.C.S.; Darrell Porter; H. Pike Oliver, Jonathan Aries and Paul Burke; Ruth Holmes, P.R. and Colorado College.

My editorial "staff" is beyond all thanking: Edna Jane Sprague, copy reader; Maxine Whitworth, typist.

CHAPTER ONE

Mountain Fever

THE PLACE TO START is at the beginning and the beginning of Colorado Springs was in the tidy, vibrant mind, the strong heart and tough body of General William Jackson Palmer.

Palmer and nobody else. Zebulon Pike had nothing to do with it, even if he did discover Pikes Peak in 1806—about a century after the Spaniards first saw it. Neither did Major Stephen Long, who came by with his Army explorers in 1820, nor the ubiquitous trapper, Kit Carson, nor the great path maker of the 1840's, John Charles Frémont, nor Julia Archibald Holmes, that sturdy bride in bloomers who out-tramped her husband to the top of the Peak in 1858 to show that whatever men could do women could do better.

Of course there was Colorado City. It set up as a mining supply center to the Colorado gold camps of South Park in 1859, but at the wrong place and the wrong time and for the wrong reasons. When General Palmer first passed the Peak in July, 1869, Colorado City was mostly ghost town because Denver had all the supply business. Only a scattering of pioneers remained among the crumbling log cabins near Fountain Creek to tell of the glorious months in '62 when Colorado City tried and failed to serve as Capital of Colorado Territory.

There is no quick way to bring General Palmer to the start of this story in '69. He was born in 1836 on a farm in Delaware near Delaware Bay, but he was raised by his parents, Matilda Jackson and John Palmer, in Quaker Philadelphia where he got a grade school education, and a touch of high school. At seventeen he was quietly precocious and only a desultory Quaker. He had a large, handsome head, curly brown hair, and a slight wiry frame

1

perhaps five feet eight inches tall. He loved cricket, pretty girls, and arguing about Abolition, anti-Catholics, and freedom of the press. He was even then a sort of self-man Philadelphia aristocrat —a bit stiff and reserved on the outside but diffident, good-humored, and kind within. He was enormously persistent to achieve his own ends which had to do with a dream of building around him a neat, trim, happy, sensible world.

He turned railroader, and at nineteen he went abroad for his coal-mining uncle to see how coal burned in English and French locomotives. He sailed home eight months later full of bright ideas and a conviction that "Paris is the most wonderful city in the world." In 1857, still under twenty-one, he became private secretary to another Quaker, J. Edgar Thomson, president of the Pennsylvania Railroad. Two years later he was out west with Andrew Carnegie to decide for President Thomson where the Pennsylvania should go next from Pittsburgh—to St. Louis or Chicago.

Soon Fort Sumter fell, postponing the question, and it took Will Palmer about six weeks to decide that he had to defend the Union even if he were a pacifist Quaker. But not as a railroader. No office war for him. He read up on pack trains, mules, and litters, got a captain's commission, and recruited a carefully-picked troop of proper young Philadelphians, the nucleus of his beloved Fifteenth Pennsylvania Volunteer Cavalry. Palmer wasn't a snob, exactly, in his recruiting. He just felt that people with superior brains and energy ought to hang together and run things.

The Fifteenth Pennsylvania was his dream of order in a military phase. The dream was a nightmare at times because the proper Philadelphians got very improper more than once—mutinied, for instance. But on the whole they covered their slim dynamic leader with glory. As fast-moving gadflies, they harried the Confederates of the western theater half to death, skirmishing, scouting, escorting, and raiding from Maryland to Georgia, from the Great Smokies to Memphis. At the end, Palmer—a brigadier general now—and his 1,200 horsemen chased Jefferson Davis for a month down the verdant spine of the Appalachians and into the arms of the Tenth Michigan Cavalry in Georgia.

The year 1866 was release time for young Americans, a time for exploding of creative energies held in check by the war. General Palmer, aged thirty, had been trained well in railroading by J. Edgar Thomson of the Pennsylvania. He knew where to explode —west of Kansas City where new railroads could turn worthless mountains and plains into high-priced real estate. He knew that capitalists were everywhere with tons of cash to invest—dollars in Philadelphia and New York, pounds in London, guilders in Amsterdam. In 1855, he had seen for himself the land hunger of Englishmen, obsessed by fears of running out of pasture on which to feed their cattle and sheep in England.

And so Palmer began his slow demarch on his future Colorado Springs by getting the job to build the Kansas Pacific Railroad west from Kansas City. This political sop of a line was projected originally to join the Omaha-based, California-bound Union Pacific in western Nebraska, but its directors soon forgot its branch role and decided to go to California, too, through New Mexico. In June of '67, these directors in St. Louis ordered General Palmer to make a survey of southern routes through the western wilderness to San Francisco from the rail head at Salina, Kansas.

News of the proposed Kansas Pacific survey got around even to an international conclave of doctors in St. Louis who were attending a lecture series on homeopathic medicine. This homeopathy was all the rage and had to do with giving to patients pills containing minute toxins to counteract the germs which bothered them. Among those at the conclave was a small, bubbling youngster of twenty-six from London named Dr. William Abraham Bell, who had barely finished his medical training. Bell had journeyed to St. Louis at his father's request. Dr. William Bell, Senior, was one of England's most famous physicians, a man whose bedside charm brought him the trade of everybody who was anybody. He wanted fresh data on homeopathy just to be sure that he wasn't putting the wrong toxins into the stomachs of England's social and business elite.

Young Dr. Bell was pure Irish by birth, but he drank his tea at five o'clock precisely like an Englishman. Medicine, oddly, did not interest him. What he loved was horses and adventure, and when the Kansas Pacific news reached him in St. Louis, he dropped homeopathy—and medicine in general, for that matter— forever. He applied at K. P. headquarters to go on the survey and took the only job open, photographer, after three days of learning how to be one. He met General Palmer in August of '67 in the Raton Mountains part of the Maxwell Grant, 140 miles south of Pikes Peak. The ensuing survey gave the K. P. party nine months of excitement, danger, and hardship. It involved Indian battles, threats of starvation, lost trails, desert heat, and sub-zero snow storms on the passes as the men moved 5,000 miles through the Southwest to San Francisco and back to Kansas by way of Salt Lake City, Cheyenne, and Denver.

Before the trek ended in March of '68, the cavalry hero, Will Palmer, and the effervescent tea-drinker, Willie Bell, had become close friends. They had become also two of the sturdiest males in the Southwest with vast knowledge of what the Rocky Mountains were all about. Back in St. Louis, Palmer urged that the Kansas Pacific should run to California over Raton Pass and on through northern New Mexico. But Congress refused to make any more huge gifts of land to help railroad promotors, and nothing came of the General's suggestions. Young Dr. Bell went back to England to report belatedly to his father on homeopathic pills and to write a remarkable book, *New Tracks in North America*. Palmer wound up unhappily building the Kansas Pacific into Denver. There, in August, 1870, it met the Denver Pacific which ran north to join the transcontinental Union Pacific at Cheyenne, Wyoming Territory.

Failure of his K. P. hopes put the General to planning a railroad of his own. It would be, naturally, a neat, trim, orderly affair staffed by Fifteenth Pennsylvania officers and other true blue friends like Willie Bell. It would be a "North and South" road, from Denver south and over the Sangre de Cristos to the Rio Grande River in the San Luis Valley and on down to Texas and Mexico, to be fed enroute by all future east-west railroads that crossed its right-of-way. It would be a complete novelty, having a three-foot narrow-gauge track which would permit it to make sharp curves and to climb steeply in the Rocky Mountains. It would be much cheaper to build than a line with tracks four feet eight-and-a-half inches apart.

But there was a great difficulty. The government's free-land-for-railroads policy was no more. Eastern and European investors would have no interest in Palmer's proposed line unless it owned a great deal of land the value of which could be expected to increase hugely when the railroad ran through it. The government's preemption price now for Rocky Mountain wilderness was $1.25 per acre—far too high for promoting a railroad. Palmer's problem, then, was to find cheaper land.

One day it occurred to him where to find it—in that Raton Pass region which he and Dr. Bell had examined during the Kansas-Pacific survey. It consisted of two Mexican estates known as the Sangre de Cristo and Maxwell (originally Beaubien-Miranda) Grants. Governor Manuel Armijo had doled them out in the 1840s before the Mexican War, and Dr. Bell's father was physician to many of the British plungers who had money in them—men like William Blackmore, a brother of R. D. Blackmore whose novel *Lorna Doone* was about to become a classic. William Blackmore had put two of his alcoholic brothers on the Sangre de Cristo Grant to straighten them out, and Willie Bell believed that many rich Englishmen would pay well for ranches where they could send their black sheep.

William Gilpin, the flamboyant Colorado booster who was first governor of the territory, had bought the Sangre de Cristo Grant in 1864 for $30,000 and had sold half of it to an Englishman, Wilson Waddingham, who brought in William Blackmore and some Dutchmen and split the grant in two—Trinchera Estate on the north and Costilla Estate on the south. It contained altogether 1,038,195.55 acres, enclosing some of the loveliest scenery and finest ranch land anywhere. It spread southward from the 14,317-foot summit of Colorado's Blanca Peak for sixty miles to Rio Costilla near Taos, New Mexico. It ran west from the crest of the Sangre de Cristos across San Luis Valley as far as the Rio Grande—forty miles.

The Maxwell Grant was still more tremendous. Lucien Max-

well, the French-Irish trader from Kaskaskia, Illinois, had inherited part of it in 1864 through his Mexican wife, Luz Beaubien
of Taos. He had paid $50,000 for the rest, thinking he had come
into a modest parcel of 32,000 acres or so. His surveyor had cor-
rected him. The Maxwell Grant, by a liberal interpretation of
Mexican landmarks, contained 1,714,746.92 acres! It adjoined
on the east the Sangre de Cristo Grant of the Waddingham-
Blackmore-Gilpin group and ran from the Spanish Peaks through
the Ratons into New Mexico almost as far as Fort Union and the
Mora River Valley above Santa Fe.

On the basis of these complicated facts, Palmer made a few
simple deductions. It was plain to him that the two grants had
cost their European owners only a few cents an acre. He had in
England two influential friends—the Drs. Bell, Junior and Senior.
Suppose the Bells called on the owners and suggested to them
that General Palmer was about to build a railroad which just
might run through the grants—if the owners took up his railroad
bonds? Surely the Europeans would see their opportunity. Palmer's proposed railroad would quadruple overnight the value of
those remote 2,752,942.47 acres along the Colorado-New Mexico
border below the Spanish Peaks. Even small mortgages on the
grants would raise enough capital to build the railroad at least
from Denver to the Rio Grande!

AT THIS CRITICAL POINT, in the spring of '69, a cataclysm
occurred. Palmer had boarded the Pennsylvania at St. Louis on
his way East to look up a friend of William Blackmore's, and he
began describing his Colorado and Mexico railroad scheme in
the palace car to a fellow passenger who introduced himself as
William Proctor Mellen, a New York lawyer. Mellen revealed
that he had studied law in Cincinnati as the protegé of Salmon
P. Chase, who became Lincoln's Secretary of the Treasury. Both
Chase and Mellen, Palmer discovered, knew William Blackmore
and other British financiers who were interested in the West.
Mellen suggested that he himself might be useful to Palmer in
his western ventures.

The two men were joined in the car by Mellen's nineteen-year-

old daughter, a small demurely-elegant, snub-nosed creature with
a low musical voice. Her name was Queen. Palmer looked at her
once and was lost—the typical total love-fall of a thirty-two-year-
old bachelor who gazes upon a soft thing of nineteen and realizes
with the suddenness of a thunderclap how empty his life has
been without her. Before the train reached Cincinnati, the
normally-composed General was just another frantic suitor.

Some weeks later Queen told him that she was his. Whether
she loved him deeply is a moot point, but there is no doubt about
her filial devotion. Queen had been raised mostly by her father,
with some help from her stepmother who was also her aunt.[1] She
knew that Mellen had made unfortunate investments after the
Civil War, that he was discouraged about his career in New York,
that he was past his prime at fifty-three years of age, and that his
health was poor. She did not mind, therefore, when Palmer combined his love-making with the acceptance of William P. Mellen
as his close business associate in the Rockies.

The wedding, Queen and Will Palmer decided, would take
place at the Mellen home in Flushing, Long Island, after Palmer
finished building the Kansas Pacific into Denver. By June of '69,
he was back at the K. P. railhead—Sheridan, Kansas—writing
sonnets by the yard and seeing Queen all over the prairie. His
world was upside down. Queen had upset it and he asked himself incessantly how he could bring a refined girl who was used
to places like Flushing, Newport, and Saratoga to the bawdy-
house environment of a place like Sheridan, or even to raw
Denver.

AND SO—by way of two Mexican land grants and a love affair—
we reach the circumstances which resulted in Colorado Springs.
Before Queen came into Palmer's life, he had visualized the
usual rough railroad towns which he would found along his
"North and South" line at intervals to be determined by prospects
for agriculture and mining. But Queen split him into two people
—the tough empire builder determined to conquer the wilderness,
and the Arthurian cavalier shielding his gentle lady from the facts
of life. The problem was intricate. Queen, he knew, held deep

prejudices against the West, derived from the frontier trials of her maternal grandparents and from the fact that her uncle, Malcolm Clarke, had been killed by Indians in Montana.

To soothe Queen, Palmer had promised to consider settling down in New York City as the eastern officer of the Kansas Pacific, even though he knew that was impossible. He had seen too much of the mountains. The tonic climate and elastic air of the Rockies, their majesty and friendliness and simplicity, the heady freedom and infinite horizons, had spoiled him forever for the cramped and soggy East.

Somehow he would have to make Queen love the mountains, too. This imperative preoccupied him in July of 1869 as he scouted for a section of his "North and South" line, circling from Sheridan, Kansas, up the Arkansas and by moonlight up Fountain Creek where the plains met the Front Range and the Spanish Peaks showed darkly to the south. On the early morning of July 27th, the General, wrapped in blankets on top of his Concord coach, passed Pikes Peak for the first time. He bathed at dawn in the sandy, ice-cold Fountain, breakfasted in moldering Colorado City, and toured that cathedral park of violent reds and deep greens which Pikes Peak pioneers had been calling the Garden of the Gods since 1859.

He loved everything—the soda springs at the foot of Ute Pass, the gray-green mesas and grassy valleys of Fountain and Monument Creeks, the deep, cool canyons smelling of spruce and pine. And Pikes Peak over all. This noble presidence, he knew, had always been the greatest of Rocky Mountain landmarks through immemorial ages of changeless mankind. It was a kingdom in itself of huge jutting spurs and majestic ridges and forested knobs, of vast secret parks and lakes. Soaring a mile above its 400-square-mile mass was the brown 14,000-foot summit, snow-streaked, friendly, placid.

On that day, Palmer believed that he had the answer to his problem. Here was the one spot in the whole wild West fit for Queen Mellen of Flushing, Long Island. And, after all, he planned to have some sort of town every ten miles along his railroad. Why not build a very special one at Pikes Peak—an attractive place for

well-to-do people, on the order of Newport or Saratoga? Next
day in Denver he wrote Queen about it, but furtively as to what
he really had in mind. "I am sure there will be a famous resort
here soon," he predicted. And, a little further on: "I somehow
fancied that an exploration of the Monument or the Fountain
might disclose . . . perhaps some charming spot which might be
made a future home."

A week later, after a second visit, he wrote her more boldly.
He described a spot which he called "Bijou" in Monument Park
near today's Air Force Academy and went on glibly about "a
great country home" and "the deer-park" and "the fountains and
lakes" and "the lovely drives" and how much they would enjoy
watching the bright red cars of the Denver and Rio Grande
rattling past their home as they sipped their afternoon tea in the
summer house. He mentioned his bay horse Don and how Queen
would love having Don for her own mount.

In September, 1869, young Dr. Willie Bell reached Kansas from
England and rode across the plains to Pikes Peak with Palmer.
Bell was full of plots to raise money abroad for Palmer's railroad.
In October, the General guided a famous newspaper man from
the Kansas Pacific railhead to Fountain Creek—Nathan C. Meeker, an ascetic idealist who was Agricultural Editor of Horace
Greeley's New York *Tribune*. Meeker could plan as boldly as
Palmer. He was seeking irrigable land on which to put a large
group of eastern farmers and artisans. Palmer discussed his
embryo Newport in the Rockies, but Meeker just looked bored,
suggesting with a bleak smile that towns where people did no
honest work were unstable and only a cut above red-light dis-
tricts. He added that the valleys of the Monument and Fountain
were too small for serious farming. But the two men parted amic-
ably at Denver. Meeker continued north to found Union Colony
and Greeley, Colorado, on the Cache la Poudre River, during the
winter of 1869-70.

By this time, rumors of the General's plans were flying fast,
and Palmer knew he must take up land before others got ahead
of him. In January, 1870, he sent one of his old Fifteenth Pennsylvania staff officers, Captain William F. Colton, to pick a town-

site at Pikes Peak. Colton recommended a tract of 320 acres five miles out on the plain at the junction of Fountain and Monument Creeks.

The General felt fully committed now and he could not let Queen hope any longer that he might settle down in New York City. He wrote her in detail about his "North and South" railroad and his resort and about their love nest, Bijou. Queen had questioned his views on the joys of trains rattling by Bijou at tea time, and he had hastened to assure her that his trains would not be "near enough to make it noisy, only near enough for the cars to look graceful across the Monument Valley from our cottage. It won't hurt, when it is our own railroad, will it?"

He asked many questions in his letters to Queen that winter as any anxious fiancé does when his beloved is noncommittal about the things closest to his heart. "Could we ever live away from the mountains?" he would ask. And "You will have plenty to do, will you not, looking after all these colonies? I wonder which will be busiest, you or I?" The word pictures which he painted for her were doggedly rosy, softening the Pikes Peak landscape, playing down the current rash of Indian troubles, playing up the weather and making El Paso County's rugged pioneers seem like Long Island gentry. And he reminded Queen again how she would love his bay horse, Don.

And, in April of 1870, the great day came. Queen and her father, William P. Mellen, reached the new K. P. railhead at Kit Carson, Colorado, and the General brought them the last 140 miles to Colorado City by coach. Poor Will! Colorado weather can be at its absolute worst in April—cold, blustery, snowy. And it seemed determined to be at its worst this time, for Queen's benefit.

Snowstorms obscured the beauties of Pikes Peak during most of her brief stay. A grass fire had blackened much of the prairie. The mesas looked as inviting as Arctic tundra. Under the circumstances, Will gave up promoting Bijou as a home site for Queen in favor of a glade at the north end of the Garden of the Gods which he called Queen's Canyon. As the visitors were led over the windy, treeless town site, a garrulous tobacco-juice-spit-

ting pioneer insisted on pointing out to Queen the exact spots
where eighteen-year-old Charley Everhart and the Robbins boys,
aged eight and eleven, had met horrible deaths at the hands of
Arapaho Indians less than two years before. For the ride over
the mesa to Queen's Canyon, Palmer put an English side-saddle
on good old Don and helped Queen mount. Good old Don disliked both the side-saddle and the flowing skirts of Queen's Long
Island riding costume. He began to heave ominously with snort-
ings and prancings and Will had to rescue his terrified bride-to-be.

QUEEN WAS TOO KIND to be openly critical of Will's dreary
dream town, and she returned to Long Island to prepare for the
wedding without saying what she thought of the place. Palmer
was too busy to wonder why. In the late spring, he was encouraged to learn that three Colorado speculators, Jerome Chaf-
fee, George M. Chilcott, and Charles F. Holly, were deeply in-
pressed by the apparent direction—toward Raton Pass—of his
proposed "North and South" railroad. As a result, they had
bought the interposed Maxwell Grant for $650,000 and had un-
loaded it on William Blackmore, Wilson Waddingham, and others
for $1,350,000. The Englishmen had mortgaged it then for
$3,500,000 to a Dutch group. To make sure that the "North and
South" railroad kept pointing at Raton Pass the Dutchmen pulled
a few strings and that's how General William Jackson Palmer
suddenly found himself to be president of the new Maxwell Land
Grant and Railway Company!
     Will Palmer and Queen Mellen were wed in Flushing on No-
vember 7, 1870, and sailed two days later from Europe on the
S. S. Scotia. Captain William Colton, Major Henry McAllister,
and other old Fifteenth Pennsylvania officers saw them off, and
they were met in Liverpool by Willie Bell, who had engaged for
them in London, as Queen wrote in her honeymoon diary, "comfortable but *not elegant* apartments at the Buckingham Palace
Hotel."
     The diary is revealing. Queen, a sweet, warm, generous girl,
loved the London theater, the symphony concerts, the opera. She
enjoyed the beautiful homes and the company of witty, well-

bred people like the great Charles Kingsley, author of *Westward Ho!* and *Water Babies,* and his daughter, Rose, and his son, Maurice Kingsley. She liked "bacon for breakfast—fried thin!" and "coppery oysters—*not broiled*" and shopping for "blue-cloth, fur-trimmed sacques." It tired her even to watch the skating in Regent's Park but she could sing arias at parties in her mezzo-soprano voice until dawn.

She hated hats which would have concealed her defiantly curly hair. She was a graceful, glowing dancer and she enjoyed dancing the "galop" with specialists like Willie Bell and getting French chocolates from Richard Ward and other young charmers with whom she flirted harmlessly while Will was tied up in the evenings with Wilson Waddingham and William Blackmore and powerful tycoons from Amsterdam and The Hague and Paris.

On Christmas day, 1870, her diary reported happily: "In the morning I found Kriss Kringle had really been to my stocking for I found a beautiful watch in it! I told Will to thank Santa Claus for me if he should ever meet him which he promised to do. Sat with Lady Augusta at Westminster Abbey who was very polite and kind. The services were conducted after the very high church customs and I did not like it at all."

But Queen could be ever so slightly waspish because the General had to do so much of his railroad money-raising at night. Sample: "In evening Will dined with Mr. Speyer. Queen remained at home and played bézique." On the whole she was sporting. She knew that Will had to find half a million dollars for his railroad from the Sangre de Cristo and Maxwell Grant crowd in Europe while her father and Will's Quaker friends raised the same amount in New York and Philadelphia. She rejoiced on January 26 when success was near ("Will busy with bankers—option one month, one half—three months, other half! Excellent!!!").

And still, Queen's omissions were odd. Not once, in twelve weeks of diary writing, did she mention Pikes Peak where she would be going soon—going to the home and the town which Will was building expressly to please her.

CHAPTER TWO

Lots of Lots for Sale

PEOPLE THESE DAYS would call General Palmer "an organization man." He made plans and picked henchmen to carry them out while he went off promoting something else. Some of his henchmen fizzled badly but he never had to complain about Alexander Cameron Hunt.

The General had met and liked Hunt in 1868 on his return to Denver from the Kansas Pacific survey while Hunt was still the Democratic governor of Colorado Territory, appointed by President Andrew Johnson. When the Republicans won the election in '68, President Grant allowed himself to be convinced that Hunt was a scalawag, removed him, and gave the governorship to an old Civil War comrade, General Edward M. McCook.

Hunt was a fascinating and attractive pioneer—a tough, stocky, rough-and-ready sort of fellow with a fine sense of humor and an inexhaustible zest for living. He looked as though he ought to have been born on a midwest farm, but actually he was a native of New York City. As a young Forty-Niner, he made a gold fortune in California which he lost playing poker one night in 1856. During the Pikes Peak gold rush of '59, he drove an ox team from Illinois to Denver, ran a restaurant briefly, and was appointed United States marshal for the region. While roaming the Territory to uphold the law, he bacame a pet of the Ute Indians, several of whom got to following him around like so many adoring poodles. In '62, he won fame by cornering and running out of town a super-desperado named Jake Slade. This Slade was revered throughout the nation because he wore as charms on his watch chain the ears of a rival whom he had murdered earlier.

Anyone who could handle Jake Slade could be useful to Palmer. Early in January, 1870, the General met Hunt in Denver and described his town and railroad dreams while a couple of old Ute chiefs squatted close by, idly fingering the Arapaho scalps which they wore as badges of valor. Soon after, Palmer asked Hunt to secure the Pikes Peak town site which Captain Colton had recommended—320 acres at the junction of Fountain and Monument Creeks.

The ex-governor examined the tract and rode over to Colorado City to discuss the matter with Irving Howbert, a slim, quiet young friend of his who had just been elected clerk of El Paso County.[1] Hunt remarked that 320 acres didn't seem like much of a town site with the railroad coming through it and all. Howbert agreed that more land was needed and Hunt hired him to help out even though Howbert protested that one more job would just about be the death of him. Hunt asked how that could be. The new county clerk explained that the other county officials were too busy or too lazy or too far away to work and had deputized him—at no extra pay—to act as county treasurer, county assessor, and all three county commissioners. Besides, he was the telegraph company's new agent and was up all night trying to learn the Morse code.

During the next few weeks, Hunt and Howbert combed the mesas and valleys and canyons and signed up everything that was loose around Pikes Peak. They filed on public land for the most part but Howbert bought out or scared out a sprinkling of squatters as well. In March, the jubilant ex-governor wired Palmer that he had built a town site headquarters on the banks of the Monument called "The Log Cabin" and had secured Palmer's 320 acres and perhaps a little bit more. The total, in fact, came to 9,312.27 acres. The town site at the creek junction had been enlarged to 2,000 acres and Palmer was about to own also a nearby ranch of 4,000 acres. The soda springs below Ute Pass had been bought, plus the 480 acres which surrounded them. So had Queen's Canyon, the Bijou tract ten miles north of it, and other bits of mesa and valley here and there.

All the tracts together, Hunt informed the appalled General, would cost around $10,000, which was that much more money than Palmer had to spare. He nearly called the whole thing off but decided to gamble on Hunt's judgment. He cabled Dr. Bell in England, wrote William P. Mellen in New York, and was assured by them that the money would be raised. Then the General reduced the cost of his land by shopping for Agricultural College scrip. This federal scrip was given to the governments of states which had no public land. They could sell the scrip to finance higher education within their borders. Each scrip unit was worth $1.25 at par and it would buy an acre of public land anywhere. In 1870, the federal government had distributed too much scrip and its unit value had depreciated. And so Palmer was able to buy most of his 9,312.27 acres with scrip units which had cost him only about eighty cents each instead of the usual $1.25.

In October of 1870, the General founded his "North and South" line at last, naming it the Denver and Rio Grande Railroad. It was the first of a maze of interlocking Palmer companies which he would create to build the road and to develop its by-products —towns, ranches, coal and iron mines, and so on. He formed a subsidiary company, the Mountain Base Investment Fund, to promote the sale of lands bordering the railroad between Denver and Pikes Peak, and he assigned his town site purchases to this company for the time being.

When the General returned from his English honeymoon in the spring of 1871, he parked Queen in Flushing and hurried to Denver. There he summoned three town site experts to a meeting on Fifteenth Street and announced the creation of another firm, the Colorado Springs Company. It would handle town site property sales to people who joined what Palmer called the "Fountain Colony." At this meeting, President Palmer of the Colorado Springs Company agreed to pay President Palmer of the Mountain Base Investment Fund $15 an acre for town site lands which had cost him eighty cents an acre. This was sound frontier finance—not skulduggery on the General's part. His railroad was entitled to profit, through his Mountain Base subsidiary, from the immense increase in value which the railroad would bring to Fountain Colony.

The General's town site experts felt that the Colorado Springs Company could easily afford to pay $15 an acre. They planned quite an initial markup of their own—the sale of 300 town site acres at about $270 an acre. These acres would be sold in the form of 616 residence lots at $50 each and 480 business lots at $100 each—the average lot being fifty feet wide and 190 feet deep. The lots would be assigned by drawings to "any person . . . possessed of good character and of strict temperance habits" who paid $100 to the treasurer of the Colorado Springs Company for membership in Fountain Colony. The membership fee would be credited against lots purchased.

The experts planned their first drawing for August, 1871, and they scheduled three more drawings at judicious intervals. They estimated that they could sell the entire 2,000 town site acres for at least $540,000, part of which would pay off the almost $150,000 due the Mountain Base Improvement Fund. Another $150,000 or so would go into streets, ditches, trees, parks, and the like. The rest would pay for administration, platting, wells, surveying, and advertising. Those who owned the Colorado Springs Company— Palmer, and true blue friends like young Dr. Bell and William P. Mellen—would get their reward in receiving free more than 7,300 acres of other Pikes Peak land not included in the 2,000-acre town site.

WHO WERE THESE "town site experts"?

You may recall that Horace Greeley's columnist, Nathan Meeker, had declined Palmer's invitation in '69 to start a colony of farmers at Pikes Peak. Meeker had founded Greeley on the Cache la Poudre River instead, and soon Palmer began hearing rumors that three of Meeker's aides were full of complaints about his puritanical and imperious disposition. The General sent Hunt to the Cache la Poudre and the ex-governor learned that the three disgruntled Union Colony officers were Chief Engineer E. S. Nettleton, Secretary William E. Pabor, and Vice President Robert A. Cameron. Nettleton was a fine water man who had concocted a device for stream measurement and had built at Greeley the first big irrigation ditch in the Rockies. Pabor was a young poetical hack writer who could make any sow's ear seem like a silk purse. But the trio's genius was General Robert A. Cameron. He was a tall, handsome, near-sighted man of forty-three with an oratorical voice like Daniel Webster's, sometimes mellifluent, sometimes booming. He was born in Brooklyn near Hunt's home but he grew up in Valparaiso, Indiana, where he practiced medicine and edited the Valparaiso *Republican*. Like Palmer, he achieved his military rank in the western theater of the Civil War.

He was an adventurer in the grand tradition and his idol was P. T. Barnum whose successful fake freaks convinced Cameron that a sucker was indeed born every minute. In late '69, Nathan Meeker's famous "call" for members to join his Union Colony appealed to Cameron and he hastened west from Indiana when he learned that Barnum had joined. Cameron did most of Union Colony's practical planning. He thought that Meeker was wise to place in the Greeley statutes a permanent ban on the sale of liquor. But he had no interest in being personally non-alcoholic, and he objected strenuously when Meeker criticized him for making speeches to the membership while under the influence. He pointed out truthfully that his optimistic oratory, whether he was drunk or sober, had kept Union Colony from falling apart in many periods of discouragement.

Palmer's agent, Governor Hunt, reached Greeley looking for town site experts at the perfect psychological moment. He offered General Cameron $3,000 a year to set up Colorado Springs on the model of Greeley and to run Fountain Colony. Cameron resigned from Union Colony within the hour to become vice-president of Fountain Colony. Early in June of '71, he climbed to the seat of a heavily-loaded wagon pulled by four mules and headed south for Hunt's Log Cabin on Monument Creek. In the wagon with him were his aides, Engineer Nettleton and Publicist Pabor.

Great projects are apt to have ludicrous origins. For weeks Cameron's little crew pottered along Monument Creek digging water wells, killing rattlesnakes, and trying to decide where to put Palmer's town. When Palmer and Governor Hunt stopped by briefly on their way to the Maxwell Grant, Palmer stood near the Log Cabin and the best well, pointed at Pikes Peak and said, "Take your center line from here to the summit, reverse your instrument, and you have Pikes Peak Avenue." By late July, Cameron had platted 1,000 acres of lots, wide streets and parks running half a mile or so east from Monument Creek and nearly two miles from north to south.[2]

On Monday, July 31, General Cameron was inspired by a jigger or two of whiskey to hold a first stake ceremony. He was inspired also by the poetic imagery of Pabor's new Fountain Colony prospectus which stirred him to the core, especially such modest lines as: "The Colony embraces a tract of 10,000 acres of arable valley lands. The mineral waters are unequalled and the scenery unsurpassed. The farming lands are equal in richness to any in the United States."

Cameron had a good first stake audience since thirty men or so were tented around the Log Cabin, mostly Greeleyites hauling in materials or helping to dig wells. Young Maurice Kingsley, Queen's friend, who had come from England to work on the Denver and Rio Grande, represented General Palmer. After Nettleton drove the stake at the plow furrow junction marking the southeast corner of Pikes Peak and Cascade Avenues, Cameron mounted a pile of lumber and for a pregnant moment cast his eyes east over the treeless, bleak, brown town site and west over the brave pygmy trickle of Monument Creek. Then he boomed out in his best vein of silver-tongued oratory while his hearers sat spellbound—at least for some seconds. But when he spoke twice of Monument Creek as "the noble Cache la Poudre" and described how "fruit groves will blanket these glorious hills," the crowd knew that the tippling orator had forgot what he had planned to say about Fountain Colony and was falling back on his old Union Colony pep talk.

Besides speechifying, platting, and killing rattlesnakes, Cameron applied his talents to naming things, starting with the prominent knob high above the soda springs just left of Pikes Peak summit which remains Cameron's Cone today. For many street names, Cameron had a point of reference even if his spelling was shaky. General Palmer had mentioned during his brief June visit an idea of Queen's—that the street names should relate to western geography and to Palmer's career as a railroad man and promoter of the Maxwell and Sangre de Cristo Grants.

We have seen that Palmer himself named Pikes Peak Avenue. For the parallel east-west streets south of Pikes Peak Avenue, Cameron picked the names of streams to the south. He called the first street "Huerfano" (Spanish, "orphan") because the Huerfano River led to several Sangre de Cristo Range passes which Palmer had examined. Cameron put "Cucharras" (misspelled) next to Huerfano, honoring the Cucharas (Spanish, "spoon") River, a Huerfano tributary. He marked the next east-west streets "Vermijo" (misspelled) and "Cimarron" (Spanish, "wild") after the Maxwell Grant streams, the Vermejo and Cimarron Rivers in northern New Mexico. "Costilla" (Spanish, "rib") was picked because Palmer at that very time was hunting a Denver and Rio Grande route from Vermejo River headwaters over Costilla Pass and down Costilla Creek to San Luis Valley and the Rio Grande. "Moreno" (Spanish, "tawny") Street referred to Moreno Creek. It was a Cimarron River branch heading at Red River Pass, an alternate gap over the Sangre de Cristos. In naming the east-west streets north of Pikes Peak Avenue, Cameron felt that Palmer's work on the Kansas Pacific and Denver Pacific Railroads in 1870 justified using the stream names "Kiowa," "Bijou," "Platte," "Boulder," and "St. Vrain"—all waterways north of Pikes Peak which had given trouble to the General.

Some of the north-south streets were named for mountain chains—Sierra Madre (north-central Colorado), Cascade (Oregon and Washington), Tejon (Southern California), Nevada (Sierra Nevada), Wahsatch (Utah). "Sahwatch" (Ute for "blue earth") is the name of a central Colorado range and also a creek which Palmer rode up from San Luis Valley when he examined Cochetopa Pass. "Weber" referred to a river, canyon, and mountain in Utah. Cameron probably pronounced it just as incor-

rectly as it is pronounced today (the right way is WEEBER—
after the great trapper of the 1820s, Captain John Weber).[3]

The name "Colorado Springs" had the vaguest of origins, having been applied for some years to the whole area around the Ute
Pass soda springs, including the Garden of the Gods, Colorado
City, and the Monument-Fountain Creeks junction. Fitz-Hugh
Ludlow, author of *The Heart of the Continent,* used the name as
early as 1867. When Palmer bought the soda springs, he tried to
give the site a touch of elegance by calling it "La Font." For the
larger site on the plains he offered the words "Monument Dells,"
which had been suggested to him in England by the good Canon
Kingsley, apparently visualizing a Sherwood Forest sort of
place with waterfalls and cool mossy glades.

General Cameron avoided this horror and when Pabor composed his flowery prospectus he called the town site "Colorado
Springs" because it had a nice rich eastern spa sound. He did it
on the sly, fearing that Palmer would object, since the only springs
were the soda springs five miles away at the foot of Ute Pass.
Palmer did object feebly, but by that time "Colorado Springs"
was entered in Irving Howbert's county transfer books and, besides, Palmer was beginning to like the clear brave ring of the
name.

Soon after the July 31 stake ceremony, Cameron received the
very first of Colorado Springs' distinguished visitors. He was
William Blackmore, the eminent English financier, inspecting his
American holdings including mines at Central City and the Maxwell Grant. Blackmore and Cameron got along well. They were
about the same age and had the same grandiloquent way of looking at life. Like Cameron, Blackmore dearly loved a spot of
whiskey now and then—preferably now.

Blackmore was interested in Indian lore and he had just discovered the poetry of Henry Wadsworth Longfellow, especially
Hiawatha. When Cameron took him to the soda springs, Blackmore noticed some Ute Indians on hand and he urged that the
name "La Font" be changed to "Manitou," the Algonquin Indian
spirit of Longfellow's epic. The Utes, he said, were probably
using the waters for ceremonial reasons, in honor of the Great

Spirit, Manitou. As far as Cameron knew, the Utes used the
waters to ease their indigestion and rheumatism and, being of
Aztec origin, they certainly didn't care two pins about Longfellow's Algonquin deity. But William Blackmore was Palmer's
patron and a stockholder in Palmer's companies. So Cameron
abandoned "La Font" and dubbed the place "Manitou." Blackmore gave names also to several Manitou springs—the Navajo,
Shoshone, Ute Soda, and Iron Ute. He named the beautiful
rushing branch of Fountain Creek "Ruxton Creek" after George
Frederick Ruxton, the young Englishman who described Ute Pass
in the late 1840s in his classic *Life in the Far West.*

Sales at the August 12 first drawing of Fountain Colony lots
were disappointing. Publicist Pabor blamed the result on disapproval of the Greeley-inspired liquor ban in all Colorado
Springs Company deeds—thus starting an endless, futile, and occasionally tragic controversy which goes on still.[4] Pabor had
strong support from a stubby immigrant named William Bennett
Iles whom Dr. Bell had imported from England to run the hotel
being built at Manitou. Iles's opinion bore weight not so much
because of his liquor experience but because he was one of
England's greatest cricketers, so good that he had been appointed
by Victoria, Queen of the United Kingdom of Great Britain and
Ireland, and Empress of India, as royal cricket tutor to Albert
Edward, Prince of Wales, later Edward VII, King of Great Britain, etc.

Not only were sales of lots slow, General Cameron found that
he couldn't even give them away. Several had been reserved as
gifts for Colorado City residents, but El Paso County sentiment
was almost unanimously anti-Palmer—a phenomenon which often
occurs whenever a newcomer tries to restore a decaying community. However, Irving Howbert, by threats and cajolements,
convinced the county's voters that Palmer's resort deserved a
decent road up Ute Pass in place of the horrendous roller-coaster
Indian trail which had been serving as a sort of road to the South
Park mining camps since 1860. A $14,000 county bond was ap-
proved. E. S. Nettleton was hired as engineer and work began

on the shelf road up the canyon of Fountain Creek around the
north side of Pikes Peak.

That road was a major triumph of Colorado road-making history. Lot sales picked up still more after the Chicago fire of
October 8 which brought several burned-out colony prospects.
And Publicist Pabor got a flurry of national publicity by issuing
phony plans which he ascribed to Palmer for moving the territorial capital from Denver to Colorado Springs. And still an
atmosphere of discouragement prevailed. It infected Palmer himself when he rode in from the Maxwell Grant with Governor
Hunt to greet the first train of the Denver and Rio Grande which
was due on October 21 at Colorado Springs.

Palmer worried mostly about the imminent arrival from Flush-
ing, Long Island, of his bride Queen. Rose Kingsley was expected
soon, too, from Baltimore, where she had been attending the
Episcopal Church Convention of the United States as a representative of the Church of England. Rose would visit her brother
Maurice whom Palmer had just made assistant treasurer of
Fountain Colony. The General had received anxious letters from
Queen's stepmother-aunt, Ellen Mellen, asking about the wild
Indians, grizzly bears, and other pioneer perils. The letters made
Palmer see for the first time the pretensions of his Newport in
the Rockies, the alleged charms of which he was promoting on
two continents. He saw what his dream town was really like—
its primitiveness, its bleakness, its raw discomfort, its burning sun,
its high thin air, its inhospitable soil. It aspired to become a great
resort for refined people, but it was going to look at first exactly
like the raw, lawless, mining camps and hell-raising supply centers which were its only neighbors between St. Louis and San
Francisco.

The new five-mile road across the mesa from the Log Cabin to
Queen's Canyon would seem very rough to his frail princess. And
the secret glen with its tangle of willows and scrub oak—he
named it "Glen Eyrie" after the eagle's nest on the great gray
entrance rock—might appear unlovely and sinister to her. Ute
Indians loved to camp in that vicinity. The Glen teemed with

rattlesnakes, though he had hauled in a dozen pigs to destroy them.

And their dream house—Queen's and his! On their honeymoon in England they had talked of building a home like Canon Kingsley's Eversley with its thick ivy, noble architecture, and gracious grounds. Palmer had had even nobler plans drawn up for a Tudor castle at Glen Eyrie, with a central stone tower four stories high.

But the noble castle would have to wait. He could not afford it, for one thing. And neither the materials nor the craftsmen existed in the Rockies for such a building. Queen would have to be content for the present with a plain clapboard house—comfortable and large, but otherwise like any other. Though this house had been going up in Glen Eyrie since July 1, it would not be completed until after the first of the year. Meanwhile, the stable below the house was just about ready. The Palmers would try sleeping in the hayloft for a while. The General wired William Mellen in New York for tents just in case the hayloft didn't work and he asked his father-in-law to "send out Victoria immediately as she is wanted badly to keep a restaurant for us."

Victoria was the Mellen cook. At least Palmer's Queen wouldn't have to prepare the meals.

CHAPTER THREE

The Earliest Early Birds

QUEEN PALMER reached Colorado Springs in late October, 1871, on one of the first regular trains of the Denver and Rio Grande. General Palmer brought her up from Denver and she was met by Dr. Bell, Engineer Nettleton, and an assortment of amazed pioneers who had never seen such a lovely young creature. As she disembarked at the Log Cabin in a mist of Parisian frills and flounces, she looked as out of place as an orchid in a corn field. Rose Kingsley arrived on November 1, a tall, angular, ruddy spinster of twenty-six properly accoutered in heavy tweeds, a shapeless felt hat, wool stockings, and stout coarse shoes.

General Cameron and William Pabor had just left the Springs for New York City to promote lot sales, which seemed an excellent idea. Queen and Rose found only twelve small buildings, mostly unfinished, on the town site as evidence of five months hard work by the two Greeley experts. At Glen Eyrie, Queen tried gamely to endure Will's stable and hayloft and then retreated to a tent near the home in Manitou which Willie Bell was having built. Later the Palmers joined Royal Cricketer Iles in the one-story, single-board shed which was called, presumptuously, the Manitou Hotel.

Rose moved into a one-room shanty lined with brown paper next to the Fountain Colony office at Tejon and Huerfano Streets. Her brother Maurice had had the shanty thrown together in two days. A tin basin on an old stool covered with calico served her as a wash stand. Maurice put up rough shelves for her books, placed a buffalo robe on the floor and yellow and red blankets on her bed. Dr. Bell gave her a pair of bright curtains. For his own room, Maurice appended a tent to the front of the shanty. In letters to Canon Kingsley, her celebrated father in England,[1] Rose described her impressions, beginning with her amazement to find in Governor Hunt's Log Cabin a public dining room with "two large tables on one side and four small on the other, with clean linen, smart waiters and a first-rate dinner" including oyster soup and roast antelope.

"This," she wrote, "is how our day goes: Get up at 7 a.m. in the cold frosty air. M. comes in and lights the stove . . . and by eight we are ready for a walk down to the Log Cabin with a fine appetite for breakfast. The food is good and plentiful. Beefsteak or venison; biscuit—as they call hot rolls out here; hot buckwheat cakes . . . and the whole washed down with bad tea or excellent rich milk. At nine work begins and I attend to my household duties . . . and then am ready to help M. in writing out agreements for lots and memberships."

She did not care for the cattle and antelope bones which dotted the town site or for the howling coyotes and flapping great horned owls and skunks which moved in at night. She hated the road to Manitou and its rickety trestle bridges and the fearsome ford over the roaring Fountain Creek. She disliked the smelly town dump on the bluff west of Cascade Avenue where General Cameron had talked grandly of putting an ornamental garden and Versailles-like fountain. She was depressed by El Paso County's scraggly graveyard which looked as though it belonged to Colorado Springs and was the first thing hopeful immigrants saw on incoming trains. It had three hundred graves which seemed a great many for a town three months old.[2]

On the other hand, Rose loved the thrilling daily arrival of the Santa Fe stage hauled by four bay horses under the majestic control of a driver in a suit made of yellow blankets. From her shanty she enjoyed the northeastward view of pine-fringed, yellow-cliffed hills—past which wagon trains hauled by oxen wended into town through Templeton Gap.[3] She liked evenings of whist with Engineer Nettleton and English friends from Denver, and she adored her dirty black-and-white kitten Tucker and her captive horned lark which she confined in a kind of cage fashioned in part out of a copy of *Martin Chuzzlewit.*

Best of all, Rose loved to scramble around the foothills. Sometimes she scrambled alone, armed with her trusty pickax which she used to loosen rare stones as well as for self-defense if necessary. Some times she scrambled with one or both of the De Coursey twins, Gerald and Captain Marcellin L., lecturing them at length on the flora and fauna.⁴ Time and again she begged Queen Palmer to go along on these strenuous hikes, but the General's delicate wife confined her explorations to the lower stages of Queen's Canyon.

Queen preferred dancing and indoor games for exercise, and it was a puzzle to her how Rose could stand to wear the same drab tweed dress and the same floppy felt hat day and night, week in and week out. Queen was fond of children and, on November 13, 1871, she began teaching school for five or six small children in a room of Publicist Pabor's house on Cascade Avenue at Bijou Street. It was an ambitious project for a bride of twenty-one years who had hardly learned to cope with her drafty tent at Manitou. She spent two hours or more five days a week riding horseback to and from her school. Children were always drawn to Queen and soon she had twenty pupils to teach, some of them almost as old as she was. There were problems of discipline. The older boys got to throwing paper wads at the girls and infuriating them by shrill references to their long flowing hair as "beaver tails." Queen stood the gaff for five weeks and took sanctuary on December 16 in Denver. She passed the school on to Rose Kingsley who lasted just two days before hurrying to Denver herself to take up roller skating.⁵

When Queen returned to the Springs after the Christmas holidays, she hired at her own expense Mrs. J. Elsom Liller to continue her free school for the rest of the term. Mrs. Liller's husband had just been brought to Pikes Peak from England by General Palmer on Canon Kingsley's recommendation to edit Palmer's first weekly newspaper, *Out West.*⁶

In her rugged ramblings, Rose Kingsley rode often through Colorado City and observed the popularity of its rejuvenated log saloons and gambling dens. She decided that all those bar flies should be improving their minds instead. On a mid-November evening she called a meeting in the Denver and Rio Grande office near her shanty of everyone interested in a reading room and library to compete with the horrid saloons. Maurice Kingsley attended the meeting and so did Dr. Bell and Irving Howbert and Matt France, Howbert's partner in a new real estate firm. France, an amiable Indianan, had edited the South Bend paper of Schuyler Colfax, Grant's first vice president, before coming to Colorado for his health. The Palmers supported Rose's reading room plan and $143 was subscribed at the meeting. Rose picked a properly august name for the organizers, The Fountain Society of Natural Science, and it was decided to give a public concert in January to raise more money for the project.

Raising money for culture by amateur entertainment has always been pursued with energy in the Springs and the tradition got a fine start with Rose's concert. The community was in a festive and optimistic mood by January of 1872. Maurice Kingsley was selling thirty Fountain Colony memberships each week. The population had reached three hundred people living in fifty-five houses. Rose was writing Canon Kingsley that "I find it difficult to keep pace with all the new arrivals, or the new buildings which spring up as if by magic." Rose exhibited also a shift in attitude toward the Pikes Peak region which was characteristic of many colonists who found it bleak and colorless at first only to change completely after a few weeks' residence. "It would be difficult," Rose wrote, "in any part of the world, to find such a series of mineral springs or finer scenery. And there can be no doubt that the prophecies of Ruxton and Frémont will be fulfilled;[7] and that the 'Fountain Colony' will answer all expectations of its promoters and become a dangerous rival to Saratoga and the Sulphur Springs of the East."[8]

Engineer Nettleton's eleven-mile ditch from Fountain Creek to the town site was in full operation. General Palmer's Colorado Springs Hotel, which carpenters from Greeley had been building since August, opened on January 1 at the southeast corner of Cascade and Pike Peak Avenues. William Pabor, who didn't believe in modest claims, billed the hotel as "the most elegant hostelry between Chicago and San Francisco." It was a handsome square frame building of two regular stories and a mansard roof with five dormer windows and a spacious porch across the entire front. Palmer had planned to put Cricketer William Iles in charge of it but Iles declared that he could not run a hotel properly or profitably unless liquor were served. The two men parted company and Palmer brought in a new manager from Denver.

All public activities in Fountain Colony from whist games to church services took place in the second floor hall of the rickety Foote Building near the Colorado Springs Hotel. Rose scheduled her concert there for January 25. By January 18, she had canvassed the county for musical talent and had worked the community into a dither of wardrobe creativity and artistic expectation. From then on she guarded the health and morale of her stars—Queen Palmer, mezzo-soprano, and Maurice Kingsley, balladeer and guitarist. She found time also to wash and press her enduring tweed suit.

The January weather had been sunny and warm but cold fog set in on Wednesday, the 24th, and the temperature fell well below zero. When Rose gathered some of her shivering artists at Editor Liller's home to practice that evening, she had to push the piano close to the stove and "between each verse I had to put my fingers in the open stove door to thaw them." Thursday, the great day, dawned warmer, but not much. The first full rehearsal occurred in the afternoon when the Santa Fe stage swept in bringing the bass player from his ranch fifteen miles down the Fountain. Rose's company consisted also of two violinists (who ran the livery stable), a Colorado City tenor and a second lady pianist —eight musicians altogether. After the rehearsal, the artists eased their nervousness by writing out programs.

"The concert," Rose wrote Canon Kingsley, "was advertised for 7:30; but we did not all get together till nearly eight; and by that time Foote's Hall was crowded with an orderly audience of about 150, of all classes, down to 'bull-whackers' who dropped in after their day's work with the ox and mule teams.

"At last all was ready. Captain de Coursey appeared with a jug of eggnog under his coat,[9] which was cunningly deposited under the piano so that as the performers went up to the very shaky platform they could stoop down and refresh themselves unseen; and the concert opened with a chorus. Everything went well. The bass viol, who I found had only tried his instrument a fortnight before, scraped away and tuned his strings, which insisted on getting out of tune every six bars.

"Our prima donna Mrs. Palmer and Maurice got rapturous applause. Mrs. P. sang a scene of Verdi's and two or three popular ballads; and Maurice began with 'The Fox Went Out on a Moonlight Night,' which was so successful that he had to sing two encores. We wound up with the 'men of Harlech' after which loud cries for Maurice began; and he was obliged to sing again. All went home delighted with their evening. The result to the reading room was most satisfactory, as after all expenses were paid we netted $60, a creditable amount for a town only five months old."

Dr. Bell could not attend the concert. He was in San Francisco with the U. S. Minister to Mexico, General W. S. Rosecrans, under whom Palmer and his Fifteenth Pennslvania had served in the Army of the Cumberland. Palmer had employed Rosecrans to get Mexican permission to build a narrow-gauge line to Mexico City from the Denver and Rio Grande's proposed southern terminal at El Paso, Texas. Willie Bell came back to the Springs just as the Palmers were moving into their Glen Eyrie home, an exciting event made doubly confusing since the whole William P. Mellen family had arrived from Long Island and moved with them into the big house at the mouth of Queen's Canyon—the fifty-eight-year-old father, Queen's stepmother-aunt, Ellen, aged thirty-five, and their six young children, three boys and three girls. Ellen Mellen was expecting a seventh child soon.

QUEEN PALMER told the General just then that she was pregnant herself, and her happy husband congratulated himself that their Glen Eyrie dream home was ready for her to await the birth of their first child. But Queen had other plans. In early March,

she refused to stay behind when Palmer and Rose and Maurice
Kingsley[10] left on railroad business in Mexico City. By this time,
Queen did not try to conceal her limitations in the role of pioneer
woman. Ellen Mellen could have *her* child at Glen Eyrie if she
wanted to. As for Queen, she would not return to Colorado
Springs until after her baby was born—in New York, with proper
medical care and all Eastern conveniences.

To this day, Queen Palmer has remained a beautiful and bitter-
sweet enigma. Life is easy to take at age twenty-one and yet,
even in 1872, Queen was unable to accept Glen Eyrie and Colorado Springs. She seemed to love Palmer and still she allowed
herself to hurt him by turning against his Pikes Peak dream which
he was realizing for her. It is hard to understand how she could
open her bride's home to the lively Mellens, to let them place
their stamp, instead of hers, on that lovely glade, including the
initials of young Clark and Chase and Nat cut on tree trunks and
Mellen names for things everywhere—Lady Ellen's Bower, the
Seven Baths, Echo Rock.

As things developed, the period from late October, 1871, to
early March, 1872—a little over four months—was Queen's first
and last serious effort to settle down in the Pikes Peak region.
Her low sweet voice graced no more Springs benefits and she
began no more Springs schools. Her sporadic appearances at
Glen Eyrie thereafter—in 1874, 1878, 1880—were butterfly visits
in effect, usually with, but sometimes without, her husband, giving gossips a rich field for speculation. In 1876, Queen lived
briefly in a house on Cascade Avenue. The Panic of '73 had
thrown Palmer's railroad projects in such financial straits that he
couldn't afford to keep Glen Eyrie open for a period. The first
Palmer daughter, Elsie, was born in New York on October 30,
1872. Dorothy Palmer was born in Colorado in 1880, Marjory
Palmer in England in 1881.

Frances M. Wolcott, in her book *Heritage of Years*,[11] hinted at
the mystery of Queen's life at Glen Eyrie when she wrote of "her
spacious room in the third story where she gathered books, heard
musicians and never permitted any but an invited friend to
enter." Queen's famous "kicking tantrum" was viewed by the

town as a demonstration of her antipathy for Colorado. The widely-circulated story went that she and the General were riding in an open carriage up Ute Pass on their way to Dr. Bell's hotel at Manitou Park north of present Woodland Park. A strong wind came up, covering them both with dust and gravel. Queen commanded Palmer to stop the carriage. She stepped from it, walked a hundred yards away, gathered up the yards of pleated tarlatan ruching and pink ribbons which constituted her costume and crawled under a mountain mahogany bush. Five minutes later she returned to Palmer waiting at the carriage. "I made the best use of my rest," she told him. "I was in a furious passion as if the wind were a person, so I lay kicking and screaming as if I were crazy."

One of the "musicians" in Queen's life was a problem. Count Louis Otto de Pourtales was the son of a French scientist at Harvard and he had come to Pikes Peak to recover from the strain of Boston high society, champagne in particular. Mrs. Wolcott called Louis "the Mute Seraph" and described him as a good horseman and dancer, born lover and indifferent guitar player. He made a game of falling in love with pretty young women but for Queen he conceived a grand passion. He would gallop in from his Florissant ranch in the middle of the night, pelt her third-story window at Glen Eyrie with rocks, and then burst into a song "of unrequited passion as persistently melancholy as the call of a mourning dove." Queen was pleased at first but decided in the end that she needed sleep more than male attention. She asked John Blair, Glen Eyrie gardener, to suggest to the Count that he do his serenading at reasonable hours.[12]

All the while, Queen and the General drifted further and further apart. Their interests had never been similar and the time came when they had nothing to say to each other or to do with each other. In 1880, the Springs heard that Queen had had a "heat attack" during a visit to Leadville, Colorado. The marriage broke up for good three years later when Queen left Glen Eyrie on the grounds that a "heart condition" required her to live at sea level. The General, people said, systematically stripped Glen Eyrie of everything that reminded him of her. Queen set up residence with her three daughters first in that resort which had inspired the General at the beginning—Newport, Rhode Island—and then in New York City and finally in England—London and Ightham Mote, near Tonbridge, Kent.

Of Queen's fashionable establishment at Ightham Mote, Mrs. Wolcott wrote in her book, perhaps spitefully: "It was our delight to arrive at the portcullis and see swan flying about the moat. . . . So draughty was that dining-hall that every chair at table had to be screened from drafts from everywhere and nowhere. Our spines were chilled. . . . I know I felt that a woman's best friend was a hot water bottle and that to jump into bed and pull up the coverlets to shut out sight and sound was but the part of wisdom. . . . A gentleman who played delightfully on a Stradivarius violin was arrayed in the mode of Oscar Wilde, in velvet jacket and knee-breeches, his patent leather pumps ornamented with large steel buckles."

Palmer adjusted his life in the eighties so that he could go abroad and visit his daughters twice a year, maintaining an English address at 2 Suffolk Lane in London. Queen died at last of heart disease in England at the sad young age of forty-four, on December 27, 1894, while her husband was at Glen Eyrie.

The General stood financially by the great and only love of his life to the end—and let her have her way. Perhaps he was as much to blame as she was for the tragedy of their marriage. If Queen hurt him by denying Colorado Springs, he probably hurt her by his utter absorption in his complicated business affairs in Colorado and Mexico—the same sort of business affairs that had kept him out so many nights during their London honeymoon while Queen stayed in their Buckingham Palace Hotel room playing bézique.

CHAPTER FOUR

Potpourri: The First Decade

THOUGH QUEEN let the General down in her lack of enthusiasm for Fountain Colony, he found that he could depend on the support of his old Fifteenth Pennsylvania Volunteer Cavalry comrades. That was his good luck because he needed them in those anxious years after the Panic of '73. He was away from Colorado Springs much of the time trying to save his railroad projects. In 1877, his desperate plight reached a climax. He had to default on the first Denver and Rio Grande bonds which William Blackmore of the Maxwell Grant had peddled for him in 1870. As a result, poor Blackmore, who had told General Cameron to call the soda springs "Manitou," became a hopeless alcoholic and committed suicide in England.

When Maurice Kingsley left the Fountain Colony board, Palmer replaced him with Gerald De Coursey, and his brother, Captain Marcellin L. De Coursey, the thoughtful supplier of eggnog during Rose Kingsley's concert. General Cameron and William E. Pabor returned to Pikes Peak from their New York promotion trip in mid-summer of '72 and Cameron wrote Palmer in Mexico asking that his $3,000-a-year contract be renewed at a higher figure. Palmer turned him down by return mail. Cameron gave up the job of director of Fountain Colony, said good-bye to his self-designated memorial, Cameron's Cone, and headed north to start his third Colorado town, Fort Collins. It was about this time that Pabor named and widely publicized a rock formation in the Garden of the Gods as "Seal Making Love to a Nun." Tourists flocked to the Garden from far and near but Palmer did not seem to be properly impressed by this triumph of publicity. He requested that his imaginative promotion man resign. Pabor joined Cameron on the Cache la Poudre.[1]

The departure of Cameron and Pabor left, as acting director of Fountain Colony, William P. Mellen, a weary and elderly parent whose hands were more than full controlling his six small children and his young pregnant wife in the rattlesnake paradise of Glen Eyrie. However, Palmer relieved Mellen soon by sending out from Philadelphia Major Henry McAllister, an old friend. Major McAllister had been one of several Fifteenth Pennsylvania comrades who had wished the newlywed Palmers bon voyage in New York as they had boarded the S. S. *Scotia* for England in 1870. By curious coincidence, Major McAllister was born on the same day and in the same year as General Palmer and in the same Kent County of Delaware. Both were Quakers. Both were a bit stern and autocratic. Both were really very peculiar because they liked poetry.

The major became director of Fountain Colony in the nick of time. On November 16, 1873, Mellen died after an apoplectic stroke while visiting relatives in Cincinnati.[2] By then, another of Palmer's Quaker friends, William S. Jackson from near Philadelphia, had joined McAllister to watch the General's interests.[3] Jackson came to Colorado Springs as treasurer of the Denver and Rio Grande Railroad. More help arrived when Dr. Willie Bell, thirty-two-years old now, returned to Manitou from abroad with his blushing English bride, the former Cora Georgina Whitemore Scovell. Next, a second Fifteenth Pennsylvania major, William Wagner, moved in as a Colorado Springs Company officer. The chin-whiskered Wagner was first mayor of the town, which was incorporated on September 2, 1872. Some months later, it became seat of El Paso County, erasing Colorado's City's last claim to ephemeral renown and forcing County Clerk Irving Howbert to move from his log cabin office to new quarters east of Monument Creek.

McAllister and the De Courseys,[4] Jackson and Wagner—all from the Philadelphia area—held things together during the financial crises and social sadnesses of the 1870s. When William B. Young's bank failed during the Panic of '73, William Jackson

continued page 51

General Palmer, a railroad ty-coon at the ripe old age of 32, loved everything on first sight —the soda springs below Ute Pass, the sparkling streams, the warm red rocks of the Garden of the Gods, and Pikes Peak beam-ing over all. *State of Colorado and Mrs. Elsie Queen Nicholson.*

Young Dr. William A. Bell, very British for an Irishman, gave up medicine forever when Palmer asked him to help build Colorado Springs. *Denver Public Library Western Collection.*

Some English money was raised by mortgaging Trinchera Ranch (part of the Sangre de Cristo Grant) in Southern Colorado. "Trinchera" means "irrigation ditch" in Spanish. *Denver Public Library Western Collection.*

37

General Palmer started his resort in the wilderness primarily as a nice place to bring his sheltered Long Island bride, Queen Mellen. *Elsie Queen Nicholson.*

Of course the village of Colorado City had been going for years before Colorado Springs. It had this log cabin, which Anthony Bott later called "Old Capitol Building," just to please the tourists. It was never any such thing. *State Historical Society of Colorado.*

The Springs pioneer of pioneers, young Irving Howbert, was not quite this dignified at the age of 24 when he helped Palmer to buy the town site. *Colorado College Library.*

Palmer's agent, Governor Hunt, built this Log Cabin in 1870. When the railroad arrived in October, 1871, it became the station restaurant and was sold later to Fred Harvey. Identified figures, extreme left to right, are: Governor Hunt, Mrs. Elizabeth Hunt McDowell (Hunt's daughter). Ed Eaton, Mrs Helen McDowell Malhern, and Major John H. McDowell (Hunt's son-in-law). The McDowell's ran the restaurant. *Pioneer Museum.*

Irving Howbert put through the building of this Ute Pass Wagon Road to South Park. Note how the new 1936 auto road joined Howbert's old road. *Colorado College Library and Pioneer Museum.*

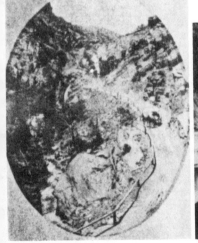

Palmer's Colorado Springs Hotel, Pikes Peak Avenue and Cascade, opened on January 1, 1872. *Colorado College Library.*

For calling this Garden of the Gods formation "Seal Making Love to a Nun," W. E. Pabor got fired from his job as Fountain Colony publicist. The name was changed to "Seal and Bear." Only a stub remains of the courting seal today. *W. H. Jackson photo, Colorado College Library.*

Palmer got his first Glen Eyrie house (towerless) finished in the nick of time for Queen Palmer was pregnant and sick of pioneering. In the late 1870s, he added the three-story tower to the house. *Fred and Jo Mazzulla Collection.*

Rare photo of Pikes Peak Avenue in 1873. The "contractor and builder" shop of W. S. Stratton, the future gold king, can be seen left foreground. *Fred and Jo Mazzulla Collection.*

Ah me! Sergeant O'Keefe, "his wife Nora," and friends mourned the death of "infant daughter Erin," consumed by Pikes Peak pack rats. *Pioneer Museum.*

Dr. S. E. Solly started this Manitou soda spring off to fame and fortune by ascribing to it healing powers which nobody had dreamed it possessed. The stream is Fountain Creek. *W. H. Jackson photo, Colorado College Library.*

The vivacious Helen Hunt was one of the nation's great writers when she came to the Springs and married Will Jackson. For his bride, Jackson bought the cottage at Kiowa and Weber which W. S. Stratton had built. The cottage was greatly enlarged after "H.H.'s" death. In 1961, Will Jackson's children by Helen Fiske Banfield sold the famous home to Colorado Springs for $100,000 and gave half of the proceeds to Colorado College. *Pioneer Museum and Denver Public Library Western Collection, W. H. Jackson photo.*

Helen Jackson loved the dramatic weather around Pikes Peak, including winds which could blow Palmer's trains off the track near town. The winds induced Major Henry McAllister to thicken the walls of his house at 423 North Cascade which he completed by January, 1874. The McAllister house, one of the oldest in the city, is owned by the Colonial Dames of America and is open to the public. *Pioneer Museum and Bob McIntyre.*

Colorado Springs was a sweet, quiet hamlet in the 1870s and 1880s when girls like Priscilla Martin were buying eels at Hooker's Grocery to please their fiancés. Almost every child possessed a burro friend for transportation. *Pioneer Museum*

In summer, tourists flocked to Manitou, arriving by rail at the Denver and Rio Grande depot, extreme lower left. The canyon of Ruxton Creek, upper center-right, provided a burro route to Pikes Peak. *Colorado College Library, W. H. Jackson photo.*

Nothing could be finer on a sunny Sunday in that happy era than a picnic in North Cheyenne Canyon. *Pioneer Museum.*

Dr. William A. Bell's home in Manitou, Briarhurst, was the focal point of Little London's society. *Colorado College Library, W. H. Jackson photo.*

Though Palmer banned liquor from the Springs, whiskey flowed freely from a barrel for tennis players and others at Dr. Bell's Manitou Park Hotel up Ute Pass. *Denver Public Library Western Collection.*

Early tourists—buxom girls and bearded men alike— flocked to the rugged Bear Creek Trail up Pikes Peak. *Pioneer Museum.*

By the late 1870s, hikers would climb the Peak and return to Lake House near Lake Moraine to spend the evening dancing the German. *Colorado College Library.*

Tom Palsgrove's Half Way House, up Ruxton Creek, had twenty-two rooms for its guests, plus a bowling alley. *Pioneer Museum.*

Helen Hunt Jackson's favorite hotel was at Seven Lakes where "a strange man of Mohammedan tendencies administered the milk cure." *Colorado College Library.*

As early as 1880, Balanced Rock in the Garden of the Gods was a photographic cliché. *Pioneer Museum.*

When Irving Howbert and Ben Crowell built their Opera House in 1881, a friend asked Ben to translate the motto on the Venetian drop curtain, "Nil sine numine." Salty old Ben, who hadn't the slightest idea, replied instantly, "No sign of a new mine." The motto—meaning "nothing without Providence"—was adopted for the Colorado Territorial seal in 1861. *Colorado College Library.*

General Palmer's first Antlers Hotel (1883-1898) had charm, distinction and worldliness. *College College Library.*

Colorado Springs' tranquil first era began to fade in 1889 with the opening of the Carriage Road from Cascade to the top of Pikes Peak. These tourist surreys were soon to be put out of business by the cog train, which transformed General Palmer's small resort into a national center of tourism. *Pioneer Museum and Stewart's.*

bought its fixtures and started the El Paso County Bank. Early in '74, Jackson, McAllister, and Engineer Nettleton induced the Colorado Council of Congregational Churches to start Colorado College on Colorado Springs Company land. Palmer gave more land at Pikes Peak Avenue at about the same time to establish the Colorado School for the Deaf and Blind.

In November of '73, the De Coursey twins made properly distinguished funeral arrangements for the Irish sheep rancher, Judge W. H. Baldwin, one of the celebrities of the mountain West, who stumbled into a shallow well and drowned at Green and Stitzer's Slaughter House. The fame of Judge Baldwin (the "judge" derived from the fact that he had judged sheep once at a Colorado Territory fair) was many-faceted. He had been scalped by Indians in South America and shot twice by Arapaho Indians near Monument Creek (the Arapahos would have scalped him if he hadn't been scalped already). He had never been seen even slightly sober. Last, but not least, he was El Paso County's only out-spoken Democrat, fond of haranguing staunch Republicans like McAllister and Jackson on the rights of man and Jeffersonian democracy.

Judge Baldwin's untimely death at age forty-six should have ended his career but it didn't. The oratorical toper lived on and on as an object lesson which kept the town in a state of division for years. The issue was the General's liquor ban, championed by the editor of Palmer's *Gazette*, J. Elsom Liller, thirtyish, of Nottinghamshire, England—Canon Kingsley's protégé. Liller, a lean, lank, frail, sallow young man, was a fair journalist even if his humor ran to ghastly puns like "Liveryman Charley Holmes is currying favor with his horses" and "Barbers on Pikes Peak Avenue are shaving things pretty closely these days."

But Editor Liller was as intransigeant as death and taxes. He simply could not understand the American spirit of compromise. He came to the Wild West from a tidy isle where law was law and order was order. When Palmer told him to uphold the liquor ban in the deeds of the Colorado Springs Company, he took the General at his word and backed the ban editorially with every ounce of his limited strength, come hell or high water and let the chips fall where they may.

There was the law in black and white. And what was the fact? The town had twice as many drug stores as were needed to meet the demand for drugs. Their main business was selling whiskey— for medicinal purposes, of course. By law each druggist was the judge of medicinal purpose. Naturally, if a customer said that he was ill because he needed a drink, the druggist was legally bound to provide the medicinal cure, even if—or perhaps especially if— the patient staggered up to the medicinal purpose counter suffering from delirium tremens.

Incredulously, Liller found himself listening to bitter complaints by these druggists that they were subjected to unfair and illegal liquor competition. They told him about "The Spiritual Wheel" at the southeast corner of Pikes Peak Avenue and Tejon Street—a storeroom with nothing in it except a hole in a wall containing a partitioned tray turning on a wheel. If a man wanted a drink he placed a coin on the tray, the wheel turned and a jigger of whiskey appeared miraculously where the coin had been. The druggists told Liller about the public bar in back of the billiard hall in the new La Font House on Huerfano Street. On Liller's charges, La Font's bartender went to police court periodically, paid a $25 fine, and hurried back to his saloon to sell more liquor.

Judicially at first, and then angrily, and at last hysterically, Liller scolded his *Gazette* readers for ignoring liquor violations, for permitting fixed juries, and for electing "Temperance Slates" the members of which were not strong for temperance. Friends began avoiding him on the street and even wrote him guarded notes of disapproval when he started to chide the Colorado Springs Company itself for not pushing its case against "The Spiritual Wheel" more aggressively toward the United States Supreme Court to test the legality of the forfeiture clause.[5]

Then came the last straw. In addition to the owner of La Font House, Liller often castigated in his columns a liquor vendor named D. W. C. Root (Root would have been called a bootlegger in a later day). In February, 1874, Root committed suicide. Did everyone regard the death of this chronic law-breaker as good riddance? Indeed not. Much of the press of Colorado Territory rose in righteous wrath to avenge Mr. Root, blaming his demise on the unjust attacks of that vicious propagandist, J. Elsom Liller, whose *Gazette* editorials had driven an exemplary citizen to his grave.

The sensitive Liller couldn't stand it. Though the Root uproar subsided soon, J. Elsom's health and spirits declined. During the winter of 1875, he took to his bed from which he dictated listless columns urging voters to elect the latest "Temperance Slate" in the city elections of April 5. He got up for part of Easter Sunday, April 4, but lay down again at 4 p.m. and seemed to fall asleep. When Mrs. Liller tried to wake him some hours later he was dead, of an overdose of laudanum. Next day the "Temperance Slate" won in a walk.

GENERAL PALMER never excelled at wooing high government officials to advance his own projects, but he had powerful friends who spoke for him. It happened that his English backer, William Blackmore, became interested in the new Yellowstone Park in Wyoming Territory and, in 1872, partly financed the second Yellowstone expedition of Dr. Ferdinand V. Hayden, chief of the U. S. Geological and Geographical Survey of the Territories. The great and brilliant Hayden and some others had pushed the bill creating Yellowstone Park through Congress to receive President Grant's signature on March 1, 1872.

Blackmore told Hayden about his heavy stake in Colorado Springs and its fiscal parent the Maxwell Grant,[6] adding that both areas would benefit if the Hayden Survey tackled them next. As a result, Hayden set up a triangulation base at Pikes Peak early in September, 1873. For two months, the Colorado Springs Hotel was gay with evening parties for these romantic geology people including such celebrities as Henry Gannett, discoverer of Wyoming's highest mountain, Gannett Peak, and Dr. A. C. Peale, the noted mineralogist. The festivities made excellent publicity, especially when Fountain Colony could announce that Dr. Hayden had bought a residence lot because he felt that "the resort would grow far beyond expectations."

On September 26, Hayden and his assistants rode up the seventeen-mile Bear Creek trail between Cameron's Cone and Mount Rosa to the top of Pikes Peak. They marked their visit by building an imposing cairn on the summit and by making the Peak's official altitude 14,147 feet above sea level (today's figure is 14,110; Pike recorded it in 1806 at 18,581).[7] A bit later, Hayden's men mapped an extinct volcano on the southwest slope of the Peak in a high summer cow pasture called Cripple Creek.

The structure of the Cripple Creek volcano convinced the Hayden experts that gold must be present there in quantity. But nobody believed them. The absurdity of their diagnosis was proved the next September when a Springs cowboy named Bob Womack guided a hundred argonauts to Cripple Creek. They located a claim called the Lone Tree Prospect Tunnel but found no gold in it, only a gray stuff which somebody said was "white iron." Probably it was sylvanite, Cripple Creek's characteristic gold ore. The claim lay in the heart of what would become, twenty years later, the richest part of the Cripple Creek Mining District.

Government windfalls came to the Springs in pairs during '73. In February, Congress approved an appropriation to build the Army Signal Corp's second largest station on top of Pikes Peak. The Army began work improving the Bear Creek trail and Western Union strung a telegraph line along it. The Signal Station opened on October 11, 1873, and from then on the nation's newspaper readers took an avid interest in the daily reports which flowed down the telegraph line about life at 14,147 feet above sea level. They learned from Sergeant Seyboth, the first chief observer, that water froze up there at thirty-four degrees instead of thirty-two; that it boiled at 178 degrees instead of 212. Potatoes had to be cooked four hours to be edible and beans never did get done.

Sergeant Seyboth was an obliging public servant and did his best to meet the insatiable demand for news by turning out bright copy on his life at the threshhold of Outer Space. But there was a limit as to what could happen. After he had described several hundred-mile gales and several nightmare bouts with static electricity and several storms with hail as big as pumpkins and several thunderclaps which left him stone deaf for weeks, he realized that his vast audience was longing for more esoteric adventures. The Seyboth report of December 6, 1873, seemed to fit the bill. It made the front pages not only of American papers but also of papers in the Loch Ness hinterlands of Scotland which had prided itself on holding a monopoly in respect to the phenomenon described.

As Seyboth and his faithful burro (he wrote) ambled down the Bear Creek trail just below timberline, they passed near the lovely cold blue waters of Lake Moraine. Suddenly, the sergeant was startled by a loud splashing sound. He faced the lake and observed moving swiftly across it an enormous something at least one hundred feet long. A sea serpent—beyond a doubt! Its horrid body, covered with great scales, was light brown. Its head, held six feet above the water by its long neck, was "large but symmetrical." The eyes were "small for such a large beast" and "seemed to glance rapidly in every direction as the slimy creature glided rapidly through the water."

The sergeant concluded his report by stating that he and his burro fled down the Bear Creek trail until they reached three Ute Indians who lay almost prostrate with fear beside a boulder. Seyboth asked their opinion of the Lake Moraine sea serpent and they replied that they had just escaped from the long claws of the monster. They added that the serpent had ruled the lake for centuries and was particularly fond of Utes, having eaten seven since March.

Chief Observer Seyboth was succeeded at his perilous Pikes Peak post by Sergeant Boehner and then by Sergeant Sackett.[8] The new reporters found much to titillate their international public. But it remained for a high-altitude scribe named Sergeant John O'Keefe to achieve the ultimate in journalistic grandeur. During the early summer of 1876, Colorado's impending Statehood was on everybody's mind until O'Keefe shocked the world with the awful news from the Peak. First, the news. Then the photograph of the pile of rocks to mark the small grave which the bereaved O'Keefes had erected in the thin air at immense

physical cost. The photograph showed the simple pine head
board, crudely but plainly lettered, near the Signal Station. The
moon-inspired epitaph:

> Fair Cynthia with her starry train
> Shall miss thee in thy silent rest,
> And waft one sweet, one spheric strain
> To Erin dear, among the blest.
>
> > Erected by Sergeant John and Nora O'Keefe
> > to the memory of their infant daughter, Erin
> > O'Keefe, who was destroyed by mountain rats
> > May 25, A.D. 1876.

Deluged with inquiries, the Associated Press man in Colorado
Springs reluctantly pressed the mourners for details. O'Keefe
wired down the pathetic message: "The wind was blowing unusually hard on May 25th. Nora and I struggled outside to put
more stones on the roof of the Signal Station to prevent the gale
from blowing the roof away. When we returned inside our dear
child was no more. The pack rats had consumed her."

What more was there to say? Well, not much. Only a final
statement from U. S. Army headquarters, and a reprimand to
Sergeant O'Keefe. The sergeant, the Army disclosed, had no wife,
Nora or otherwise. He had no infant daughter. He had a black
cat named Erin, the gift of Dr. Henry K. Palmer of Colorado
Springs, who had given it to him and to his three assistants to
assuage their loneliness on the Peak. When Erin died, May 25, of
natural causes, the four officers had buried him or it with full
military honors, beneath the cairn of rocks which Dr. Hayden and
his men had built in September of '73.

THE PANIC OF '73 brought business growth to a dead halt almost everywhere in the United States. But, as the depression
deepened, Fountain Colony flourished like a weed patch, gaining
five hundred residents and half as many buildings each year. Engineer Nettleton finished a second long irrigation canal. Director
McAllister planted 5,000 round-leafed cottonwoods along the
ditches lining the main streets.[9] In '74, a smart young carpenter
from Indiana, Winfield Stratton, bought a Colorado Springs Com-

pany lot (offered originally at $50) for $288 and sold it two months later for $800.

When President Grant stopped overnight—October 9, 1875—at the Manitou House and muttered one of his stirring one-minute speeches on the porch of the Colorado Springs Hotel, he was surprised to see that the new resort was full of visitors.[10] Most of the prosperity was caused by a rumor seeping through the East and Europe, that the Pikes Peak climate would repair any crock, however badly cracked. And there was truth to it. The visitors seen by President Grant were mainly happy lungers who had come to Fountain Colony in the terminal stages of tuberculosis and were now on the mend. The rumor was pushed hard by two ardent boosters, Dr. Boswell P. Anderson, a suave Virginian, and Dr. Samuel Edwin Solly, a suave Britisher. Dr. Anderson was born in 1847 and fought the Civil War galloping over the Alleghenies with Mosby's guerrillas. He reached Manitou in '72 to run the soda springs bath house for General Palmer. Dr. Solly was born in 1845, educated at Rugby, and graduated from the Royal College of Surgeons in 1867. Then he went from one European spa to another seeking health. In 1874, he arrived at Pikes Peak to give the place a try.

Both men were exceptionally good looking, tall, courtly, with rich soothing cultured voices and lively intelligence. However, they were too young to know much about general medicine. They knew still less about "consumption"—tuberculosis, the bacillus of which had not been isolated yet. But they noticed that tuberculars improved rapidly in the high altitude Pikes Peak air if fed well and given rest and exercise. Also, the invalids seemed responsive to a little romance—not too strenuous—and to bedside manners exuding cheer, confidence, and deep personal interest. Drs. Anderson and Solly learned how to mix their lady and gentlemen patients and the two physicians improved their naturally perceptive bedside manners. Before they knew it, they were ranking specialists in "consumption."[11]

In important addition, they had the foresight to promote a mass of attractive medical facilities which culminated in such establishments for long-term patients as Glockner and St.

Francis Hospitals and Cragmor Sanatorium.[12] As a starter, Dr.
Solly went to work on the various soda springs at Manitou.
Some of these vaunted waters had a nauseous taste and some
smelled like rotten eggs and all presented problems because of
conflicting claims about their miraculous healing powers. In
1875, Dr. Solly wrote a pamphlet, "Manitou, Colorado, Its
Mineral Waters and Climate," which cleared all confusion. It
explained why the waters which smelled and tasted worst were
best for you and it described many healing powers which nobody had dreamed that the springs possessed.

The Navajo, for instance, bubbling from a ledge on the right
bank of Fountain Creek, was found by Dr. Solly to be a splendid
water for drinking to ease bronchial catarrh, and even catarrh
of the bladder or genito-urinary passages. It soothed derange-
ment of liver or kidney or spleen, phthisis, cancer, gout, and
gravel, to say nothing of corpulence, flatulence, and waterbrash.
Shoshone waters near the Navajo reduced ague, gall-stones, and
hemorrhoids. The Iron Ute up Ruxton Creek was superb in
treating chronic alcoholism, uterine affliction, and green sick-
ness. Bathing in such waters was as salutary as drinking them
in the cure of atonic gout, muscular rheumatism, or leucorrhea.
Near the pamphlet's end Dr. Solly thoughtfully pointed out the
curative advantages of patronizing Manitou's five hotels, bowling alleys, billiard parlors, croquet grounds, band concerts,
theatricals, hiking trails, and trout streams.

LONG BEFORE Dr. Solly's medical masterpiece was printed,
the marvels of Manitou reached the ear of a famous lady writer
who lived at Newport, Rhode Island, and who didn't feel well
at all. Her pretty name was Helen Hunt, born Helen Maria
Fiske in 1831 at Amherst, Massachusetts, and therefore as New
England as Pinkham Notch and Walden Pond. She had had a
sad domestic career—both of her young sons dying and her
husband of eleven years killed in an accident. She had moved
to Newport in 1866, discovering there a facility for writing
saleable poems and articles for the New York *Independent,* a
liberal weekly which some critics called "an infidel sheet" be-

cause so many Unitarians wrote for it. After Ralph Waldo Emerson praised Mrs. Hunt as "the greatest poet in America," her market extended to *The Nation, Atlantic,* and *Scribner's Monthly* and she began hauling in as much as $3,000 a year. This income put her in a class with her friends Harriet Beecher Stowe and Louisa May Alcott, and financed her European trip of 1869-70.

She spent the spring of '72 in California, returned East, and started having spells of bronchial catarrh which reduced her production drastically. She believed in the homeopathy which Willie Bell had studied in St. Louis, though little good came from the homeopathic pills of her family physician in Amherst, Dr. Cate. At last, in November of '73, Dr. Cate took her to Pikes Peak to see if the waters of Manitou really could cure bronchial catarrh. He set her up in genteel rooms on the north side of Kiowa Street between Cascade Avenue and Tejon Street. This north side was composed of portable houses from Chicago and was called "Dead Man's Row," in honor of its invalid population.

Members of Fountain Colony were not unused to writers, but they were awed by Mrs. Hunt's literary stature, fabulous earnings, and rumored disinterest in attending church. She was a plump, round-faced, forthright, vivacious woman whose graying curls were usually covered by a silvery scarf. Of course the waters of Manitou cured her bronchial troubles at once and the gossips reported delightedly that she was nursing the ailing bachelor and civic leader, William Sharpless Jackson, unchaperoned, in his room at the Colorado Springs Hotel. At the same time she was taking buggy rides to Cheyenne Mountain with Mr. Gerald De Coursey, who already had a wife.

If there were competition between Mr. Jackson and Mr. De Coursey for Mrs. Hunt's affections during the next year or so, it ended in July, 1875, when De Coursey died of a lung hemorrhage. Helen wrote a broken-hearted poem about his death and burial near Cheyenne Mountain, "Flowers on a Grave," for the New York *Independent* of September 16. Then she married Jackson, aged thirty-nine, on October 22, 1875. The ceremony was performed in Wolfeboro, New Hampshire, by her brother-in-law, Everett Colby Banfield, attended by a brace of Banfield offspring including Helen's sixteen-year-old niece, Helen Fiske Banfield.

Helen Hunt, the famous poet, and Will Jackson, the small-town man of business, made an odd couple. She was a New Englander of the Emersonian school—an unpredictable woman of bright dancing light and purple shadow, pixeyish and metaphysical. Jackson was of William Penn's Pennsylvania—upright, conscientious, methodical, humorless, heavy, and with a beard thick enough to raise mice in. He was a factual person, serenely sure that two and two equalled four, whereas his bubbling bride knew it never did where human beings were concerned. Frances Wolcott called the union "the wedding of a skylark to a turtle" and yet the reasons for it were plain. At forty-four, Helen Hunt was weary and frightened, even though she was writing profitably again—as much as $575 in one fortnight. She yearned for the wealth and security and comfort which a staunch man like Jackson could give to her. For his part, Jackson was thrilled to win such a brilliant wife, and he found relief in her from the monotony and confinement of life at the El Paso County Bank on South Tejon Street. He was pleased also to be tied to a woman who could earn $575 in a single fortnight.

For two or three years, Helen Hunt Jackson was very happy in the Springs. Will Jackson, a thrifty Quaker, bought her a small cottage at Weber and Kiowa Streets which the smart carpenter Winfield Scott Stratton had built—with Pikes Peak visible only from the kitchen window. Before Will knew it, Helen had torn out the kitchen and begun expanding in all directions on a plan which eventually transformed his little gray home in the west into a rambling New England mansion as be-gabled as Nathaniel Hawthorne's place at Salem.

By 1878, she had written seven books in the cottage, and many glowing articles and poems on Colorado which informed her millions of readers that their favorite author had moved from Newport, Rhode Island, to that upstart "Newport" in the Rockies. She enjoyed the breath-taking wildflowers of July which carpeted her little private park above the falls of South Cheyenne Creek in sight of Gerald De Coursey's grave. She liked dramatic weather—the rolling thunders of August and the deep dazzling snows of April. She was excited by the fantastic January winds which once blew two Denver and Rio Grande coaches and two baggage cars off the track five miles south of the Springs.

But the idyll didn't last. Helen Hunt Jackson was not a mixer. She kept away from the social set—the Dr. Bells, the Wagners, the McAllisters. Since people didn't know what she was about, they invented things—she was an atheist, a free-lover, a New England witch with gray-green eyes who chanted over her brews in Sanskrit. Like Sergeant Seyboth on Pikes Peak, she found that there was only so much to describe in the Rockies. For the first time in her life, her editors began complaining that she was repeating herself. She was homesick for those pygmy highlands of her youth—the White Mountains of New Hampshire, all chiaroscuro and drip.

More and more she wanted something new to write about, something new to think about, something different from wifely duites at Weber and Kiowa. In the early fall of 1879, while Coloradans boiled with hypocritical rage over the murder of Palmer's old Greeley friend, Nathan Meeker, by Ute Indians, she left town for respite in Maine. The Colorado Utes had complained of white iniquity for years but Helen had given them little sympathy. They were too close to home. In November, she attended a lecture in Boston by the Ponca heroine Bright Eyes, detailing crimes committed against her tribe. Helen was transported. Here was her new interest, her cause. She hurried to New York and in four frantic months researched and wrote a passionate indictment of American Indian policy which was published in '81 under the title *A Century of Dishonor*.

It was a bitter, slashing, murderous diatribe and it set official Washington on its ear. Overnight Helen Hunt Jackson became the heroic rallying point for the defense of all red men. She journeyed far and wide as a government investigator. In the winter of 1884, during a few weeks of frenzied creation in New

York, she wrote a tragic novel about a Mission Indian girl of Southern California, *Ramona*. She felt that this fictional treatment would stir more readers than the non-fictional first book. It did. With sobs and tears, America clutched *Ramona* to its heaving bosom and made it a prime classic of American literature.

It became, naturally, impossible for the world-renowned champion of the American Indian, Helen Hunt Jackson, to resume normal domestic life on Weber Street. She tried it in the summer of '84, and succeeded merely in falling down stairs and breaking a leg. She left on crutches in the fall for more Indian investigations in Southern California just as Will Jackson was named receiver of the Denver and Rio Grande Railroad, from which Palmer had been ousted by the wily railroad manipulator, Jay Gould. Helen worried about leaving Will but she could console herself that he was not alone. Her favorite niece, Helen Fiske Banfield, who had attended her wedding, had arrived at Weber Street as Will's ward to recover from an illness which occurred after her graduation from Vassar.

The broken leg did not heal properly. Before Helen finished work in Southern California, cancer developed. In April of 1885, she went to San Francisco. She knew that she was dying and discussed the matter calmly for months with any friends who dropped in. On August 2, 1885, Will Jackson arrived at the request of her doctor. Helen lived until August 12, 1885. Her last act was to write a note to President Grover Cleveland thanking him for helping her Indians.

William Jackson moved his wife's body to Colorado Springs and placed it in her private park above the South Cheyenne falls on land owned by the James Hull family. Thousands of her admirers climbed up there and paid their respects by placing stones on her grave. In 1891, Mrs. Hull began charging tourists ten cents to visit the huge pile of stones. Jackson tried to buy the plot but could not come to terms with the owners. In '92, he moved the remains of Helen Hunt Jackson to Evergreen Cemetery.[13]

Will had remarried in the meantime. Three years after Helen's death, he wed her niece and his ward, Helen Fiske Banfield, aged twenty-nine years. Will was fifty-two himself but he had no fear of criticism. President Cleveland, aged forty-nine, had only recently married *his* ward, twenty-two-year-old Frances Folsom, in the White House while the whole nation cheered.

LIQUOR, INVALIDS, HELEN HUNT—all very well. But what was Colorado Springs really like, say around Thanksgiving Day, 1880?

Well, it started snowing on the Sunday before and by Tuesday the depth was seven inches. Sleigh bells jingled merrily up and down Pikes Peak Avenue. Ladies in buffalo robes, goat button boots, and seal sacques met in Robinson's Drug Store and discussed the drunk found frozen in Shook's Run and the eighty-pound wolf which J. F. Seldomridge shot near his place. Mr. Robinson interrupted the ladies to recommend Shiloh's Vitalizer for Thanksgiving Day after-effects. The label guaranteed that Shiloh's Vitalizer would cure their indigestion, consumption, cancer, yellow skin, and premature child birth.

After Tuesday night's bitter cold, residents began running out of coal. A rumor arose that a nasty row over coal had taken place at Grace Church and that vestrymen were resigning in shame, having counseled that no coal be bought until late December. Grace Church burned its last lump of coal at noon Wednesday. The Thanksgiving service was cancelled. Episcopalians were urged to attend the union service which the Reverend Cross would conduct at the Baptist Church, Weber and Kiowa.

Wednesday's *Gazette* announced the impending marriage of Mr. Peter Mariani to a young lady from Kankakee, Illinois, Miss Priscilla Martin. Priscilla had just completed Professor Connor's course in penmanship, receiving second prize, *Tales of Hiawatha*. On Friday evening she would appear at the Congregational Church musical and literary entertainment in a recitation, "The Lost Heir." She had induced her fiancé to appear also on the program in an original monologue (Priscilla's), "A Bachelor's Reasons for Taking a Wife."

64

Priscilla knew how to play a melodeon.

Since Priscilla had asked Mr. Mariani to her mother's home for Thanksgiving dinner, she was seen shopping on Wednesday. She bought York State cider, Boston brown bread, and nic-nacs at Pascoe's Bakery; two pints of solid meat oysters at the North End Market; fresh mincemeat, figs, saratoga chips, and some fried eels at Hooker's Grocery. In an emotional moment, she entered the Pikes Peak Dry Goods Emporium and bought for Mr. Mariani, at $15, an Egyptian straw overcoat which could be worn turned inside or outside.

Enough of Priscilla for the moment. On Wednesday night, delighted residents witnessed Zamloch, the conjuror, at Courthouse Hall. He was fascinating. For instance, he placed on the stage a large wicker basket, donned an orange domino, crawled into the basket, raised a hand high, and fired a pistol. An instant later, with a cheery "Hello!" he climbed into the hall through one of the windows facing Nevada Avenue.

Thanksgiving morning was warm but the ice was still good for skating on Monument Creek below the Denver and Rio Grande depot. The town's sporting element went to the turkey shoot in Hermann's beer garden, Manitou. Members of Company A, First Battalion Cavalry, State Militia, attended a target shoot at their rifle range. From noon on the Methodist Church served Thanksgiving Dinner at fifty cents each (children, half price). A great day. Topping it off was Company A's annual gala ball at Courthouse Hall, with music by Hull's eleven-piece society orchestra. Prizes for the target shoot were distributed and there were more prizes for guessing the ages of General Grant, General Sherman and General Phil Sheridan. Prize for the best joke went to Mr. W. R. Roby with the bon mot, "Miss Lily Langtry is so beautiful that she is head and shoulders above any adornment of dress."

Mr. Peter Mariani thought this very funny and laughed loudly until restrained by his fiancée, Miss Priscilla Martin, who thought it quite vulgar.

By Saturday, the Springs had recovered from its Thanksgiving Day, 1880. The afternoon paper announced that the engagement between Mr. Peter Mariani and Miss Priscilla Martin was off. Some guessed it was the melodeon and some said fried eels and some said it was the Egyptian straw overcoat.

But nobody ever really knew why.

CHAPTER FIVE

Little London

A LUCKY STAR has always cast its light over Pikes Peak. It was pure luck that the most revered man-of-letters in Great Britain and Ireland, Charles Kingsley, Canon of Westminster Abbey, should catch cold in the fogs of San Francisco in June of '74 and should be ordered to Colorado Springs to get over it.

The great man hadn't cared to come at all, even if Fountain Colony was beginning to be called "Little London" because of so many tea drinkers in the landscape. For him, it was either Colorado Springs or Denver—and Denver was no place for the head of the Temperance Society. And when the canon got to Pikes Peak, he couldn't wait to get away. But Dr. William A. Bell, who had assumed Pabor's duties as press agent, didn't mention that detail in his reports abroad informing the English, the Irish, the Scots, and the Welsh that Colorado Springs was the high point of Kingsley's American tour and was, furthermore, the one place on earth where a man could recover from a cold in proper British fashion.

The canon's tour had been a spectacular success. In February, the Lotus Club in New York had overwhelmed him with honors. In March, Longfellow and Whittier had toasted him in Boston, which he had admired even though "Americans make themselves ill by hot air and foul air and want of exercise." Back in New York, William Cullen Bryant and John Hay, Lincoln's ex-secretary, had called on him and he had lectured at the Opera House to four thousand people. In April, he had dined in Washington with President Grant and had spent hours with F. V. Hayden talking about the Rockies. He was feted at Baltimore, at Niagara Falls, at Detroit, at St. Louis, at Omaha. He had enjoyed the scenery of Salt Lake City in May but was aghast at Mormon disinterest in monogamy. "What horrors this place has seen!" he said. "Thank God we in England know what love and purity is."

At Pikes Peak, Dr. Bell and his bride bedded the canon down tenderly with hot bricks in their new "Briarhurst" home in Manitou and he was soon over his cold. Rose Kingsley was along—a twenty-nine-year-old spinster now and still ready to climb a cliff any time. In late June she took her father up Ute Pass to stay at Dr. Bell's ranch at Bergun's Park where the Union Jack flew proudly. Kingsley studied the insects and wild-flowers of July, though distracted by Bell's English foreman, "Chumley" Thornton, a huge Cambridge graduate who instructed the canon on everything—in a voice like the bellows of a bull defending his harem—from lettuce-culture to why peat-fired malt makes better Scotch whiskey.

After some days of "Chumley," Kingsley wrote Fanny, his wife: "Oh my Love, Your birthday-letter was such a comfort to me for I am very home-sick and counting the days till I can get back to you. . . .This place is like an ugly Highland strath, bordered with pine woods. Air almost too fine to breathe." He was not much happier on July 11 as the Palmers' guest at Glen Eyrie: "Thank God our time draws nigh. I preach at Colorado Springs tomorrow and lecture for the Church on Wednesday; Denver Friday and then right away to New York, and embark on July 25th. . . . Tell G. I have seen no rattlesnakes; but they killed twenty-five here a year or two ago, and little Nat Mellen, twelve years old, killed five. . . . We are trying to get a horned toad to bring home alive. . . . Tell G. that I will write again before we start over the plain. Oh! happy day!"

It was in Manitou that Kingsley composed his eerie poem which opened: "Are you ready for your steeple-chase, Lorraine, Lorraine, Lorree? Barum, Barum, Barum, Barum, Barum, Barum, Baree." Englishmen from all over El Paso County attended his famous lecture on Westminster Abbey. And yet, such is human perversity that Kingsley lives in Little London history neither for his poem nor for his lecture, but because a bug lighted on his manuscript during the talk.

As one anonymous writer described it: "Mr. Bug sat still a moment or two, during which space the speaker improved the occasion to study his peculiarities of form and structure . . .; but while these investigations were in progress, and his language rolling right along to the delight of his hearers, the insect began to expand his wings as if anxious to fly away. The reverend speaker saw the motion, and deftly caught it in his hand. Going right on with his line of argument, he continued his examination until, having settled everything to his own satisfaction, he let it buzz away about its own business."[1]

Dr. Bell exploited in full Kingsley's month-long stay, to strengthen the "Little London" idea and to lend prestige to his advertisements in British dailies on the wonders of Pikes Peak for sheep and cattle ranching. His promotion then and thereafter was perfectly timed. He had known for years that British farms were no longer able to grow enough food to support the British population. By 1874, he was aware that British emigration was approaching flood tide. Thousands of tenant farmers and younger sons of large land owners were on the move to the American West.

William Blackmore and his Maxwell Grant friends had been only the vanguard of British capitalists with excess money to invest in the Rockies. Bell saw to it that the Pikes Peak region got its share both of British emigrants and British pounds. Before the movement faded in the late 1880s, Little London and El Paso County had close to two thousand residents with assorted British accents. As Frances Wolcott said, "Colorado Springs took to tea and crumpets every afternoon at five ahead of Boston and New York."

If General Palmer composed the strong melodic line of Colorado Springs, Willie Bell contributed at least the grace notes. He was an attractive man with the elusive fay quality of the Irish—eager, impulsive, and pure. Palmer's love for him was the delighted puzzled love of a father for a precocious son. The General was the stern military commander to most of his associates, requiring and getting obedience and punctuality. But Bell was special. When he did some fool thing against orders—like selling Helen Hunt Jackson's private park up South Cheyenne Canyon to the James Hull family—Palmer just looked pained and let it pass.

And the General envied Bell's emotional balance, his ability to attend to business as varied as Palmer's without getting too absorbed, his refusal to let his ambition interfere with his hobbies. Palmer envied Bell's religious fervor, his view of Heaven ruled by happy pink cherubs and a friendly God in a beard who, Bell was sure, came to Manitou personally in '73 to bless Briarhurst when Willie christened it with Church of England rites. Most of all, Palmer envied Bell's domestic bliss with Cora Georgina Whitemore Scovell and their five children born in the 1870s. Life at Briarhurst was cheerful bedlam, managed by bevies of English servants who seemed forever tangled in romance with Palmer's Glen Eyrie people. The Bells gave frantic Christmas parties, flowery Easter parties, gay anniversary parties, huge summer lawn parties. Guests were never introduced—they just circulated. Confusion at the lawn parties was increased by the presence of the children's ponies, donkeys, and pet skunks and Willie's pack of hounds.[2]

The Bells, in short, were characters and Little London watched their ways with endless pleasure during the 1870s and 1880s. When the first horse-drawn cars reached Manitou, Bell showed his loyalty to Queen Victoria by always waiting for them on the left, as in London—and protesting bitterly to the mayor if the horse refused to recognize his wrong-side signal. Mrs. Bell played the piano quite well, but she thought she played even better because she had been kissed as a child in Berlin by Giacomo Meyerbeer, the great composer. She was as High Church as her fond husband. In the 1880s after phones arrived, she phoned her children if in Denver on Sunday to hear their prayers over the new invention. She loved correct English and when she observed that some of Little London's ladies were a bit ungrammatical, helped Mrs. Solly and others to found the

Tuesday Club so that the ladies could improve. The Tuesday
Club meets still, its fundamental purpose unchanged.

Mrs. Bell's endearing absent-mindness achieved the stature of
a Pikes Peak legend. Friends whom she asked to dine always
checked an hour in advance to make sure that she had remembered her own invitation. There were many stories on the
theme. A friend and his wife were waiting for the Bells to
arrive at their house for dinner at 6:30 p.m. At that exact moment, Mrs. Bell phoned. "Ida," she said, "don't come to dinner
before seven, please. Willie's playing chess." One evening a
friend rode in her carriage on her way to dine with the Bells at
Briarhurst. She passed them in *their* carriage going the other
way. "Having dinner in Manitou, I see!" Mrs. Bell called cheer-
ily. "How nice! Willie and I are dining at the Town and Gown."
Frances Wolcott has supplied two of the stories:

> One night at a meeting-house a dance was given in honor
> of the wedding anniversary of Dr. and Mrs. Bell. . . .As
> dawn was breaking, Mrs. Bell and I walked to the dressing-
> room to put on our wraps. She said she felt uncommonly
> tired. As she lifted her white satin wedding dress to put
> on her overshoes, lo, she had never removed them! I ought
> not to have been astonished, as a few days previous she
> had come to pay me an early morning call. Putting her
> baby in the middle of the bed to run on an errand, she had
> not returned until nightfall, when, remembering the child,
> she ran lightly up the steps waving her hands and exclaim-
> ing: "Can a mother forget her child!"[3]

For the most part, Palmer trusted his mercurial business associate, but he felt a trifle uneasy about what was going on at
Bell's 10,000-acre ranch up Ute Pass in which Palmer held a half
interest. The General saw nothing wrong with the cattle operation under "Chumley" Thornton and he endured the lumbering
project with its mill and eight-mile railroad to the Ute Pass
road near present Woodland Park. What worried him was Bell's
Manitou Park Hotel which opened in 1873, and continued with

a new manager almost every summer until it burned down in 1886.

During a week end in the summer of '77, the General found Bell's hostelry to be a square, comfortable, two-story log building with porch on three sides and Mansard roof. Near it were several cottages and twenty tents. The setting was a spacious valley—Canon Kingsley's "strath." Inside the hotel was a commons room brightened by red cotton curtains, a fireplace, and halves of barrels for seats. The chambermaid was a busty yellow-haired Denver lass in a jaunty sailor hat with blue ribbons. She spent much time squirting Persian Insect Powder over everything to subdue the bedbugs, and much more time, Palmer observed, flirting with the freckled, sandy-haired porter, Dawson, who, Palmer knew, had a perfectly serviceable wife in Colorado City.

The Manitou Park did not have a saloon exactly, or a bartender. But Palmer found in the kitchen a barrel of Scotch whiskey attended by an English dandy in a spotless white flannel suit with pearl buttons and stylish blue monogram. On his head, he wore a blue monkey-cap and he held a volume of poetry by Baudelaire. He told Palmer that Dr. Bell's lessee gave him his room free in exchange for his services which consisted of selling whiskey by the cup as a convenience to the guests. The whiskey, he explained, was of the best, in spite of its red color caused by nails which had fallen into the barrel by accident.[4]

THOUGH DR. BELL was the social leader of Little London through the Seventies and Eighties, its most conspicuous member was the prodigious Francis Cholmondeley Thornton. "Chumley's" parents were Irish and he was born in London in 1850. He would have been (he said) the Marquis of Cholmondeley if his elder brother hadn't been blessed with a male heir just before he died. The new-born Marquis was cared for by a pretty Swiss nurse named Elizabeth Fanny Fabre and "Chumley" fell noisily in love with her. His relatives were enraged but, instead of firing Elizabeth Fanny, they shipped "Chumley" off to Colorado Springs in '73 to work for Dr. Bell.

"Chumley" looked every inch a marquis even if he weren't quite one—"a lean, straight-backed man with a bristling, sandy mustache and prominent, piercing eyes." His brogue was so thick that people had trouble understanding him, which was sad because he loved to talk, usually at the top of his lungs—and anywhere, on the horse car, in church, at concerts.[5] He did well ranching for Bell at Manitou Park, accumulating enough money by '78 to send for his own true love Elizabeth Fanny and to marry her. By this time, his standing in the community had risen so high that most residents addressed him respectfully as "Lord Thornton."

Thornton succeeded at ranching, but other Britishers who responded to Dr. Bell's glowing advertisements in the mid-Seventies were less fortunate. They started sheep and cattle spreads along the Monument north of the Springs and westward up Ute Pass to South Park, and learned what Nathan Meeker could have told them in 1869—the Pikes Peak region is not prime ranch country, at least not for amateurs. It was astonishing how many of them there were—Welshmen like the Gwillim brothers and Thomas Davies on the Monument; Septimus Ackerman, son of a Strand bookseller, on West Creek; Pat Murphy, the ex-steamer steward, and Gordon Scot and the Donnellys in the Black Forest; the Prings at Husted and the Finlaysons at Palmer Lake and the Mathesons near Limon and Hollis Mills and the Chalmers family and Joel Rogers in South Park. Among them was a twenty-two-year-old Scot from Edinburgh, J. Arthur Connell, who arrived north of town with a trainload of Galloway cattle which he had nursed across the Atlantic from County Kircudbright, with a stop-over in Iowa. Connell believed that his black hornless wonders would revolutionize the American beef industry. However, the last of his Galloways expired during the herd's second Black Forest winter, and the bereaved owner gave up the struggle, to become a prosperous member of the real estate and poker fraternity on Pikes Peak Avenue.

Ranch life was too rugged for practicing all the social niceties of British custom, but these were rigidly observed in Little London. Dr. and Mrs. Bell set a high standard and so did

William Blackmore's sister, Madame Margaret Hamp, who lived at first on Bijou Street. She was called "Madame" to distinguish her from the wives of her sons in the Springs. One son, Sidford Hamp, had been with Dr. Hayden on the Yellowstone expedition of 1872. Another stickler for the niceties was Captain J. Lees Armit, former member of the Queen Victoria Guards who came to the United States with Lord Kitchener under whom he had served. The handsome Armit set up as a mining attorney after winning a high place for himself as the man who brought the whiskey sour to Pikes Peak.

Still another was the cricket expert, William Iles, who, after resigning as manager of the liquor-less Colorado Springs Hotel, opened a hotel of his own in Manitou where a gentleman could have a drink if he wanted one. Of course there were those who laughed at tradition. Tom Walsh, a genial Irishman, didn't care a hoot for tea and crumpets at five or any other time though in the end he got closer to the fountainhead of British custom than anyone else. Tom was a Springs carpenter briefly and later became the multimillionaire owner of the Camp Bird Gold Mine in Western Colorado. Near the turn of the century he was presented at the Court of Edward the Seventh. His daughter, Evalyn Walsh McLean, was often seen in Washington, D. C., wearing quite a large diamond called the Hope.

There is something infectious about ancient custom, and that is why many Americans in Little London during the 1870s and 1880s behaved as British as the British who composed only twenty per cent of the population at most. The old story went that two Americans stood chatting in the sunshine on Tejon Street. One carried an umbrella and had his trousers rolled up. The other asked, "Why are you walking around with an umbrella and your trousers that way?" The reply: "Just got a cable from London. It's raining cats and dogs there." Everyone enjoyed Boxing Day after Christmas and more Union Jacks flew from Little London flagpoles on Queen Victoria's birthday than American flags on the Fourth of July. Policemen were "bobbies" instead of "cops," and they wore helmets and brass buttons. English dog-carts with bob-tailed ponies in tandem

made pretty plumes of dust as they moved along Pikes Peak
Avenue. Children had to be raised by pink-cheeked governesses
from England or Scotland or Ireland. Since some of these young
ladies were very pretty they often married into the best Nevada
Avenue families and became the grandmothers of today's elite.[6]

Captain Charles Stearns who, like Palmer's John Blair, hailed
from Perthshire, Scotland, opened a tailor shop affiliated with
London's Bond Street. Stearns dictated male fashion at Pikes
Peak, forcing men to accept trousers with cuffs and to wear
knickerbockers and plaid stockings at cricket and rugby. White
tie and tails were obligatory at even informal dinners, where
the menus usually included roast beef or mutton or broilers in
paper pantalettes and some times jack rabbit made to simulate
English hare—all prepared according to recipes in *Warne's
English Cook Book*. Of course the fox hunting set rode to
hounds on the plains east of town in full red-coated panoply
with Tanzt breeches, Busvine habits, and expensive English
saddles. Members gathered often at the home of Madame
Hamp who owned one of the finest packs. After the hunt—some
times drag, some times coyote—there was a hunt breakfast with
bowls of steaming claret and Glenlivet on the table and an air of
heartiest good fellowship as everyone sang "Do Ye Ken John
Peel," eyes brimming with happy tears. And a final "God Save
the Queen," to be sure.

Much of the architecture of Little London was derived from
England—Bell's Briarhurst, General Palmer's Glen Eyrie, Irving
Howbert's gracious stone pile on Weber Street near the New
England cottage of Will and Helen Hunt Jackson. The old
Grace Church built on Pikes Peak Avenue near Weber in '73 (a
restaurant now) was English Gothic and so was the main
Colorado College building (today's Cutler Hall). Homes by the
dozens on North Weber Street and elsewhere featured Tudor-
inspired towers and cupolas, and gables with exposed beams.
However, there were important American modifications inside
them. Little Londoners accepted central heating, with pleasure
preferring the risk of illness "by hot air" (in Canon Kingsley's

phrase) to such cold as Frances Wolcott endured at Queen Palmer's Ightham Mote, Tonbridge.

The Little London period of Colorado Springs history began when William Blackmore arrived in '71 to pick a name for Manitou. It began to fade after 1890 when Dr. and Mrs. William A. Bell returned more and more often to England with their children, their ponies, donkeys, pet skunks, hounds, and such pink-cheeked governesses as had resisted matrimony at Pikes Peak. But its aura remains, like the odor of moth balls, musty but unmistakable and, furthermore, imperishable. Other influences have followed, and persist; strong tinges of Philadelphia, Boston, New York, Chicago; fugitive traces of Peking, Dallas, and Honolulu. But Colorado Springs began as Little London and it will never really get over it.

CHAPTER SIX

The Tourists, Bless 'em

GENERAL PALMER conjured up Colorado Springs for Queen Mellen with only a vague idea of what he had in mind when he wrote "there will be a famous resort here soon." He knew next to nothing about the resort business. His trip to England and France at the age of nineteen was a working, not a pleasure, tour. The years after were so full of fighting and railroading that he had no chance to gad about seeing what people did in their spare time, if any.

He knew only from hearsay what the word "resort" meant. Tourism, the business of going somewhere purely for the fun of it, was a brand new concept in the United States which began at the close of the Civil War. Before that, Newport and Atlantic City and Saratoga and the Springs of Virginia served a miniscule few. In '69, Helen Hunt's favorite White Mountain resort, Bethlehem, New Hampshire, was a frail infant. Florida was swamps and alligators. Southern California slept in the sun. Though palace cars rolled between Omaha and San Francisco (and would roll soon between Kansas City and Denver), the travelers who got off them had to stay in "white-washed Mugby Junctions"—Henry M. Stanley's phrase. The fact is that, as Palmer passed Pikes Peak in 1869 wrapped in blankets on top of his coach, he dreamed of a kind of place for the pleasant employment of leisure which had not proved itself even in the East.[1]

The spa aspect was easy to plan. After all, people had been drinking and bathing in stinky waters under expensive auspices for centuries. Dr. Anderson got the soda springs off to a splendid start in '72. And he was abetted by the suave super-expert,

Dr. Solly, who had bathed in style all over the Continent. Even before Solly's prose poem on mineral waters hit the stands, the form of address of strangers meeting in Manitou at the Navajo or the Iron Ute was "And what is your complaint, Sir?"

But invalids alone couldn't bring prosperity to Palmer's resort and to his railroad which carried them to El Paso County. What did the region have to attract healthy visitors? A great blue ocean to gaze at? No. Pounding surf beaches for bathing? No. Artists' colony? No. Concerts? For all of Rose Kingsley, no. Well, what then? Pikes Peak, of course! And what would this new kind of traveler make of a monumental bump like that?

The General could only try to imagine. He had no precedent (except the hardy hiker Miss Kingsley, who was scarcely typical) to tell him how people would take to 400 square miles of rugged crags and gulches lying as high as 14,147 feet above sea level. But he was sure that what moved him would move others. Human beings thrilled to noble height because it was like their own aspirations. The great isolated uplift above Fountain Colony was unique for its variety of scene and for a drainage structure which gave it long, cool, deep, canyons, clear rushing streams, and superb virgin stands of spruce, yellow pine, and Douglas fir. The mountain was the home of exotic birds—big black-headed Steller jays, western tanagers in bright red, yellow and black, ptarmigan, black-and-white nutcrackers, and huge dour ravens. Its 8,000 feet of vertical rise duplicated the entire range of plant life from Mexico to the Arctic. There was creamy yucca in the Garden of the Gods and little red elephant in the higher parks and blue fringed gentian around Lake Moraine and rose crown in the alpine meadows.

Palmer had intended to promote his Pikes Peak wonderland and to educate tenderfoot visitors in the art of roughing it, but he had neither the time nor the opportunity. From the start, the tenderfeet took over the task of educating themselves, pouring out of Palmer's little trains in cumulative volume and scurrying into the foothills like ants toward a honeycomb. The creeks and canyons provided narrow corridors which led them to the shady secret interior of the mountain. South of Ute Pass, these

creeks in order were Ruxton, Sutherland, Bear, and the two
Cheyennes, North and South, which split away the jutting bulk
of Cheyenne Mountain from Pikes Peak proper. North of Ute
Pass were Williams Canyon, Black Canyon and then, just beyond the Garden of the Gods and Glen Eyrie, Queen's Canyon
cut by Camp Creek. The mouths of all these canyons reached
the plain within a stretch of ten miles from Queen's Canyon on
the north to Cheyenne Mountain on the south.

Before the 1870s ended, the eastern and southern slopes of
benign old Pikes Peak teemed with male and female explorers,
from June to October, from dawn to dark, and often all night
long—tourists mostly young but some far from it, tourists on
foot, tourists on burros and horses and mules, tourists at last in
carriages, in the usual progression of taming the wilderness.
They were happy and excited tenderfeet, thrilled by the novelty
of their experience, for terrain like this and tourists like themselves were utterly new on the American scene. Each Nebraska
farmer and Iowa school marm and Ohio soda jerk felt touched
with the glamour of the pioneer. And each had a right to feel
proud, for he or she was the prototype of those countless millions
who compose Rocky Mountain tourism today—from Glacier and
Yellowstone National Parks south to Mesa Verde and Bandelier.

The speed of their conquest of Pikes Peak derived in part
from knowledge which they received from Colorado's argonauts.
After 1858, tens of thousands of miners had combed the Colorado Rockies for gold, learning how to build safe trails, where to
stand in electrical storms, what to do about mountain fever and
other tricks of high-altitude travel. These latter-day mountain
men created vast numbers of mountain-trained animals for
transport and they taught eastern manufacturers to make
saddles and vehicles suited to mountain conditions. General
Palmer's agent, Governor Hunt, was such an expert mountain
man, and so was E. S. Nettleton, the Fountain Colony ditch-
builder. Nettleton gave direction continuously in the development of the first trail up Pikes Peak—the seventeen-mile Bear
Creek Trail. The trail was begun in 1871 and improved in '73
so that the Signal Station sergeants could pack their supplies

on burros past the Lake Moraine sea serpent to their small stone house with its hungry pack rats on top.[2]

The trail started at Colorado City and tenderfeet from Colorado Springs and from Manitou commenced at once to follow it. By the summer of 1874, forty or fifty of them daily were hiking at least seven miles to a pretty forest glade at 9,000 feet called Jones Park (J. C. Jones filed on the glade that year and built a log shack in which travelers could have a bite to eat or get out of the hail). Some climbed four miles farther to Lake Moraine where Dr. H. Huntington built his Lake House with bunks for forty hikers who might want to rest overnight before tackling the last six miles above timberline to the summit.

In his *Pikes Peak Atlas*, Robert Ormes tells how a party of twenty pioneer tourists from Manitou House walked up the Bear Creek trail to Jones' shack and the Lake House, and how the hikers met a pair of hunters with grouse hanging from their belts, a pair of miners with ore samples and picks and shovels, and a party of yodelers with guides returning from the peak. Next morning, the group pushed on to the top where they discussed year-around living conditions and storms over a cup of coffee with Signal Corpsman Brown. Back at Lake House in the evening, the hikers found another crowd of pioneers dancing the German to the music of the Colorado Springs Orchestra.

Manitou tenderfeet soon discovered that for them it was seven or eight miles shorter to the summit if they clambered up the steep slope of Mount Manitou and then joined the Bear Creek Trail near Lake Moraine.[3] But the initial climb was unpopular and the route was abandoned entirely by 1882 when a shelf for a toll road was blasted by Alfred Cree for three miles straight up Ruxton Creek out of the granite walls of Engelmann Canyon. This steep shelf road, for burros only, cut the length of the summit trip to ten miles. Its attraction was increased when a Pennsylvanian named Tom Palsgrove built a comfortable log hotel in a grove of evergreens at the forks of Ruxton Creek. In 1884, the Palgrove family owned 640 acres up there. The hotel had twenty-two bedrooms, a bowling alley, a shooting gallery, and about fifty burros in good working order. Tom Palsgrove called the hotel Half Way House, which was not accurate as it stood less than a third of the way to the summit.

From Lake Moraine, a two-and-a-half mile trail was cut southwesterly over a divide to a group of bright blue ponds called Seven Lakes, which hung on the south side of the mountain at almost 11,000 feet looking as though they would drain away if somebody pulled the plug.[4] Meanwhile, George Baird began building a toll road for tie-cutters and cattlemen around the north side of Cheyenne Mountain. Others pushed this road on through Rosemont, site of the present Broadmoor Hotel Reservoir, toward Seven Lakes. Beyond Rosemont, the road climbed along East Beaver Creek and over steep ridges ("The Seven Steps") and through two delightful little valleys to reach Seven Lakes in 1878.

All told, the distance from Colorado Springs on the Cheyenne Mountain road was twenty-two miles and tourists liked it, since they could ride all the way in wagons. From Seven Lakes it was a mere five-mile hike to the top of Pikes Peak. By then a Mr. Quincy King and a Mr. Welch had put together a sort of hotel at Seven Lakes, forty-six feet wide and twenty-four feet deep which managed to contain, somehow or other, twenty rooms. Mr. King was a gifted namer of lakes, even seven lakes. The largest—the eighty-acre one by the hotel, he called "Minnetonka," or "Sparkling Water." The next nearest was "Minnehaha," which meant, obviously, "Laughing Water." Beyond Minnehaha was Lake Lenore and over a knoll was Lake Pontchartrain, so called, Mr. Quincy insisted, "from its resemblance to the lake of the same name in Louisiana." Farther away was Bear Lake (scene of a bear's suicide), Lake Carrie (honoring Mr. King's lady friend) and Lake "Larry." This Larry was sports editor of the *Colorado Springs Gazette*—and Seven Lakes editor also. One of his reports described how a cinnamon bear crossed the Cheyenne Mountain Toll Road in front of a tourist wagon. "The ladies," Larry wrote "fainted and the gentlemen got under the seats and the driver swooned. The bear was frightened most of all and at last account was seen near Canon

City, still running, all in a perspiration and his hair partly turned white."

Another Seven Lakes press agent was Helen Hunt Jackson who visited the hotel after Quincy King sold out to Mayo Smith in 1881. Mrs. Jackson was entranced by the new manager whom she called "a strange man of Mohammedan, sacred dervish tendencies who practices semi-medical, semi-religious medicine by the laying on of hands and administering the milk cure." Mrs. Jackson's Pikes Peak dervish confided to her that he was over seventy and that his wife was in her twenties, but he kept younger than springtime by galloping on his own feet down to Fountain Colony and back to Seven Lakes every second Tuesday.[5]

The pioneer tourists of Pikes Peak were quite late in stumbling upon one of its secret valleys. Crystal Park is a tidy little bowl which sits out of sight, like a bird's nest in a lilac bush, in front of and under Cameron's Cone. Prospectors began staking gold claims up the steep gulch of Sutherland Creek in the mid-Seventies. Tom Wanless, a Springs merchant, thought enough of the claims and of the crystals scattered all over to homestead Crystal Park and to build a seven-mile trail which a strong horse could negotiate. The toll in '79 was twenty-five cents per horse and before the summer ended a couple dozen tourists daily were getting up to Crystal Park, 2,000 feet above Manitou. Two years later, a group of St. Louisans bought the park's 1,400 acres from Wanless and transformed the trail into a frightful wagon road with nearly seventy-five hairpin turns in nine awful miles. A small hotel was built and cabins sprinkled in secluded spots among the spruce and purple beardtongue. From the hidden porches of the cabins there were superb views of Colorado Springs, of the bright red rocks of the Garden of the Gods, of the green edges of Manitou, and of the jagged yellow gash of Williams Canyon.

Seclusion was something which was being searched for desperately just then by a man named John George Nicolay, aged fifty, who had been struggling for ten years to finish a writing job in collaboration with an old friend, John Hay, aged forty-two.

During the Civil War, Nicolay and Hay had formed a unique team as private secretaries to Abraham Lincoln. After the President's assassination, the Century Company had paid his two secretaries a huge advance and the whole world waited breathlessly for the fruit of their labor—a ten-volume *Life of Abraham Lincoln*. They worked on it off and on through the 1870s organizing their material and writing some of the books. But they were far behind schedule, being exceedingly popular and important men who were distracted constantly by diplomats, politicians, editors, historians, and ladies of very high society.

Nicolay visited Crystal Park on horseback in '79. He went up in a wagon in '81 and the road scared him so badly that he saw the solution to his problem of finding seclusion for himself and John Hay. He rented a Crystal Park cabin for the summers of '82 and '83, certain that up there in the sky at the end of such a road he and his friend Hay would be able to finish *Lincoln* without the slightest fear of interruption. And they did finish the ten volumes in the Crystal Park cabin so that the work could begin to run serially in *Century Magazine* in 1886, with book publication in 1890. And John Hay returned to the cabin now and then and arranged at last to have General Palmer buy it for him, plus most of Crystal Park around it.[6]

IT SHOULD NOT BE THOUGHT that all pioneer tourists were mountain goats. Many explored in the muggy lowlands at no more than 6,000 feet, which meant a comfortable carriage ride of four or five miles through the 640-acre Garden of the Gods. The route ran either from Colorado Springs on Palmer's Glen Eyrie road over the mesa or from Manitou on the twisty road past Balanced Rock which John Blair built for General Palmer. The Garden remains relatively pristine still and can be a very rare sight, especially when the afternoon light has a soft touch of mist and mystery in it. Such light brings out the emerald green of the grasses and the stunning reds and whites of the uptilted sandstone slabs which once lay flat over the granite of Pikes Peak in the days long ago when all was ocean here.

The Garden of the Gods has always been hard to describe. Helen Hunt Jackson called it "a supernatural catastrophe." Much later, Julian Street called it, weakly, "a pale pink joke." Legend has it named in 1859 while Melancthon Beach, founder of Colorado City, was showing it to his friend Rufus Cable. Beach, the legend goes, was raised in Milwaukee, and as the two men surveyed the glorious scene he remarked, "Don't you think, Cable, that this would be a great place for a Milwaukee beer garden?" Cable replied indignantly, "Beer garden! Why this is fit for a Garden of the Gods!"

Since Melancthon Beach was raised in Sparta, New Jersey, the legend is dubious. When General Palmer patented Glen Eyrie, he had no interest in the Garden because it lacked water.[7] Parts of it were patented in the early 1870s but the owners did not care if tourists used it as a public park. Meanwhile, General Palmer was on terms of friendship with another railroad builder, Charles E. Perkins, vice-president of the Burlington line. Palmer kept urging Perkins to build a home in the Garden of the Gods and to bring the Burlington from Chicago to the Springs. In 1879, Perkins did buy, for $4,000, the 240 acres which surrounded the main Gateway rocks. He continued to buy parcels until he had 480 acres (total cost, $10,500). Somehow, he never built the home, and the Burlington never reached the Springs directly.

The Garden in the 1870s was a perfect place for a young man to take his best girl on a Sunday afternoon. And, some people, as Earl Pomeroy points out in his *In Search of the Golden West*, were attracted by their interest in the grotesque, visiting Pabor's sandstone "Seal Making Love to a Nun" and all the other mystic confections—"The Eagle With Pinons Spread," "The Angry Dolphin," "Elephant Attacking a Lion," and so on. Pomeroy adds that the Garden of the Gods tourist could pretend that he "saw the Old World as well. He might 'pass under the shadow of China's great wall, muse among Palmyra's shattered columns, stand face to face with the Sphinx of Egypt, gaze upon the Temples of Greece, or the Castles of England or the old Abbeys which pious monks upreared.' The exchange of Western curiosity for European antiquity had become almost literal."[8]

THE PIKES PEAK HOTELS multiplied through the 1870s—rambling friendly frame monstrosities dripping with bay windows and gingerbread. Most of them were girdled by broad shady porches where the children tumbled and slid and shrieked all day in perpetual games of hide-and-seek. Manitou had its Cliff House and the Beebee and the Manitou House. In the Springs Palmer's Colorado Springs Hotel had to compete soon with Pascoe's and with the National and the Central and the Spaulding. One hundred and forty guests were capacity for the largest hotels. Rooms in summer rented for $2 a night and up. Underneath the placid surface of hotel life flamed incessant rivalry between managements. When the Colorado Springs Hotel installed fans in its dining room "to keep the pesky flies off the tables," the Beebee put in a bowling alley which forced the Cliff House to buy a fountain and so the Spalding House countered (a bit apathetically) with ornamental brass spittoons. Managers raided each other's staffs with the result that waiters—white waiters in particular—became impossibly arrogant and had to be fired in a body at intervals and replaced by new crews rushed up from Denver.

Guests were fully occupied, what with whist and fan-tan for the ladies and billiards and poker for the men by day and progressive mixed eucre or dancing the German by night. Sometimes a wealthy guest—Mr. Orlando Metcalf, the Pittsburgh steel magnate, at the Manitou House, for instance— gave a dance for all the guests, paying for everything including stringed orchestra, cigars, and punch. Once at the Colorado Springs Hotel guests corralled a wandering Italian street harpist and viol player and held their own impromptu "hop" on the piazza. There were day-time picnics for young people in the Garden of the Gods with games like the one "Chumley" Thornton was said to have invented at Manitou Park called "a snake scramble." This game required the young ladies to scramble through the scrub oak and when they saw a rattlesnake they had to scramble back to their starting place. The last girl in had to kiss somebody.

Most popular pastime of all was watching and gossiping about the celebrities who were constantly appearing, as General Grant appeared at the Manitou House in '75 and at the Beebee in '80. In August of '75, attention at the Beebe centered on a tall, lean, shrewd-faced young man named John D. Rockefeller who was known to be in his mid-thirties though he looked younger. He wore a no-nonsense economy suit and everyone was aware that he was worth several million dollars as president of some sort of odd business in Cleveland called The Standard Oil Company. He blessed the Springs by giving a handsome Sunday School library to the Baptist Church. A month later, Mr. Jefferson Davis from Memphis, Tennessee, turned up at the same hotel with his son, Jefferson Davis, Jr. The Civil War was ten years by the board but many Northerners still growled at even the sound of the name of the President of the late Confederacy. A reception at the Colorado Springs Hotel was spoiled by an invited guest who greeted the Southern leader with "I will not shake hands with a rebel." And the *Gazette* had encouraging words for his enemies: "Mr. Davis looks sadly broken in health. Whatever slumbering fire may be enclosed in his brain, physically he appears like a man from whom little harm is feared."

And so the world's great paraded for the tourists and departed to spread the fame of General Palmer's dream resort. The merchant prince from Chicago, Marshall Field, and his sister stopped at the Beebee and gulped down Navajo waters for a week. Oscar Wilde arrived at Briarhurst in '82 as the guest of the Bells and gave a well-attended lecture on literary falsehood which the *Gazette* critic approved with the parting shaft: "But the question arises whether Mr. Oscar Wilde's truths would not be just as true if he dressed like other people." In '83, tourists were among the huge crowd which gathered to hear the Reverend Henry Ward Beecher speak on "Moral Uses of Luxury and Beauty." The crowd hoped that Beecher might mention the moral uses of his alleged love affair with Elizabeth Tilton—the great scandal of his era. But the eminent divine switched topics

and bored his audience with a windy talk on "The Reign of the
Common People."

ON THE EVENING of April 17, 1881, Dr. Solly and Will Jackson and Orlando Metcalf and Hanson Risley, General Palmer's
lawyer, and almost everyone else who was anybody held a town
meeting in Courthouse Hall. The air was full of expectant
excitement because the future of the Pikes Peak region as a
resort seemed to be at stake. Colorado Springs had grown to
4,500 people but its facilities for tourists were behind the times.
Manitou had no more room for expansion.

Two citizens could not attend the meeting because of pressing
theatre business. The pioneer Irving Howbert and his bachelor
friend from Colorado City, Ben Crowell, had struck it rich (with
Joseph F. Humphrey) in the fantastic silver boom at Leadville.
They had spent $80,000 of silver profits to build the Colorado
Springs Opera House, a copy of the Madison Square Theatre
in New York. The lovely new structure on Tejon Street with its
Venetian drop curtain, its two-hundred-and-sixty-one softly
sizzing gas jets, and its elegant decor was scheduled to open
the very next night, April 18, starring the famous Maude Grang-
er in *Camille*.[9]

Those at the town meeting knew that the ultra-modern Opera
House accentuated the inadequacy of the Colorado Springs
Hotel and other faded properties of the Colorado Springs Company. Not that anyone blamed General Palmer. In the past
decade, he had authorized at least $200,000 in improvements
for Fountain Colony and had not permitted the declaration of
a single dividend by the Colorado Springs Company. He would
have replaced the frame shack at the corner of Pikes Peak and
Cascade long ago if the complicated affairs of the Denver and
Rio Grande Railroad hadn't kept him strapped all through the
1870s.

Things were different now. The General was getting rich for
a change. He had given up pushing his railroad to Texas but he
had won from the Santa Fe Railroad the right-of-way through
the Royal Gorge of the Arkansas and his tracks ran to Leadville.

His successful $10,000,000 bond issue in '79 had given him capital to triple his trackage in Colorado—from 300 miles to 1,200 miles, over Tennessee Pass to Red Cliff, to Wet Mountain Valley, to Espanola in New Mexico, to Gunnison, and well along toward Durango and Silverton over Cumbres Pass. Although the railroad wasn't making him wealthy of itself, it boomed the value of subsidiary properties—his town sites and ranches, coal beds, steel mills, and iron plants.

Dr. Solly presided at the town meeting and told the crowd what it wanted to hear. He had been pressing a scheme on the General for months and the General had approved at last. The scheme called for building the finest resort hotel in the mountain West—$100,000 worth. The Colorado Springs Company would contribute the site—four acres at the end of Pikes Peak Avenue. Palmer would arrange a $50,000 loan and would buy $25,000 worth of stock if other residents would buy the same amount. Other citizens took up the subject after Solly. Will Jackson called it a sound proposition. Dr. Anderson said it might help to get the State Capital away from Denver. There was no opposition at all. The town meeting ended with the hotel scheme approved and most of the stock pledged.

The hotel was two years a-building. It had no name until the spring of '83, when Palmer called it The Antlers, partly because "Chumley" Thornton kept sending him deer and elk trophies from Manitou Park and the hotel seemed a good place to park them. It was a noble structure, created by Boston architects on Solly's English designs. Gray Castle Rock stone formed the exterior of the three lower floors. The top two floors were of wood. It was one hundred and one feet high. There were gables galore and turrets and towers and cozy balconies and gay awnings and porches on three sides. It cost $125,000 in the end but Palmer took up half the difference and the main bondholder, James K. Caird of Scotland, took up the rest.

On June 1, 1883, the proud residents of the Springs flocked to the hotel opening and found that the Antlers was everything Dr. Solly claimed it to be. It had a hydraulic elevator and public rooms with tons of Gothic walnut furniture upholstered in

leather. It had billiard rooms and children's play rooms and
Turkish baths. The beautiful carpets, table linen, and bed linen
had been selected at Arnold Constable and Company in New
York by Ed Giddings. It had central heating and gas lights.
There were seventy-five guest rooms with two baths (hot and
cold water) on each floor. The bridal suite had blue Turcoman
curtains, its own bath, blue Wilton carpets, and an open fireplace.

There are hotels and hotels. The rare good ones have an in-
herent personality and taste which is as accidental as personality
and taste in people. The first Antlers (1883-1898) had this
personality. It had charm and distinction and worldliness. As
is the case with all great hotels, the tourists who could afford to
stop there were inspired by its flavor to be more interesting,
more attractive, more intelligent, more tolerant and out-going
and gay than they were normally. Its fame spread, removing
from the national mind any lingering doubts about the quality
of General Palmer's Newport in the Rockies.

Forty years later, a deeply-perceptive novelist, Willa Cather,
was writing a book, A Lost Lady, about the 1880s. She sought
a device to stamp her central character with the special elegance
and relaxed morality of the period. Her solution was significant.
Her bewitching young Mrs. Forrester, "with skin the fragrant
whiteness of white lilacs," always wintered fashionably with her
aging husband at the Antlers, sipping old fashioneds on the
western terrace at sunset and dancing the evenings away.

CHAPTER SEVEN

Soaring Rails

THE ANTLERS, as it turned out, opened at the worst possible time. Colorado Springs was in the throes of a five-year doldrum, matching the State-wide lull in mining. The Springs population was static at 4,500—just too few people to support all those seven Antlers bathrooms and all that leather upholstery. Within a year, the hotel was unable to meet Mr. Caird's eight per cent interest and it went into the trusteeship of Hanson Risley, Palmer's official receiver. Dr. Solly and his friends despaired. They could not know that help was arriving in 1884—prodigious help which would invigorate the town beyond imagining. It came in the form of two remarkable men. One (a guest at the Cliff House in Manitou) was a forthright multimillionaire, Zalmon G. Simmons, from Kenosha, Wisconsin. Another was a hopeless invalid, James J. Hagerman, from Paris, France.

Hagerman was born in Canada in 1838, grew up on the St. Clair River, graduated from the University of Michigan in '61, and rose in the iron business to become head of the Milwaukee Iron Company. In 1876, the demand for Bessemer steel was outstripping the supply of suitable ore. Hagerman began working the vast Menomenee deposits of northern Michigan which made good Bessemer. In four years he amassed a very large fortune which was lucky because he had developed consumption. He moved to Europe in 1881 with his family to get well.

Like Andrew Carnegie, his business colleague, Hagerman was a small pepperish person. He weighed less than 120 pounds and seemed to feel best when angry about something. Even as an invalid he was in a constant state of diminutive uproar, railing at the alleged idiocy of his doctors and nurses and castigating the comfortless design of his cast-iron bed pan. His condition worsened in Europe and so, in October, 1884, he had himself and his wheel chair shipped to Pikes Peak where he expected to die in a few weeks, protesting the process up to his last breath. Sick as he was, he found strength, as he wrote twenty years later, to blast Colorado Springs for being "as dead as Julius Caesar" with "no business worth mentioning and little hope for the future. . . . Although I liked the climate, the town was so depressingly dead that we almost decided to try Denver..."

To his surprise, Hagerman's health started to improve. To pass the time, he began acquiring claims in the new silver camp of Aspen, Colorado, plus Western Slope coal lands and stone quarries. He erected on North Cascade Avenue a stone mansion which cost $110,000 and made General Palmer's wooden Glen Eyrie look like a gardener's cottage.[1] And he began listening to a grandiose scheme outlined by Irving Howbert to build a standard-gauge railroad from the Springs up Ute Pass, across South Park to Leadville, over the Continental Divide to Aspen and on toward Salt Lake City. The scheme had a corporate name, The Colorado Midland Railway Company, and it seemed to have derived from Willie Bell's poignant wish to connect his toy eight-mile railroad at Manitou Park to a real line. Irving Howbert, a plunger on occasion, was in it with several wealthy men including the Manitou party-giver, Orlando Metcalf, and Jerome B. Wheeler, a stylish New Yorker who owned mines in Aspen and half a department store in New York called R. H. Macy & Co.

The plotters were inspired by a heady dream of railroad conquest based on the financial weakness of the Denver and Rio Grande, and of the Union Pacific which ran the Denver and South Park Railroad in the Colorado mountains. The wily financier, Jay Gould, was causing the weakness for his own obcure purposes by stock manipulation. When Gould had forced General Palmer out of the Denver and Rio Grande in 1883, construction westward had stalled at Red Cliff just over Tennessee Pass twenty-five miles beyond Leadville. In 1884, the railroad went bankrupt and Helen Hunt Jackson's husband, Will Jackson, became receiver and then president.

In its course westward, the Denver and Rio Grande rambled like a cow path. From Denver it ran south through Colorado Springs to Pueblo—one hundred and twenty miles. Then it ran west up the Arkansas to Salida—ninety-six miles. Then it ran north still up the Arkansas to Leadville—fifty-six miles. The track distance from Colorado Springs to Leadville was one hundred and ninety-six miles. From Leadville to Aspen would be one hundred and eight miles more—if Receiver Jackson could get permission from his English bondholders to build on from Red Cliff.

Irving Howbert explained to Hagerman that, by contrast, the Colorado Midland would run from the Springs up Ute Pass to Leadville in one hundred and thirty miles, and to Aspen in two hundred and four—one hundred miles shorter than the narrow-gauge Denver and Rio Grande tracks to the same place. Furthermore, the standard-gauge Midland would be able to handle freight without trans-shipment. Plainly such a line would cash in on the wealth of Aspen. It would also win the only direct route west between the Union Pacific in Wyoming and the Santa Fe in New Mexico.

James J. Hagerman accepted the Colorado Midland presidency in June, 1885. He was inspired by the same dream of conquest that excited Howbert, and, besides, he needed only one look at the somber Quaker countenance of Will Jackson to know that a scrap was coming; and Hagerman loved a scrap above all else. The corporate battle between the Midland on one side and the Denver and Rio Grande and Union Pacific on the other ran through most of 1886. Hagerman blared and blandished by turns as he sought capital for the Midland and low rates from the Denver and Rio Grande for carrying construction crews and materials. Jackson faced the miniature tempest with stolid determination to earn for the Denver and Rio Grande as much Midland-derived freight revenues as he could while giving the upstart road just enough rope to hang itself.

As the fight progressed, business titans like Lord William Lidderdale, Governor of the Bank of England, became commonplace in the Springs—either meeting Hagerman at the Antlers if he was

up or at his Cascade Avenue mansion if he was sick in bed. Hagerman's picturesque ire—coattail flaring like the tail of a bantam
rooster—amused the town and his vituperative comments brightened life along Pikes Peak Avenue. No rival escaped his frequent
invitation to "migrate to a climate too hot for comfort"—not even
the Honorable Charles Francis Adams, head of the Union Pacific
and son and grandson of two American Presidents. To Hagerman, Adams was "sophomoric" and Will Jackson "talked like a
boy" and "their minds conformed to the narrow gauge of their
railroads." He wrote later, "If God Almighty had given them a
quit-claim deed to Colorado, I had not heard of it and would not
recognize it." Ex-Governor John Evans, the Denver patriarch,
was "an old fox" and Hagerman mentioned "the oily way" of Mr.
Kimball, the Union Pacific traffic manager, who was identified
as "that venerable but mild-mannered and astute twister of
people's necks. Like Ah Sin's, his smile was childlike and bland."
Hagerman's wrath spread to his own partners. "Jerome Wheeler,"
he complained, "talks too much. Howbert is as timid as a boy.
Humphrey says nothing but 'yes,'" As for Orlando Metcalf, "he
shirks every question and wants to spend half his time in Manitou Park."

It seems unlikely that any one, Hagerman included, took his
invective to heart or worried seriously about the peculiar business
ethics which were a feature of the battle. After all, Hagerman
and Jackson and their associates were like men playing poker
with cards not of their choosing, for Jay Gould supplied the deck
and it was stacked. In any case, Hagerman did raise $7,000,000
to build the Midland to Aspen and on to his coal deposits on the
Colorado River (the Grand River then). Jackson was able to
extend the Denver and Rio Grande to present Rifle, also on the
Grand, with a branch which reached Aspen on November 7,
1887. That date was six weeks before the Midland got there
from Colorado Springs but the moral victory was lost in the widespread astonishment that Hagerman's road made Aspen at all.

The Colorado Midland was an epic effort to defy the laws of
gravity. It began on the banks of Fountain Creek near its junction with the Monument, ran to Manitou, curled around Iron

Springs and shelved its way frighteningly up Ute Pass on a maximum four per cent grade to Divide. It entered the spacious grass lands of South Park through Eleven Mile Canyon of the South Platte River after passing the honorary depots of Metcalf, Lidderdale, and Howbert. It crossed the blue Mosquito Range on the easy grades of Trout Creek Pass and ran up the bewitching Arkansas in cozy companionship with its blood enemy, the Denver and Rio Grande.

The Rocky Mountains achieve a climax of height, ruggedness, and complexity near Leadville and it was precisely there that the Midland plunged west up the Lake Fork of the Arkansas heading straight at a high gap in the Continental Divide on the north slope of Mount Massive. The gap became Hagerman Pass. Just beneath it, at an above-timberline altitude of 11,528 feet, the 2,200 foot Hagerman Tunnel was driven through to the Western Slope at Loch Ivanhoe. The tunnel workers created a shanty town called Douglass City which roared the alpine nights away during the summer of 1887 and earned its proud reputation as the drunkenest, gamblingest, most lecherous spot in the West, winding up in a blaze of alcoholic glory when the Midland powder house blew up. From Loch Ivanhoe, the railroad and its long snow sheds descended the lovely Frying Pan River past Hagerman's "peachblow" stone quarries to present Basalt where an eighteen-mile branch doubled back up the Roaring Fork to Aspen. The main line met the Colorado River at Glenwood Springs and stopped at present New Castle twelve miles down the river.

The project as a whole was at once foolhardy and wonderful. It was conceived in Colorado Springs and directed by Springs residents against implacable opposition. During the two years of its construction, many Midland workers lost their lives and the rest of the crew seemed to stick with the dangerous job for the pure satisfaction of completing the most technically difficult and scenically overpowering two hundred and forty miles of full-sized railroad on earth. And the crowning wonder was that the Midland was slammed through by the sheer driving will of a

small and very sick man who had come to Pikes Peak expecting
to die.[2]

WHILE IRVING HOWBERT and his friends were cooking up
the Midland scheme in the early 1880s, other rash dreamers were
plotting to lay rails to the top of Pikes Peak. Professor James
Hutchinson Kerr, a Yale graduate who taught science at Colorado
College when the spirit moved him, organized the Pikes Peak
Tramway Company. He was a man of means and financed sur-
veys in 1883 for the construction of a thirty-mile railroad which
promised to please everybody. It was to start at Manitou, run
up to Crystal Park by way of Iron Mountain, continue climbing
around the north side of Cameron's Cone to Lake House and
Lake Moraine, cross over to serve Seven Lakes Hotel, and then
snake along past Sackett Mountain to the top. The maximum
grade would be six per cent and the cars would be hauled by
special twenty-ton locomotives. In '84, Kerr spent $40,000 build-
ing grade on the Crystal Park section[3] and sold bonds to Manitou
investors including Major John Hulburt. The canny professor
distrusted Springs banks because of local hard times and con-
sequently placed his bond money in a New York bank which
went bankrupt the very next day. The fiasco ruined Kerr financially and ended the career of the Pikes Peak Tramway Company.

Major Hulburt continued to believe in the Pikes Peak railroad
idea in spite of his losses and promoted it to any one who would
listen including Edward E. Nichols, Sr., owner of the Cliff House.
Nichols' hands were full keeping his waiters in order, but he
introduced Hulburt to his favorite guest, the Kenosha tycoon,
Zalmon Gilbert Simmons, who heard the major's piece and promised to think about it. This Simmons, aged fifty-six, was a striking character—a short, powerful, warm, impulsive fellow with a
flowing white beard and invariable silk hat and cutaway. He had
made money faster than he could bale it in all kinds of ways—
fanning mills, telegraph companies, gambling in stocks. He was
a founder of the Unitarian Church in Wisconsin. Although not
particularly pious, he despised profanity. Once when he said

"Damn" over the telephone, he apologized quickly into the mouthpiece, "Oh, excuse *me*, but there's a burglar in the room!"

In '84, Simmons had come to Nichols' hotel to rest after a period of work transforming his cheese box factory at Kenosha into a revoluntionary plant for the production of better beds. It happened that he had developed a sturdy wooden insulator for telegraph lines and had supplied his product to Western Union for its new line up Alfred Cree's Ruxton Creek toll road and on to the U. S. Signal Station on the Pikes Peak summit. He decided to see how his insulators were standing the weather above timberline. Nichols arranged for him to make the trip to the top on a popular Cliff House mule named Balaam. Between the mule's razor back and the rugged topography, the short-legged Simmons and his cutaway and silk hat had a very rough time of it. When he and Balaam returned to civilization two days later, he discovered that he was too stiff and too sore to sit down or even to lie down and he spent some days of painful recovery in a Cliff House Turkish Bath. When he felt a little better, he summoned Major Hulburt and announced that he was ready to spend a million dollars so that he and the rest of the soft-bottomed human race could ride up Pikes Peak "in the greatest comfort that technology could provide, specifically a Cog Railroad."[4]

During the next few years, Simmons' absorption in the cog project equalled his passion for building better beds. He realized that he was creating a sensational tourist attraction which deserved the support of all railroads bringing tourists to Colorado Springs. To promote, therefore, the interest of rail officials in his Manitou and Pikes Peak Cog Railway, he assigned minor blocks of stock to David Moffat, president of the Denver and Rio Grande after '87; Jerome B. Wheeler of the Midland; and R. R. Cable, head of the Rock Island Railroad which reached Colorado Springs from Chicago in '88. To clinch Cable's devotion, Simmons put in his twenty-three-year-old son, Hiram S. Cable, as superintendent of the cog road. Hiram applied himself with special fervor, having met, wooed and married along the way one of Jerome Wheeler's charming daughters.

The line was patterned after Sylvester Marsh's Mount Washington Cog Railway in New Hampshire, a three-mile road which had begun running to the top of New England's highest hill in 1869. The Pikes Peak version consisted of a teapot of an engine with an absurd perky tilt to it pushing a glassed-in car up a maximum grade of twenty-five percent. Engine and car ran on light rails but the crux of the matter was a very heavy double toothed rail in the center by which the cog wheel in the engine, turning, engaged the cog rail and inched the engine and car up the track. The pushed car was not coupled to the engine, since the line was all upgrade. The car had its own engaged cog wheel so that it could be stopped almost instantly by its brakeman if the engine got loose from the rack somehow and slid off down the grade by itself.

Grading started in August of 1889 after Simmons got permits for a right of way and station acreage on top from the Secretary of the Interior. By Christmas some 800 workmen, mostly Italian, and one hundred mules had advanced grading well along but at tragic cost. Three men were blown up by dynamite, one crushed by a boulder, and two had fatal heart attacks in the exhausting high altitude. Water officials in Colorado Springs threatened damage suits every few days because rocks kept falling into and muddying Ruxton Creek which carried the city's water supply. In the spring of 1890, the impatient bed improver hurried back west from Kenosha to help his Italians personally to shovel snow off the route. His first engine, named "John Hulburt," arrived from the Baldwin Works in May and had its test run in July—a bitter disappointment since it ran out of steam and died a few hundred yards up the grade. But Simmons' engineer, Thomas F. Richardson, solved the problem by enlarging the boiler and building three water tanks along the line.

Meanwhile, gaily-painted cars with narrow seats upholstered in gold plush—"Leadville" and "Colorado Springs" and "Denver" —appeared from the Johnson Car Works in Pennsylvania. Starting August 16, 1890, "John Hulburt" pushed one of them daily as far as Tom Palsgrove's Half Way House. In mid-October, the second engine, "T. F. Richardson," struggled up to the top in an after-season trial. Simmons bought a third engine, "Pikes Peak," that year. The engines had to be faster and more powerful than Mount Washington's famed engine, Old Peppersass, because the Pikes Peak run was nine miles instead of Washington's three and Simmons insisted on making the longer distance in about the same elapsed time of an hour and a half. The vertical climb was 7,539 feet as compared with 4,684 feet to the top of Washington.

The day of triumph for the promoters and for most Coloradans who had followed events with intense interest, was on June 30, 1891, when the "John Hulburt" set off jerkily up the awesome grade pushing the "Denver" loaded with city officials and reporters. Departure time from the pretty stone-and-wood depot in Manitou was 8:23 a.m. "John Hulburt" belched smoke and its whistle shrilled and there were alarming bangings and squeakings as the new cogs ground in the rack. But Simmons (in silk hat and cutaway) and Hulburt and E. E. Nichols and the rest sang and made jokes and acted as though they had been riding trains to the top of the world all their lives. They quieted down as the "Denver" moved higher on its tiny shelf far above the flashing flow of Ruxton Creek. Some of them closed their eyes and prayed in the close canyon short of Butterworth Flat. (Butterworth was a greenhorn engineer who had got that far on his first run and then had walked to town, having decided that piloting Pikes Peak cog trains was not for him).

At Artists' Glen the officials admired the peephole view over Manitou backward through the slot in the canyon. In Ruxton Park beyond Hell Gate they gasped at the stunning complexity and lonely grandeur of the Pikes Peak country south and east of the summit as the train began its six-mile sweep to the top. Eastward they saw Lake Moraine huddled under Cameron's Cone and the south-curving ridges of Mount Garfield and Arthur and Almagre, with Seven Lakes peeping from behind. They picked up a hitch-hiker at Mountain View and then the train ground above the forest into the eerie, tense rock world above timberline where fat marmots and conies squealed at them and

the wind screamed. Rounding the dramatic curve of Windy
Point, they suddenly saw below them the plain stretching off in
the gray-green infinity toward Kansas.

They also saw a rock slide on the track ahead, two miles short
of the top, and workers frantically trying to clear it. Nothing
could get through until late afternoon and it was cold up there.
Simmons apologized to his guests and ordered the train back to
Manitou. And so the second train—carrying sixty-one members of
the Highland Christian Church Choir from Denver—had the thrill
of being the first to reach the summit—at 5:25 that same afternoon. The choir members felt exhilarated though queasy, and not
too interested in the view. After half an hour they were glad
to return to the "Denver" and start the creaking descent.

It was after dark when they arrived, sooty and tired, back at
the Manitou depot. The trip had pleased them hugely, but what
pleased them most was a surprise Zalmon G. Simmons had arranged. The surprise was a free steaming-hot full-course late
supper for the whole Highland Christian Church Choir at the
Iron Springs Hotel.[5]

THE RESTLESS ENERGY of Hagerman and Simmons set forces
in motion which changed General Palmer's resort in a few years
from a quiet village for the exercise of genteel indolence to a
bustling—though still genteel—city, hell-bent on progress with a
Board of Trade and everything. Bank deposits increased by five
times. The population soared from 4,500 in 1884 to 11,200 in
1890. Marcellin De Coursey received $15,000 in the latter year
for a Tejon Street lot which had cost him $500. Five railroads
pounded along Monument Creek. Electric street cars replaced
horse cars. The summer congestion at Manitou ended as new
resorts appeared in Ute Pass along the Midland line—Cascade,
Green Mountain Falls, Woodland Park, Ute Park (later Chipeta),
with hotels like the Ramona, the Cascade, and the Woodland
Park. In town, the old Colorado Springs Hotel, once the pride
of the Rockies, succumbed and was buried without mourners.

The Antlers was enlarged and new inns built—the Alamo and Alta Vista and Elk.

So much building! Since Will Jackson headed a bank (the El Paso County), Hagerman had to head one, too, the First National, and his first presidential act was to put up a new bank building, using his "peachblow" sandstone from the Frying Pan, of course, and plate glass from France. The same "peachblow" went into General Palmer's Out West Building on Pikes Peak Avenue and into parts of the Hagerman Building at Tejon and Kiowa. John Hundley, a young livery stable owner, built a seventeen-mile carriage road up Pikes Peak and opened it for tourists in '89. Four of his four-mule surreys met the Midland train at Cascade every morning at 8:10 a.m. and got to the summit and down again easily before dark (at $2.50 per person). While Hundley was building the carriage road, his rival, G. R. Fowler of El Paso Livery, stole a march on him with a $12,000 brick barn at 9 North Cascade—"the finest west of New York City." It featured a white pine lounge where ladies could freshen up and "remove the stains of travel." It had stalls for one hundred and nine horses and an up-to-the-minute ventilating system so that sweating horses wouldn't catch cold. John Hundley wasn't taking this lying down. Before 1889 ended, he completed, at 21 North Cascade, a *$20,000* brick barn with hydraulic elevator and a *carpeted* panelled lounge with mirrors, settees, and hair brushes for the ladies. Hundley's ventilating system (*for one hundred and twenty horses*) had been inspected by Francis B. Hill, secretary of the Humane Society who certified that no sweating Hundley horse would suffer from drafts.

The new spirit of enterprise was dramatized when a local sign man put a billboard on top of Pikes Peak to herald the arrival of Adam Forepaugh's Circus. A nautical expert launched on Prospect Lake the steamer "Chicago"—almost as big as the lake itself—for excursionists. Industry bloomed in Colorado City with the huge Midland shops and Jerome B.. Wheeler's Glass Works which made beautiful light green pickle jars and whiskey flasks. Wheeler[6] formed also the Manitou Mineral Water Company and soon the miraculous seltzers which Dr. Solly had praised in '75 were available in the Waldorf Hotel in New York.

All this progress was not accepted with universal joy. Some residents condemned the increase in smoke and burglaries, the scarcity of house maids, and the destruction of Rainbow Falls in Ute Pass caused by blasting for the Midland. More serious was the state of things in Colorado City—Old Town—which had come to life with a vengeance. Bob Ford, Jesse James' killer, lived there much of the time and could be seen dealing faro in Laura Bell's dive or in the Crystal Palace dance hall. Colorado City's constable seemed to encourage beer mug battles between laudanum addicts like Minnie Davenport and Hazy Maizie. Law enforcement just didn't exist. When the notorious prostitute Blanche Barton was hauled into court for running a house of ill fame, the judge released her on the grounds that she couldn't run a "house" because she lived in a tent.

But most people didn't waste time talking about Colorado City.

There were happier subjects. They discussed how old Chauncey Depew and his crony Cornelius Vanderbilt looked walking arm-in-arm along Pikes Peak Avenue. And General Sherman rubber-necking through Manitou Grand Caverns just like anybody else! And President Harrison when he came to town—so glum and small and pasty-faced! It was lucky that no one was hurt at his reception on the Antlers piazza when a part of it dropped eight feet.[7]

And what about this Count Pourtales and the "City" which he was building called Broadmoor?

CHAPTER EIGHT

A Sunny Place for Shady People

FROM THE START, Colorado Springs tended to orient itself westward and northward toward Pikes Peak and the Garden of the Gods and Glen Eyrie, and eastward toward Austin's Bluffs. Only a few residents noticed the buffalo shape and strange romantic texture of Cheyenne Mountain four miles to the southwest. Fewer still went up that way past Bachelors' Flats and through the mesa fields above Cheyenne Creek except tourists and peculiar people like Helen Hunt Jackson.

But Irving Howbert used to go up there in the late 1860s to bind wheat on Burton C. Myers' seven-hundred-and-twenty-acre farm near the site of present Cheyenne Mountain Country Club.[1] Myers had fashioned a pond at the springs of Spring Creek and had planted a few cottonwoods. Besides wheat, Burt grew broom corn which he used to make brooms for sale in his Colorado City store. In 1875, he sold the Spring Creek farm to a Connecticut visitor, Frederick W. Pitkin, who was to become governor of Colorado four years later.

In 1881, the Burt Myers property, plus eight hundred and eighty more acres around it, was purchased by an amiable young Philadelphian, William J. Willcox, son of a wealthy paper and cement manufacturer. Willcox was, for a wonder, neither a Quaker nor a member of Palmer's Fifteenth Pennsylvania, even if he was a Philadelphian. He had come to Colorado Springs in 1880 to recover from tuberculosis, bringing his wife and children. With much vim and no experience, he had transformed Myers' place into what he called the Broadmoor Dairy Farm.[2] He had bought twenty Jersey and Swiss cows, dug ditches, put up an ice house and spring house and enclosed everything in twelve miles of barbed-wire fence. He had built three cottages for the milkers and a handsome stone sixteen-room house for his family, complete with central heating, hot and cold water, and hardwood floors.

His health became better and by June of 1885 he wanted to return to Philadelphia to engage in some less baffling business. Most of his Broadmoor cows had some grave disease, seemed reluctant to settle on schedule, and gave less than a gallon of milk each day. His butter was of low quality. His total production was not even paying the wages of his four employees. As a result, he asked Marcellin De Coursey to find a buyer for the Broadmoor Dairy Farm. De Coursey had no luck but in December, Dr. S. E. Solly turned up at the big stone house and presented to Willcox a smiling, well-built man in a green Bavarian hunting jacket whose name was Count James M. Pourtales.

This doughty European had a complicated background. The Pourtales clan were Huguenots originally who had cleared out of France at the time of the Revocation of the Edict of Nantes in 1685 and had settled in the principality of Neuchatel, which fell under the rule of Frederick I, the first king of Prussia. Jacques-Louis de Pourtales piled up one of the great fortunes of Europe during the eighteenth century and used it to strengthen the hold on Neuchatel of the next Prussian king, Frederick the Great, who elevated him to the nobility and dubbed his sons counts. In 1814, the people of Neuchatel succumbed to democratic sentiment and joined the Swiss Confederation and it was clear that Prussia would lose its principality in time. The several Pourtales counts in Neuchatel were strong Prussian royalists now—diplomats, financiers, fighting opponents of Swiss Republicanism—but they saw the end coming and began transferring their assets to more congenial environments—to France and Alsace and Bohemia and Prussian Silesia (now in Poland). One of them, James Pourtales' grandfather, bought in Silesia an elaborate old monastery estate, Glumbowitz, comprising nine villages, and other lands near it. James Pourtales' father married Princess Putbus

of the Baltic principality, Rugen. The Pourtales title of count
lapsed and became a polite form of address after 1857 when
Frederick William IV of Prussia renounced sovereignty over
Neuchatel.³

James Pourtales inherited Glumbowitz from his father and was
increasingly disturbed in the early 1880s as bad harvests, floods,
irrigation restrictions, and low interest rates reduced the value of
all his German investments. He was an admirable young Teuton,
very sturdy, large-sized, thorough, decisive, stubborn, a trifle
pompous and yet warm and kind. Nothing could affect his loyalty
toward his friends. He loved the outdoors and excelled as a
hunter. Politically, he was more of a Bismarck imperialist than
a Wilhelm royalist, and he admired the way the English and
Dutch and even French had gone to the United States to make
fortunes for the enrichment of themselves and their own country.
He believed Germans should follow suit, building up a fleet in
the meantime and winning colonies for the Fatherland.

In the spring of 1884, and again the next spring, Count Pourtales scoured the United States for sound mortgages paying eight
per cent or better to restore his ailing Glumbowitz. On both
trips he stopped at Colorado Springs, though his business there
had nothing to do with mortgages. Pourtales was a bachelor just
turned thirty and susceptible to any pretty woman, let alone such
a lovely, slim, intoxicating creature as his French cousin, Countess
Berthe de Pourtales, an unhappy divorcée who lived with her
two small daughters in a cottage on Pikes Peak Avenue. Berthe's
father, Count Louis Francis de Pourtales (of the old Neuchatel
Pourtales tribe) had emigrated from France to the United States
in 1847 to join the Geodetic Survey in Washington. Later, in
1867, he moved to Boston to help the Swiss-American naturalist,
Agassiz, at Harvard College. Berthe was born in Washington.
As a teen-ager in Cambridge, she wrecked the calm of undergraduate life just by propelling her slender figure through Harvard Yard. She married Sebastian Schlesinger, a wealthy Boston
music patron, but the marriage failed and Berthe came West seeking health and new scenes. She chose Colorado Springs since her

brother Louis Otto, Queen Palmer's adoring "Mute Seraph,"
lived nearby on his Florissant ranch.

When James Pourtales met Willie Willcox in December of '85,
he was already in love with Berthe and longed for an excuse to
stay near her. He felt affection for Willcox on sight and believed
him to be an honest, if inept, business man. Willie had changed
his mind about selling his Broadmoor land and wanted a working
dairy partner instead. Pourtales had dairy troubles enough at
Glumbowitz but he had an eye for scenic as well as feminine
pulchritude and he could not keep his eyes off Cheyenne Mountain and the empty mesa stretching eastward from it for two
miles or so to the Canon City road. Furthermore, the sad condition of the Broadmoor Dairy Farm was a challenge which was
hard for a Prussian agriculturist to resist. Though Pourtales was
a great admirer of American energy and progressiveness, he was
somewhat irritated by American brashness and appalled by the
chaotic waste and corruption which seemed to go with American
democracy. The task of making a success of the Broadmoor
Dairy Farm was a chance to show these cocksure people what
wonders a disciplined German intelligence could perform, helped
by the latest scientific advances of the Kaiser's orderly empire.

THUS JAMES POURTALES embarked, in all innocence and
with the best of intentions, on what he thought was a short-term
venture, requiring not more than $25,000—a small diversion which
would use his talents pleasantly while he improved his bad
English and waited for Berthe to say yes. But the diversion
didn't turn out that way. Instead, when the Count became the
dominant partner in Willcox's Broadmoor Dairy Farm, he en-
meshed himself in a nightmarish labyrinth of endless crises which
would absorb his whole disciplined, scientific intelligence for
seven desperate years and dissipate most of his resources down
to Glumbowitz and the last of his nine Silesian villages.

First, Pourtales bought two cows in Denver, installed them in
the barn behind his rented house in the Springs, and, during
January and February of 1886, made a thorough study of the

problems which they presented—their consumption of carbohy-
drates, their water and sex needs, their health, freight rates for
their alfalfa, and so on. While his beloved Berthe sat watching
on a stool in her Worth Père red cloak and gray fur collar, the
Count practiced churning, weighed out feed, and timed with a
stop watch how long it took his Negro hand to milk a pail full.
Later, for personal comfort and social prestige, he bought a lot
between the homes of Dr. Solly and Dr. B. P. Anderson on the
west side of Cascade Avenue at Kiowa Street and built a $20,000
house on it. He sold the worst of Willcox's twenty cows, acquired
eighty new ones, ordered a centrifugal churn, planted alfalfa, and
began irrigation to water it. Then, in September, 1886, with
Broadmoor in promising shape, he put Willie Willcox in charge
and left the Springs, intending to spend a year rejuvenating
Glumbowitz.

Six months later, he hurried back to Pikes Peak. Willie was
in trouble. The Broadmoor company was bankrupt. The eighty
new cows had contracted contagious abortion. A rash of dairy
farms had popped up, driving the price of a quart of milk from
eight cents to seven. Vicious competitors were dumping oil in
Broadmoor milk cans. The centrifugal churn had cracked. Nobody would buy Broadmoor "Gilt Edge" butter. The alfalfa was
dying from lack of water.

The unjust catastrophe enraged Pourtales like a fat custard
pie thrown in his face and brought out the full force of his immensely combative spirit. While Willcox watched in fear and
bewilderment, the Count went furiously to work to create a better
dairy farm. He increased its size to 2,400 acres. He acquired important Cheyenne Creek water rights, planted more alfalfa,
bought 2,000 sheep to consume extra feed, and built new barns.
He set up a model cheese factory and imported a cheese genius
from Philadelphia's famous Darlington Dairy. He hired the advisory service of the world-renowned German chemist, Professor
Emil Wolff, who cabled feeding instructions from Berlin each
month. He sold all eighty sick cows and bought two hundred
fine new ones. Instead of cocktailing at tea time with Berthe,

he toured private barns in the Springs hunting exceptional high
altitude milkers. If he saw a cow giving more than twenty quarts
of milk a day, he would pay $100 for her. Such quality cows de-
served quality service. He found in the East five imported Swiss
bulls, though he winced at their names which honored William
Tell, the mythical anti-Pourtales hero of Swiss Republicanism.
One bull, William Tell, Jr., cost him the awful price of $1,000.
Other bulls were named Thaddeus Tell, Prince Tell and Duke
Tell (or "Do Tell!" as old Ben Crowell referred to him). He in-
stalled a Dutch foreman and Swiss and Dutch hands. In order
to keep tab on things, he moved into Willcox's stone house at
Broadmoor and moved Willie and his family into his place on
North Cascade Avenue.

Finally, as El Paso County land values shot up with the build-
ing of Hagerman's Colorado Midland, Pourtales formed a small
real estate firm—the Cheyenne Lake, Land and Improvement
Company—to which he contributed two hundred and forty acres
of dairy farm land and $9,000 cash. Willcox put in $3,000. An
El Paso County judge and Baptist Sunday School teacher, Ernest
A. Colburn, gave eighty acres—the core of the development (the
Lake Avenue frontage today). Pourtales hadn't cared much for
Colburn, but he needed those eighty acres which the judge con-
trolled as trustee for three minor children who owned them.
Colburn would not permit the tract to be sold except to himself,
with the further condition that Pourtales make him a partner.[4]
In the spring of 1889, Pourtales spent most of the real estate
firm's capital building Cheyenne Lake, planting two thousand
trees, and marking out radiating streets with a plow. He was
glad to secure as general manager of the separate Boardmoor
Dairy Farm a highly-regarded Scotsman and man-about-town,
Duncan Chisholm. This left Willie Willcox free to concentrate on
bookkeeping. And so Pourtales departed for Glumbowitz (with
a happy pause in New York to marry Berthe de Pourtales), feeling that he had conquered Broadmoor, though he had $180,000
tied up at Pikes Peak instead of the maximum $25,000 which he
planned to invest in 1885.

His honeymoon with Berthe was brief. Duncan Chisholm's reports were more dismal than Willcox's had been in '87. During the very dry summer, the City of Colorado Springs had begun stealing Pourtales' Cheyenne Creek water. Cheyenne Lake had disappeared and his two thousands trees had died. Cheap oleomargarine was being used in Colorado to make cheese and was ruining the Broadmoor pure cheese market. Willcox had discovered pressing business which required his presence in Philadelphia indefinitely. Broadmoor lots were not moving because there had been a rash of fatal accidents at the unguarded Nevada Avenue railroad crossing and prospective buyers of lots were afraid of the buggy ride out from town.

In the fall of '89, Pourtales returned to Broadmoor and rushed into the breach once more. After two months of incessant toil, he forced Colorado Springs to leave his water alone. He paid $20,000 for a pledge by the new electric street car company which was replacing the horse-drawn Tejon Street line to extend its tracks to Cheyenne Canyon through Broadmoor.[5] The street car company arranged a safe Nevada Avenue underpass. And then, in the winter of 1890, the Count reached a momentous decision. El Paso County population and land values were still rising so rapidly that he decided to combine the Cheyenne Lake, Land and Improvement Company and the Broadmoor Dairy Farm into one huge 2,400-acre development, the Broadmoor Land and Investment Company. He drew up an elaborate plat for "Broadmoor City" which started around Cheyenne Lake and ran eastward along the main thoroughfare, Lake Avenue, which was bisected by numbered streets. From Lake Circle, avenues such as Hazel, Maple, Beech, and Walnut radiated and were tied together by Broadmoor Avenue on the south, Berthe Circle on the east, and Mesa Avenue on the north. He projected his own power plant and water system. He planned initial lot sales covering six hundred acres at from $1,500 to $2,000 an acre which should result eventually in large revenues for his utilities. And, as his ace in the hole, he proposed to build a beautiful palace of refined pleasure, the Broadmoor Casino, in the grand European manner, the likes of which had never been seen in North America. The Casino would draw the attention of residents away from real estate projects in the North End and would greatly enhance the charms of Broadmoor City as a place to live.

In the spring of 1890 on his way back to Glumbowitz, the Count stopped at the London and New York Investment Company in New York, a Scotch-English syndicate, and contracted to borrow—with all of Broadmoor as security—$250,000, payable to him at any time up to December 1, 1890. This brought his total Pikes Peak ante up to $450,000, from $25,000. When his plans were made public, a *Gazette* reporter described Broadmoor City as "A sunny place for shady people" and the phrase stuck for a while.

WHILE POURTALES was in Europe, Duncan Chisholm nearly unloaded the entire Broadmoor Land and Investment Company on the Chicago palace car inventor, George Pullman, for $350,000, which would have brought the Count a net profit of $120,000 for his four years of struggle. But at the crucial moment—in mid-November, 1890—the great English banking house of Baring Brothers failed. Pullman lost interest, claiming that Colorado Springs and its impoverished English colony faced hard times. Pourtales went ahead with his $250,000 loan from the London and New York Investment Company and by Christmas of 1890 was back at Pikes Peak toiling day and night on Broadmoor City.

A central problem was Cheyenne Lake. The idea of giving waterless Coloradans a real lake to look at, and even to row a boat on, had seemed superb in 1888 when he had spent $9,000 on an earth dam twenty feet high and one hundred and ten feet thick. The ten-acre lake, filled with Cheyenne Creek water conveyed through a ditch, was an enchanting sight framed against the mountain. But when Pourtales rose one morning to savor it, the lake had leaked away through prairie dog holes. With infinite patience, Princess Putbus' dogged son and his crew plugged three hundred holes with clay and refilled the bathtub. It drained again. They plugged one hundred more holes. Still the lake drained. Then Pourtales pastured eight hundred sheep for two months on the bed, counting on the tramping and messy habits of the sheep to close the leaks. No luck. After more drainings and fillings, the exasperated Count coated the whole ten acres with liquid clay. And so Cheyenne Lake held water at last—at a total cost of $30,000.[6]

And how did the Pikes Peak public respond to Pourtales' heroic effort to give it a unique aqueous facility?

Condemnation was universal. Prospective buyers of lots told the Count that he was preparing Broadmoor for another Johnstown Flood. In that Pennsylvania catastrophe of May, 1889, three thousand people had drowned because a dam—just like this one—had burst. Pourtales explained over and over that, even if his dam did burst, Cheyenne Lake held hardly enough water to lay the dust on the flat thirsty mesa below it. Nobody believed him until, in an inspired moment, he began building his Broadmoor Casino right on top of the dam—indisputable proof of its stability.

And still more trouble. As construction commenced in mid-February of '91, Pourtales collapsed with tuberculosis. For eight weeks he had to supervise all the work from bed—first at the dairy farm and later in the Casino's annex. Willcox was in New York hiring a Casino staff. Chisholm was busy with the dairy farm. Somehow, the sick Count got ten thousand new trees planted along Lake Avenue and elsewhere during April. An eight-acre elliptical park took shape in front of the dam. The $50,000 Casino itself went up rapidly, designed by a Philadelphian, Lindley Johnson, who had helped create Winter Harbor, Maine. It was an imposing white birthday cake affair two stories high which spread along and concealed the Cheyenne Lake dam for two hundred and fifty feet. Graceful open verandas girdled it and the four pillars of its stately front portal rose to the gabled roof. Inside was the usual European arrangement of elegant dining and ball rooms, paneled bar, game and billiard rooms, reading room, and ladies' salon.

The furniture arrived on schedule and an early June opening

seemed certain. Pourtales located in San Francisco Rosner's Hungarian Band, one of the best in the land, which agreed to reach Broadmoor on June 1. From New York, Willcox reported jubilantly that he had engaged Mâitre d'Hôtel W. A. Kelly, late of the Lotus Club which had made such a fuss over Canon Kingsley in '74. Willie added that the French chef would be the renowned Emile Hertzog, formerly of Delmonico's. Pourtales began to feel strong again, and even optimistic.

He should have known better. The French chef came and wouldn't so much as boil an egg except on his own imported *fourneau de cuisine*, the delivery of which was delayed. Mâitre d'Hôtel Kelly turned out to be temperamental and imperious, demanding costly changes so that the Casino could run like the Lotus Club. When the *fourneau de cuisine* arrived, the Casino chimney to which it was attached would not draw. Pourtales had to tear out one whole side of the building to redesign the chimney. As a result, he had to postpone the grand opening until July 1,1891, his thirty-eighth birthday.

The members of Rosner's Band, of course, turned up punctually on June 1 to start drawing their salary of $375 a week. There were ten—Hungarians, Austrians, Germans. Pourtales had bought gorgeous Hussar costumes for them—blue and gold coats, cream-colored trousers, patent leather shoes, and military caps. Five had American wives along and it seemed that each of the ten musicians and each of the five wives had to have his or her own special kind of diet. Pourtales housed them in the Casino annex and hired an extra chef to prepare their assorted meals. Then a morale problem arose. The musicians said that they were going stale for lack of an audience while waiting for the Casino to open. Pourtales was able to arrange one free concert in Colorado Springs. During the rest of June, he and Berthe dressed in evening clothes each night and served as an adoring audience of two at the concerts of the resplendent Hussar-garbed Rosner's Band.

There were no more immediate problems. The grand opening itself was a glorious, a joyous, a complete success. And all through

July of '91 the people of Colorado Springs displayed genuine pride in every part of the Casino, its décor, its dance music, its fine food and wines, its flashing fountain. They supported it well and Pourtales began to feel that Broadmoor had been worth all the misery it had caused him even if it had come close to killing him literally. His cup of happiness ran over on July 11, 1891, when the town leaders, led by Thomas C. Parrish and Will Jackson, gave a banquet honoring William Willcox and himself.[7]

THE JULY PHASE, unfortunately, was a flash in the pan. Because of the Baring bank failure, nobody wanted to risk capital on Broadmoor lots. The Casino's August inventory showed that liquor worth $3,000 was missing. The help, Pourtales discovered, had drunk the liquor during wild parties at the Casino after the midnight closing. Much silverware had been stolen or tossed out with the garbage—some of it reappearing in the Broadmoor Dairy Farm pig pen. Mâitre d'Hôtel Kelly had a habit of currying favor with pretty women clients by giving them expensive Casino spoons as souvenirs. Pourtales fired Kelly and his fancy New York crew and lost trade by hiring more honest if less glamorous help from Denver. The Casino was $25,000 in debt on October 1 when the worn-out Count closed the place for the winter and took a month's rest cure with Berthe on a hunting trip in the Marvine Lake country of Western Colorado.

The summer of 1892 was no better. Pourtales was shattered at the start by the death of his good friend and partner, Willie Willcox, in a riding accident. Duncan Chisholm gave notice that he was quitting the dairy farm in the fall. The Reverend L. L. Taylor of the Presbyterian Church in the Springs attacked the Casino violently in the *Gazette* letter column for giving Sunday concerts at which wine was served. A weak rebuttal, signed "Justice," argued that the Casino's customers were mainly lungers who needed a drink now and then to make them more cheerful, and anyhow "Christ himself changed water into wine and countenanced its use in moderation." Pourtales met the reverend's attack by calling his Sunday concerts "sacred music" and slipping in gay waltzes when the coast seemed clear. He raised needed cash by selling for $18,000 his Cascade Avenue house to Sam Altman, the first miner to strike pay dirt at Cripple Creek's new gold camp just over Pikes Peak.

The Count raised $35,000 more—for a proposed hotel directly across Cheyenne Lake from the Casino—from some young Springs friends of his who agreed to be his partners in place of Willie Willcox and to handle the Casino's promotion. The results of their eager enterprise were wonderful. A lady balloonist parachuted into the lake by mistake and almost drowned. A tight-rope artist set off firecrackers from his high perch and nearly set fire to the Casino. The row boat races which they organized on Saturdays ended in fights. The indoor parties for the kiddies brought no revenue while wrecking the Casino furniture. The hotel did not get built. And, when Pourtales checked the unpaid Casino bar bills of his partners, they almost equalled their total investment— or so the Count said.[8]

The end came a year later, the end of Pourtales' anguished pioneer role in the Broadmoor Land and Investment Company, in Broadmoor City, in the noble Casino. The Count was at Glumbowitz when the mints of India stopped coining silver and the Panic of '93 began. He left Berthe in Silesia and arrived at Pikes Peak as Colorado's main industry, silver mining, ceased. The Casino was open, but besieged by creditors. Money could not be borrowed, even at fifteen per cent interest. On August, 17, 1893, the Count admitted defeat and sadly turned over everything to a receiver, the International Trust Company, representing the London and New York Investment Company.

THE CASINO LIMPED along thereafter without Pourtales under various lessees. A small hotel was added west of it just before the Casino burned to the ground on the early morning of July 19, 1897. Within a year, the London and New York Investment Company replaced Pourtales' noble white birthday cake of a building with a less inspired copy. By then several large homes were rising among the trees which the Count had had planted from his sick bed in 1891. And so, modestly, "A sunny place for shady people" caught on, though the Count's flaming dream would not really come true until Spencer Penrose took hold of Broadmoor many years later.[9]

And what of Pourtales? Something about the United States, its illogical, compulsive, disorderly, unpredictable, luxuriant, thrilling growth, can be surmised from this tale of a cautious Teuton of Gallic ancestry by way of Switzerland who invested an initial $25,000 in Burt Myers' wheat field under Cheyenne Mountain. The Count had meant to be shrewd and conservative, but his disciplined German intelligence was unable to resist the charms, the excitement, the infinite, beckoning horizon, the magic of America. He wound up wildly gambling, and losing at Pikes Peak, almost everything he owned. Though he suffered terribly in the process it is a question whether he regretted the vivid experience.

At all events, he made out well finally. In 1896, he invested his last bit of money in an Arizona gold mine, the Common Wealth, and won back all he had lost in Broadmoor and much more.[10] He died at peace in 1908, aged fifty-five, in his restored Glumbowitz. You can think of this pleasant, courageous man, if you like, and of his slender, distinguished Countess as you stroll along Pourtales Road and Berthe Circle in today's elegant Broadmoor under Cheyenne Mountain.

CHAPTER NINE

The General's Second Chance

FAILURE OF BARING BROTHERS, the English banking house, in 1890 and the Panic of '93 hurt General William Jackson Palmer temporarily almost as much as it hurt Count Pourtales. As in 1876, when he had closed Glen Eyrie briefly to live on Cascade Avenue, Palmer cut his personal expenses, and these included the separate establishment in England of his wife Queen and their daughters, Elsie, Dorothy, and Marjory. Since the late 1880s, Palmer had maintained for Queen a large place, Loselev Park, Guildford, Surrey, where she had entertained literary and artistic people like the widowed novelist, George Meredith, and the young American painter, John Singer Sargent. In the summer of '93, while Pourtales was giving up Broadmoor, Palmer was in England arranging for Queen and the girls to give up Loseley Park. In its place, they took a cottage at Frant, Sussex.

Through the 1880s, the General had lived the strange, hectic, lonely life of an international promoter. He had moved restlessly and constantly from his New York office at 11 Broadway to his London office in Suffolk Lane to conferences in Rotterdam and Paris and Mexico City and Denver and on back to 11 Broadway. His business concerned his railroads in Utah and Mexico and his property at Wagon Wheel Gap on the Upper Rio Grande and his Trinchera Ranch (part of the old Sangre de Cristo Grant) in San Luis Valley and his Colorado town sites and his steel and iron mills and mineral lands. He did not have the gold-seeker's wild gambling spirit and took no interest in the mining of precious metals except as freight revenue for his railroads. When the

continued page 131

114

James J. Hagerman was a small, pepperish dynamo weighing less than 120 pounds and seeming to feel best when angry about something. *Colorado College Library.*

While convalescing, Hagerman amused himself by building a stone mansion at 624 North Cascade Avenue which made Glen Eyrie look like a cottage. Later, the gables were faced with stone. *Pioneer Museum.*

Hagerman's Colorado Midland was an epic effort to defy the laws of gravity. It got over Hagerman Pass of the Continental Divide through a tunnel at 11,528 feet to reach Aspen from Colorado Springs in late December, 1887. *Pioneer Museum, W. H. Jackson photo.*

The Midland brought summer resorts to Ute Pass, including Green Mountain Falls, the big hotel of which shows beyond the train. *Pioneer Museum.*

After a painful ride to the top of Pikes Peak on the Cliff House mule, Balaam, Zalmon A. Simmons, the bed tycoon, vowed to build a Cog Railroad up there to alleviate the suffering of the soft-bottomed human race. The painting of Balaam was by Charles Craig. *Pioneer Museum, Grant G. Simmons, Jr.*

Jerome B. Wheeler gave this Italian clock to the Town of Manitou in 1889. *Colorado College Library.*

The first cog engine, "John Hulburt," had its test run in July, 1890, but it ran out of steam a few hundred yards up the canyon of Ruxton Creek. *Pioneer Museum.*

The Cog Train put an end to the old Bear Creek Trail as a popular route to the summit and few tourists hiked to Lake Moraine any more when it could be seen from a train window. *Stewart's.*

Some of the passengers looked a trifle bilious from the altitude
on the summit. The handsome man with the posy of asters was
William Jennings Bryan. *Pioneer Museum.*

The Cog Road put men to devising ways of sliding down the rails at speeds of sixty miles an hour and more. Several were killed sliding down the rails. *Pioneer Museum.*

Count James Pourtales was an admirable young Teuton, who came to Colorado Springs looking for twelve-per-cent mortgages and a girl named Berthe. *Pioneer Museum.*

Berthe de Pourtales had grown up in Cambridge where she had wrecked the calm of undergraduate life just by walking across Harvard Yard. *Pioneer Museum.*

Pourtales built a fine home at the west end of Kiowa Street. The connected cottages at **right** were known as "Dead Man's Row" because so many invalids, including Helen Hunt, had lived in them. *Pioneer Museum.*

The structure at right in the three-building photo was the Broadmoor Casino annex for Rosner's Band. The building to the left of the Casino was the old Broadmoor Hotel which was built just before the original Casino burned to the ground in July, 1897. The present Broadmoor Hotel exactly occupies the site of the Casino. The old Broadmoor Hotel was still standing in 1961, called the Colonial Club and used for employees and overflow guests of the Broadmoor. *Broadmoor Hotel and Denver Public Library Western Collection, H. S. Poley photo.*

A smaller Broadmoor Casino replaced the original during June of 1898. When the present Broadmoor Hotel was built, this second Casino was moved a bit south and serves today as the Boardmoor Golf Club. *Denver Public Library Western Collection, H. S. Poley photo.*

In his later years, General Palmer was still small, neat and wiry. He rode horseback with the same loose rein and long stirrup of his cavalry days when he had chased Jeff Davis through the mutilated South. *Fred and Jo Mazzulla Collection, Elsie Queen Nicholson.*

Palmer's monuments were Colorado Springs and the Denver and Rio Grande Railroad. One of his trains was photographed moving down from La Veta Pass and Trinchera Ranch on a roadbed which forms today's beautiful highway U. S. 160. *Denver Public Library Western Collection, W. H. Jackson photo.*

For many years after the shattering of his dream of a domestic idyll at Glen Eyrie, Palmer was an unhappy man. Better times began in 1894, when his eldest daughter, Elsie, joined him on his private car, Nomad, for a ramble all over the United States. This portrait of Elsie, at eighteen, was painted in England in 1890 by Queen Palmer's friend, John Singer Sargent, who titled it "Young Lady in White." The Palmers owned it until 1925 when it was purchased by Col. Charles Clifton and presented by him to the Albright Art Gallery, Buffalo, New York. The painting is reproduced through the kindness of the Albright Art Gallery. A sketch for the painting is in the Fogg Museum of Art, Harvard University. *Colorado Springs Fine Arts Center.*

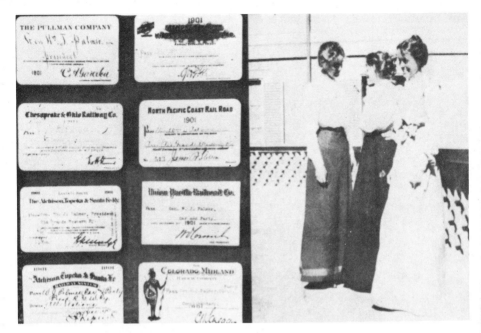

What did it cost to travel by private car all over the United States? Nothing, if you were General Palmer and had a pack of railroad passes like these. *Pioneer Museum.*

Three English - reared daughters— Marjory, Elsie, Dorothy! Sons Palmer could have handled, but girls were something else. *Elsie Queen Nicholson.*

The first Antlers Hotel burned in 1898, but Palmer had the new Antlers completed by August 1, 1901, when this crowd gathered around Pike's statue to watch the arrival of Vice President Theodore Roosevelt. *Photo through kindness of W. G. Hutchinson.*

126

Glen Eyrie remains still the most distinguished estate in the
Rockies. In the scene photo, Major Domo appears left with the
stables beyond and then the castle. Queen's Canyon cuts it way
up the center and in the middle of it can be seen the stack
which carried off smoke from the castle and released it far from
the smoke-hating nose of the General. *Pioneer Museum.*

Charles Elliott Perkins, Palmer's railroad friend, who had owned the Garden of the Gods since 1879, died in 1907, and his six children gave it to Colorado Springs two years later. The formal ceremony of acceptance occurred on October 3, 1912. *Fred and Jo Mazzulla Collection.*

When Palmer finally bowed to "progress" and bought a car, he acquired a huge White Steamer, painted a peculiar white with bright red seats. In the talented hands of Chauffeur Glen Eyrie Martin, shown here, it hauled the adventurous invalid about everywhere he wanted to go. *Pioneer Museum.*

In August, 1907, the Fifteenth Pennsylvania Volunteer Cavalry, the godfather of Colorado Springs, came to town for a week at the expense of its commander. In the reunion at Glen Eyrie, Palmer and his daughters sat in the center with the Great Dane, Yorick, posed conspicuously in front, as usual. *Colorado College Library.*

During the reunion, Mrs. Joel A. Hayes, daughter of Jefferson Davis, complained about an 1865 Palmer handbill offering $360,000 for Jeff Davis' capture which the Civil War veterans posted in the Antlers. This photograph of Mrs. Hayes and her grandchildren was taken at the same time in her Cascade Avenue home—the Hayes House at Colorado College today. The painting above her was of Mrs. Jefferson Davis. The grandchildren were Marka, Gerald and Robine (the baby) Webb, offspring of Gerald B. and Varina Webb. *Gerald B. Webb Collection.*

Marjory Palmer was photographed in her wedding dress when she married her true love, Dr. Henry C. Watt, at Glen Eyrie in the summer of 1909. *Pioneer Museum.*

Nothing in Springs history was as incredible as the discovery of the richest gold field in the world on the southwest slopes of Pikes Peak. Within a few years, the bleak Cripple Creek cow pasture became one of the state's largest cities. *Colorado College Library.*

Pikes Peak residents never did get used to Winfield Scott Stratton, the $3-a-day carpenter who became the most important mining man alive. *Fred and Jo Mazzulla Collection.*

Instead of buying a palace in Spain with some of his millions, Stratton moved into an old frame house on Weber Street across from Will Jackson's place. *Denver Public Library Western Collection.*

Stratton spent $2,000,000 to give the Springs the best trolley system that money could buy. He created Stratton Park at one end of his line, a paradise where plain people could picnic in his gardens and listen to the Colorado Midland Band. *Pioneer Museum.*

Nellie V. Walker's statue of Stratton was placed in Stratton Park in 1906. It stands at Stratton Home today. *Stewart's.*

Cripple Creek gold excitement began in '91, he sent Leroy Case up there to investigate but he took no action.

Once in a great while, the General appeared publicly in Colorado Springs when courtesy required him, as Town Founder, to greet some important visitors like President Benjamin Harrison. His few friends were mainly male and mainly business associates. One of them was Colonel D. C. Dodge, his railroad aide from the earliest days. Another was the New York banker and philanthropist, George Foster Peabody, who handled the financing of his Utah and Mexico railroad ventures. Quite often, the General managed to stop for a rest—incognito—at Glen Eyrie, but normally he lived in a glorified suitcase, his private railroad car. This car after 1890 was the Nomad—standard gauge, since by then even the Denver and Rio Grande had to broad-gauge its main line. The Nomad was a comfortable custom car, made to Palmer's own meticulous order, with an interior of dark green woodwork, a richly upholstered observation room, three bedrooms, bath, kitchen, and bunkroom for the crew of cook, valet, and porter. The cook was always George Motley, the same colored man who had prepared the General's salt pork on his surveying trips in the late Sixties. In the summer of '94, the Nomad had a novel experience—the presence of a female passenger. There was perfume in the air, powder spilled about, dainty bits of intimate clothing hanging in the bath to dry. The lady was Miss Elsie Palmer, slender, dark-haired, very British, very pretty. Elsie had come of age recently and thought it was jolly well time to have a vacation away from England and her mother and to see something of her famous father's world. Father and daughter had a long grand tour in the Nomad—a leisurely ramble from New York through the Southern states to Florida and west to Texas and north to Colorado Springs and Denver and on to Oregon and California and back East again so that Elsie could sail to England in September.

On the day after Christmas, 1894, the General received at Glen Eyrie the news that changed his bachelor life utterly. Elsie cabled that Queen could not live more than a few hours

(she died on December 28th, aged forty-four). Palmer hurried
to New York and caught a steamer for London on January 2,
1895. After Queen's funeral, he spent most of that winter in
England closing up her affairs, finding governesses and other
women employees to educate and take care of Dorothy, aged
fourteen, and Marjory, thirteen, and preparing to return to
Colorado with his family of three daughters who had never really
been his family. Three English-reared daughters! Sons he could
have handled. Glen Eyrie would have made a perfect peace-time
barracks where he could have run things with the same military
firmness and wisdom which had marked his command of the
Fifteenth Pennsylvania Volunteer Cavalry. But girls were something else. What little he knew about women he had learned
from Queen and that education had ended long ago.

His new life at Glen Eyrie began in the summer of '95. For
many months he stumbled along blindly while Elsie, a wise, forthright young lady, managed his big household. She looked after her
younger sisters and saw to it that they learned their lessons from
their governesses in the school room which the general set up
for them near the red stone spire, Major Domo, in the Glen. And
Elsie had other problems. Palmer's years of loneliness had increased his natural shyness and reserve. Unconsciously he had
raised a wall between himself and his townspeople. Perhaps he
did this to conceal how badly he had been hurt by Queen's in-
ability to be a vital part of his old romantic dream for Colorado
Springs.

His power in Pikes Peak affairs was almost absolute since he
controlled the Colorado Springs Company which still owned half
of the land of the city and its environs. Because of the power, he
had become an awesome figure to most residents—a man to be
approached with fear, or, better yet, not to be approached at all.
The situation made Glen Eyrie a dull place at first for Dorothy
and Marjory, two friendly, warm, teen-age girls with strong
British accents. But somehow Elsie broke down the barrier bit
by bit, with the sympathetic help of Palmer's old friends like the
Sollys and Edmond Van Diests and McAllisters and their chil-

dren. After a year or so, Glen Eyrie and Queen's Canyon rang
again with the racket of young people enjoying themselves as had
not been the case since the Mellens' stay there in the early 1870s.

And Palmer himself began to be more at ease with more and
more local people. He gave more and larger lawn and dinner
parties and found pleasure in showing off his possessions from all
over the world, his superb cuisine, his fine wine cellar, his stable
of horses and pack of tumbling, clumsy jovial Great Danes. And
at some point he seemed suddenly to realize that Elsie and
Dorothy and Marjory were filling the place in his Pikes Peak
community that he had wanted Queen to fill when he had written
her in 1870 just before their marriage: "You will have plenty to do
will you not, in looking after all these colonies? I wonder which
will be busiest, you or I?" The General of the 1890s hadn't
changed. He remained a dual personality—a creative business
leader and a human being needing to love and be loved. Through
the girls, he found himself getting this second chance to live
fully, to combine in a single framework his love of his family and
his pride and renewed interest in the town which he had made.

The strength of his renewed interest had a severe test on the
early afternoon of October 1, 1898, when fire broke out at the
Denver and Rio Grande freight station during a fifty-mile gale.
It spread with terrifying speed to nearby lumber yards and on to
the Antlers Hotel when a freight car of giant powder exploded,
filling the sky with blowing embers which threatened even Colorado College a mile to the north. A college football game was
called in the third quarter and the teams rushed down to help as
Mayor Irvine warned that the whole town was in great danger of
being destroyed. Hundreds of volunteers struggled to keep the
south end of the Antlers damp. Denver and Pueblo firemen arrived by special express trains. The town was saved but not the
hotel. It burned to the ground soon after the wind subsided that
evening.[1]

General Palmer learned of the fire and of his $250,000 loss by
cable while he was in London on business. He did not hesitate,
but announced at once that work would begin as soon as possible

on a larger and more costly hotel. And the new two-hundred-
room Antlers did open on July 1, 1901, a handsome fireproof
structure in which modernity and a great many bathrooms replaced the subtle charm and distinction of the old building.

The wealth of the General had grown steadily since 1883 in
spite of his troubles after the Baring failure. And, a week before
the new Antlers opened, he had a windfall. George Jay Gould,
son of the financier who had forced him out of the Denver and
Rio Grande, paid him $6,000,000 for his three hundred and forty
mile Rio Grande Western (this Palmer railroad extended the
Denver and Rio Grande from Grand Junction west to Salt Lake
City and Ogden). Palmer had expected no more than $5,000,000
so he peeled off the extra million and had it divided without
publicity among Rio Grande Western employees. Many section
hands received several thousand dollars each. One unprepared
passenger agent almost died from the shock of opening his mail
and finding Palmer's check for $35,000.

This windfall, plus the half million which he had earned in
Mexico plus apartment houses in London, plus the Antlers Hotel,
plus dozens of other Colorado properties had a net value of well
over $9,000,000. It was an estate which required little attention
and it brought him a steady income of $30,000 a month. And
the item in it which gave him most satisfaction was the hundreds
of acres of lots in Colorado Springs which he had watched grow
from a population of nothing to twenty thousand people. Among
those eighty-cent acres which Governor Hunt and Irving Howbert had bought for him in 1870 were quite a few worth $15,000
and more each.

THE RIO GRANDE WESTERN SALE in 1901 marked the end
of Palmer's active business life as a builder of the West. It was
the end of a career which had begun with his wilderness wander-
ings with Dr. Bell in the Sixties and had reached a peak of adventure in '79 when he had commanded a small private army in
the forcible seizure of the Denver and Rio Grande from the
Santa Fe. [2] He was sixty-five years old now, and a bit thicker in

the middle, though still small, neat, and wiry. He carried himself still with military straightness, and he rode horseback with the same loose rein and long stirrup of the Fifteenth Pennsylvania days when he had chased Jeff Davis through the mutilated South in the sad spring of '65. His graying hair was still curly, his long face tanned and weather-beaten, his large hands freckled. His characteristic expression was one of alert repose, with a hint of sadness in the gray eyes. He was more than ever the self-made aristocrat and yet his autocratic manner had great kindness about it. Once on the Nomad he spotted a hobo riding his rods. He invited the man into the car and told William Postlethwaite, his private secretary, to clean him up and to try to hide him from the train's conductor. "But," Palmer added, "if the conductor spots him, I'll pay the fare." Politically he had become a gold-standard conservative in a Silver-Republican State. He opposed jingoism and the Spanish-American War and he was no more than coldly polite to Vice President Theodore Roosevelt when the glamorous head of the San Juan Hill Rough Riders came to town briefly for the Colorado Quatro-Centennial celebrations, August 1-3, 1901.[3]

The General had no trouble adjusting to his life of leisure at Glen Eyrie. He increased his large correspondence with surviving members of the Fifteenth Pennsylvania and he resumed the reading of poetry. He kept a wary eye on affairs affecting the Garden of the Gods which his friend Charles E. Perkins of the Burlington had left open to public use ever since he had bought it in 1879. Palmer and other horsemen thwarted a scheme to extend the street car line along their bridle path up Camp Creek to the Garden. Palmer vetoed also a suggestion in 1903 that mammoth busts of Presidents Lincoln, Garfield, and McKinley be carved on North and South Gateway Rocks (Gutzon Borglum didn't get around to carving his heads of Washington, Jefferson, Lincoln, and Theodore Roosevelt at Mount Rushmore until 1927). The General inclined to such sentimental acts as finding in Ute Pass a large block of Pikes Peak granite for use in its untrimmed state as his tombstone in Evergreen Cemetery. He shipped a similar

granite block to Congressional Cemetery in Washington, D. C.,
to mark the grave of his colorful fellow pioneer, Governor A. C.
Hunt.[4] He rode hatless to town often from Glen Eyrie over his
mesa road past the grounds of Colorado College and on down
Cascade Avenue. His costume was always the same—smart, well-
pressed tweed jacket, shirt and sober tie, new tailored breeches,
and a pair of cracked, scuffed, and well-oiled riding boots—very
old and shabby. He usually left his horse at Fowler's elegant El
Paso Livery next door to John Hundley's even fancier livery. He
liked to feed sugar to Fowler's tame gray wolf at the stable door.
Palmer rode scrub horses much of the time so that his guests
could ride his English hunters.

His effect on his town after thirty years was to stamp it with a
quiet disciplined personality quite like his own. Following him
(and the English whom he had encouraged to settle), Colorado
Springs had come to believe in standards, in gentility, in culture.
It admired wealth, but not unreservedly. It resisted—though by
no means with complete success—cheapness and greed and dis-
honesty and the unhappy products of ignorance. Like Palmer,
it was tolerant and avoided fetiches. The godly and ungodly
lived in peace together, the teetotalers and the drinkers, the mor-
alists and those not so good.

All in all, Palmer could feel that he had achieved a reasonable
percentage of his young dream and perhaps that is what promp-
ted his next dramatic move. He began in 1901 giving away his
money and his property in a vast program of civic improvement.
He had made large gifts earlier—Acacia (North) Park in '71,
twenty acres for Colorado College and five acres for the Deaf
and Blind School in '74, Antlers Park in '82, the sites of Prospect
Lake and Mesa Reservoir in 1890, Alamo (today's Courthouse)
Park in '99. Now he really opened up by purchasing Henry
Austin's Bluffs (seven hundred and fifty-three acres), a delicious
cliff-mesa wilderness overlooking the city which was named
Palmer Park in 1902.

Thereafter his gifts poured in like flood tide: Thorndale Park
to the west, Dorcester Park (improved), roads and lands around

Bear Creek and North Cheyenne Canyon, the right-of-way of today's Municipal High Drive, Manitou, Palmer Lake and Paseo Boulevards, Cascade Avenue's center parking, endless hiking trails to Cutler Mountain and Crystal Park. The capstone was his Monument Valley Park—a strip of one hundred and sixty-five acres on both sides of Monument Creek through the middle of the city. The strip had been reserved hitherto as the last resort of tin cans, sasparilla bottles, worn-out bed springs, cracked pots, and all the other urban has-beens. Out of the ugly mess, Palmer's engineer, Edmond C. Van Diest, created a series of charming gardens, winding walks, and picturesque bridged ponds which were ready for public use in November, 1907.[5] Charles E. Perkins died in Massachusetts in that same month, leaving the Garden of the Gods to his two sons and four daughters. Two years later these six children gave the Garden to Colorado Springs, influenced by their father's wish, by his friendship with Palmer and by the example of Palmer's multimillion dollar park system totalling 1,638 acres.[6]

While Engineer Van Diest toiled at Palmer's parks, the Denver architect, Frederic J. Sterner, struggled to keep afloat in the churning ocean of Palmer's desire to improve Glen Eyrie. The large wooden building which Queen had come to as a fearful bride watching for Indians had burgeoned through thirty years into an extremely impressive manor house. But the Palmer of 1901, with $30,000 a month to get rid of, was hardly in the manor class. He felt that Glen Eyrie was no longer a credit to himself or his town. Both deserved a princely castle, a public show place of imperishable stone, which would be second to none west of the Mississippi, if not in the entire United States.

For two frantic years Sterner, and Van Diest, too, worked up the preliminaries. They bought green roof tile from an ancient English church and sent crews into the hills above Blair Athol to cut lichen-crusted blocks of Pikes Peak stone for the walls. They ordered a custom-built four-story elevator and steam generators for the electric power plant and washing machines and ironers for the new laundry and a complicated telephone system and refrigerating equipment to produce a ton of ice daily. They made plans for the latest in stalls (including a hospital stall) for the general's forty horses and a twenty-two cow dairy barn (with cow baths) and assorted homes for the army needed to run such a principality—cottages for the engineer, superintendent, gardener, caretaker, electrician, gateman, stableman, and the rest. They invented a living room weather register hooked up electrically to a weather vane on a distant cliff. Since Palmer had become a smoke hater while working on the railroad, they designed a rock tunnel which took the castle's chimney smoke and released it far away. They acquired hydraulic cement for a projected swimming pool one hundred feet long by sixty feet wide. To supply water for it and for twenty castle bathrooms and kitchens, stock tanks and lily ponds, they spent a quarter million dollars on Camp Creek and pipe lines to provide 1,150,000 gallons of water a day. They worked on Palmer's specifications for a wine cellar, properly cool and dark with sturdy labelled racks at convenient height to hold the General's prized vintage Bordeau and Burgundies, Mosels and Rhines, Rhones and Loires and Chiantis and Tokays and champagnes and heavier sherries and Madeiras and Malagas. Such wines required a small decanting room which was spotted just off the dining room.

Architect Sterner hired platoons of decorators and sent them abroad to gather ornamental stone for forty fireplaces and Chippendale furniture and prints and paintings which would not clash with the general's menagerie of hunting trophies. The decorators bought oriental rugs and red burlap wall coverings and tons of paneled oak and leather upholstery and a one-ton silver-alloyed bell to hang in the top of the four-story crenelated stone tower. The bell was cast by Krupp at Essen, Germany.

The actual construction was done during 1903-04 while Palmer and the girls cruised the Mediterranean and toured Europe. They returned to Pikes Peak in April to find the Glen incredibly transformed. Its lawns and gardens were larger and more formal. Camp Creek flowed tidily now as it emerged from Queen's Canyon and rippled through the Glen's rock-bound intervale of scrub oak and spruce and willows and wildflowers. The brown Tudor castle against its great hill was a stunning sixty-seven room affair, hidden from the public road. An enormous wing contained "Book Hall" for large gatherings, with vaulted ceiling twenty-five feet high. It was big enough to seat three hundred people. At one end was a high gallery for observers. In the basement under the hall were billiard rooms and a bowling alley.[7]

But somehow all this grandeur scared nobody. Public attitudes had changed a lot during the decade of Palmer's second chance to be a family man. Colorado Springs had learned to relax with its founder and to take him for granted. Its residents were as pleased and as proud of the new Glen Eyrie as he was.

CHAPTER TEN

Death of a Patriarch

AND, FOR ALL of its baronial splendor, the new Glen Eyrie had an easy air. Even the swarm of secretaries, butlers, cooks, upstairs and downstairs maids, valets, and seamstresses seemed to have a good time. Tourists driving through soon stopped talking in whispers. There was no fixed routine. The girls woke and breakfasted in bed, rode, swam, lunched, went to town in their big Mexican hats, suppered, partied, and retired when they felt like it. The General worked for hours teaching his Great Dane, Yorick, to heel. Teasing the girls was his favorite indoor sport. Elsie had a smelly, irascible, and incontinent half-breed collie bitch which she loved irrationally. After long and delicate negotiations, Palmer managed to have an official letter from the Secretary of the American Collie Society posted to Elsie begging for male off-spring with which to improve the collie strain. One day Marjory demanded that Palmer ban the public from Glen Eyrie; a pair of tourists had peered in the Louis XV drawing room where she was sitting with a young man. Palmer suggested that she arrange to be made love to in a less prominent place.

Christmases at the new Glen were gay though the General's philanthropy was not overwhelming. His note book of cash gifts for one Yule recorded: "Gave Elsie from Pocket, $20; for Mary (cook), $5; Emma (downstairs), $2; Margaret (upstairs), $1; Grace, $3; Marie Thornton, $3; Rowena's Babies, $3; Margaret Bell, $2." Even more than he disliked smoke and (more recently) automobiles, he despised being lionized. At local events like the opening of the enlarged Van Briggle Pottery plant in 1903, he was apt to drop in unannounced. He watched with anonymous amusement as the Manitou Cliff Dwellers Ruins Company

140

hauled forty carloads of prehistoric Basketmaker apartment houses from Southwestern Colorado for reconstruction near Manitou as a tourist attraction.[1] Early in 1906 he gave his reluctant consent to President William F. Slocum to have his portrait hung that fall in Palmer Hall, Colorado College. The portrait had been painted earlier in England by Sir Hubert Von Herkomer, the German-born British artist who had done such famous portraits as Richard Wagner's and John Ruskin's.[2]

And then tragedy fell. It was inexplicable, insensate, and in the least likely of all possible forms. The date was October 27, 1906, a few weeks past Palmer's seventieth birthday. The time of day was a little after high noon. The Gateway Rocks of Mr. Perkins' Garden of the Gods were bathed in sunlight but clouds hung around Pikes Peak and the air felt as if snow might be coming. The General, Dorothy, Marjory, and a friend named Miss Miller had been riding their horses in the Garden. Nothing could have been nicer, more sweetly full of life's pleasure, as they rode through the delicious air in that golden setting with copper oak leaves rustling and the juncos flicking and squeaking just out of sight. Marjory, twenty-four years old now and the beauty of the family, was especially happy, having just become engaged to Captain Richard Wellesley of the British Army. The three girls and the General had left the beautiful Gateway which framed the Peak and had turned north along the road to Glen Eyrie where they expected to lunch around one o'clock. They were headed for home. But everything in sight was home to Palmer—his Peak, his town, his valley, his mesa—the whole delectable spot which he had seen first by moonlight from the top of a coach in 1869 where he had dreamed his dream for Queen.

The girls were riding English hunters. Palmer's mount was nondescript—a small cow pony named Scrub Oak, fifteen hands high. Scrub Oak was no particular kind of animal—not specifically good or bad or indifferent. He was just a horse. A mile or so from Glen Eyrie there was a gate to open. As the horses ambled up to it, Scrub Oak stepped on a rock and stumbled. Palmer fell off Scrub Oak. The Civil War cavalry leader and explorer of the

West who had ridden half a million miles on horseback in every sort of violent, perilous circumstance fell off a small walking pony who had merely stumbled. Palmer landed on his head on the road. He lay still, feebly reassuring the girls who fluttered about him. Within minutes, the Cleveland millionaire, Will Otis, drove up with friends in his big new automobile. The helpless General would have to ride in a hated car whether he liked it or not. The Otis party lifted him from the road into the car and drove him to Glen Eyrie, while the frightened girls followed on their horses leading Scrub Oak.[3] Dr. Will Howard Swan, Palmer's physician, examined the General within the hour.

Palmer's fall had broken his neck in three places—fourth, fifth and sixth cervical vertebrae. It had injured his spinal cord. His case was utterly hopeless. All any one could ask for him was quick death, blessed release for the inert shell. Dr. Swan's diagnosis, published later,[4] began: "The subject . . . had always been remarkably active physically and mentally. He had been for years harassed by a gouty eczema and had been treated for arteriosclerosis some years before. About seven months prior to to the injury, after a hard day's ride and tramp in the mountains, he had acute dilation of the heart, from which he suffered up to the time of his accident, though he persisted in long rides and unwarranted exercise." The report added that Palmer could move his head and neck freely, move his shoulders, and bend elbows slightly. The rest of him was completely paralyzed. Dr. Swan, an able medical man, placed him at once on an india-rubber water-bed (like an air mattress, in effect). The bed forestalled the bed sores which would have developed in those days before antibiotics were discovered to prevent infection. A young English doctor, Henry C. Watt, who had come to Colorado Springs in 1904 for his health, moved into the castle to watch over the General.

The huge establishment in the Glen waited drearily for the end. Discipline and order disintegrated. Elsie Palmer had a contingent worry for she expected to marry at Glen Eyrie soon an old English suitor, Captain Leopold Hamilton Myers. Elsie was thirty-four years old—no time to be delaying wedding plans. Palmer slept through most of November, and lay on his water-bed for more weeks looking blank. Dorothy read the *Gazette* to him each evening, and Marjory read letters from her Captain Wellesley about British Army life. Palmer seemed inattentive. When Elsie brought the great Philadelphia neurologist, Dr. Silas Weir Mitchell, to Glen Eyrie, Palmer refused to see him at first, telling Elsie grumpily that he was not insane. Mitchell, who had revolutionized the treatment of nervous diseases since his Civil War days as an Army surgeon, had had a second famous career as a novelist. He hung around the Glen for a week working on a book and sent in a very high medical bill for doing nothing. Palmer glanced at the bill and then admitted the specialist, who could add no more to Dr. Swan's diagnosis. But, as an international expert on Madeira wine, Mitchell chided his patient for the poor quality of Madeira which he claimed to have seen in Palmer's wine cellar. For a moment, the General showed a flickering interest.

AND THEN ONE MORNING, just before Christmas, 1907, Elsie came in to find her father incredibly changed. His gray eyes were alive again. He remarked brusquely that it was time for him to be up and doing. He dictated a long list of Christmas presents. He asked for Yorick to see if the monster dog had forgotten how to heel. He instructed Elsie to discuss her wedding plans with the Reverend Arthur Taft of St. Stephen's Episcopal Church. He called for young Dr. Watt and told him to examine Marjory who, he said, had looked peaked since her engagement to Captain Wellesley. He summoned one of his secretaries, Cecile Jacobeit, and began answering get-well letters from Fifteenth Pennsylvania friends. The General had a busy day.

As Robert E. Lee said, the human spirit is equal to any calamity. Palmer decided on that December morning to live again. He decided that invalidism was fear incarnate, the sad and fatal symptom of defeat. The resolute mind always triumphed over the puny body. The will, the brain, the soul, the soaring

imagination—these were the marvelous and irrepressible powers
which gave life its vitality and zest, even on a water-bed. The
General resumed militant command. Soon Glen Eyrie was running smoothly. He demanded and got a wheel chair and was
pushed around outside daily. Then he told Elsie to go down to
Strang's Garage and buy one of those new electric autos—com-
promising his hatred of cars, since electrics didn't smell, at least.
C. G. Strang sent the electric to Glen Eyrie, driven by a teen-aged
mechanic who had been christened, coincidentally, Glen Eyrie
Martin.

Many years later, Glen Martin, in a mood of reminiscence,
recalled his months as the General's chauffeur[5]: "That night Dr.
Watt told me, 'If you jolt him, you'll kill him.' I didn't want any
part of such a job but Mr. Strang had told me I'd have to drive,
so I did. We put up a charger for the battery. The charge was
capable of driving the machine for only twenty or twenty-five
miles. We'd go out and the General would always pick the hills
and of course the electric couldn't make the distance he wanted
to go. We were loaded. Sometimes there would be two nurses
on the side, and Dr. Watt. The charge would run out and there
we'd be, stopped up in some canyon. We'd have to send somebody back to get horses. Finally, Miss Marjory conceived the
idea of having a motorcycle follow the car to run back for horses
when the charge played out. The General did not like the
motorcycle's noise and smell and dust and he made its rider stay
a long way off.

"About this time there was an automobile show in Chicago
and they were showing a White Steamer, painted a peculiar
white. It was a gaudy thing with bright red seats, and larger
than any automobile today. The General thought this would be
a fine thing, so he bought it, paying a terrible price. Since it was
built for show purposes, it had a lot of bugs in it and when it
got here there were only four men in Colorado who could operate
it—Clarence Sly, Frank Stockdale, a man from Denver, and my-
self. It had a flash boiler made with a coil of steel and the firebox
was as big as the coach top and you sat on top of the whole thing.

It ran on seven hundred and fifty pounds of steam. In addition the coil was heated red hot. The water in the condenser was practically steam and heated this coil. But it could not blow up. At least it never did.

"The General had bought this Steamer so that we could go anywhere. The house men would carry him to the wheel chair, wheel him to the car and fit him into a case made for the car— a sort of seat, like a spoon case, made of hair and feathers. It just fitted the General. We started out on extended cruises. The General wanted to go to Palmer Park. I thought we'd go out to the spring in Willow Lane at the foot of Austin's Bluffs and turn around, because that was the end of Paseo Road. General Palmer said, 'Let's go up there to Grand View Point!' I said, 'How?' He said, 'Up that bridle path.' I told him that wasn't a road, and he said, 'Couldn't this Steamer go over that thing?' I said, 'Yes, it has the power but it probably would tear the tires to pieces.' The tires cost $95 each. The General said, 'I want to go up there.' So we did, but all the tires were ruined. We finally got to Grand View Point. The General sat there a long time looking at the beautiful view. When we came back to the lodge gate at Glen Eyrie, Perley Nichols, the General's road man, was there. The General said, 'How many men would it take to build a road up to Grand View Point?' Perley said, 'I would need enough for ten or fifteen teams and scrapers, and they would have to have a chief and a cook.' The General said, 'Get those teams and men and go out there and make camp tonight.' And Perley did. He built the road to Grand View Point and another to the north of it and the Palmer Park roads today still follow his grades."

Glen Martin continued: "A short time after this, the General wanted to show Blair Athol to Mr. Kendrick of Denver. There was a sort of road up Blair Athol and at the end of the canyon it just quit. It was almost straight up and down but this great big Steamer went up that little horse-and-wagon road just because the General wanted to go. Kendrick and the girls were so scared they walked down! That night Miss Elsie scolded me

very much and said, 'Don't you ever drive to Blair Athol again!'
The very next evening we started out and I said, 'Where to?' The
General said, 'Blair Athol.' Every time after that for a month
we had to drive up Blair Athol. By that time I had worn a fairly
good automobile road up there.

"The General had never been through the Cave of the Winds
and he thought he'd like to see it, although no automobile had
ever been driven up there. We took a doctor, two nurses, the
valet, and two or three helpers and started up Williams Canyon.
At the Narrows there was just enough room to allow a carriage
to go through. The top of the car was down and bulged out. I
saw that both sides were touching and I said, 'What will we do?'
The General said, 'Tear the top off!' and we went right ahead.
The bows of the top just stayed there. In his form-fitting case
he was lugged through the cave and got stuck in a place called
'Fat Man's Misery.' The General ordered a saw and had the
ledge cut off for his release.

"One day, Ringling Brothers Circus was in town, camped near
the Colorado Avenue viaduct. Two little English girls were visiting at Glen Eyrie—grand-nieces of the General.[6] Relatives were
usually around. In fact, all the family lived on the General.
When we drove past the circus tents, the little girls wanted to go
and so did the General. We stopped and I explained to the circus
manager that we would have to bring the Steamer inside because
the General couldn't be put in a seat. The manager said, 'Well,
buy a section of seats and we will tear them out, but you'll have
to buy them for both afternoon and evening shows.' I think the
section cost $368 or $378. The manager gave me several hundred
tickets for both shows and we drove the Steamer in under the tent
in the afternoon and the General had a wonderful time. I handed
out the evening tickets to the Glen people and gave all the rest
to kids down town."

FOR ALL HIS DERRING-DO, Palmer was not improving. He
was steadily sinking. But he sank carrying the banner of his
valiant personality high. Late in May, 1907, he received notice

of the thirty-fifth reunion of the Fifteenth Pennsylvania Volunteer Cavalry to be held in Philadelphia during August. Dr. Watt informed him that he, Palmer, could not attend. Palmer threw a conniption fit. After Marjory calmed him down, he assembled his Glen Eyrie and Colorado Springs Company staffs from William Postlethwaite and Cecile Jacobeit on through Glen Martin and John Mathys, his valet, and the gardener, Bill Burghard. He told them that Dr. Watt refused to let him go to Philadelphia. Very well. Then the week-long reunion for the entire regiment would be held at Colorado Springs at the General's expense. The two staffs would be his reunion task force.

It seems probable that nothing in Palmer's career thrilled and stimulated him more than that Fifteenth Pennsylvania celebration—not his espionage for General McClellan after Antietam or his three months' imprisonment as a Union spy in Richmond or his Rocky Mountain treks with Willie Bell in 1867-68. The drama of it caught the nation's attention and gave it something felicitous to talk about all summer. Americans everywhere applauded. The country's railroads were eager to help Palmer, one of their pioneer builders. They arranged to pick up veterans at any whistle stop and to carry them to cities along the route of the ten-car Pullman special which the General ordered to leave Philadelphia for Colorado Springs on August 17, 1907. The veterans headed for Pikes Peak in glows of anticipation. The two hundred and eighty of them ranged from fifty-nine to eighty-two years. Many had seen nothing of the world since Palmer disbanded the regiment in '65. Though the majority were Philadelphians, others hailed from Ohio and West Virginia, Indiana and Illinois and Nebraska, California and Washington.

The special train reached the Denver and Rio Grande depot—site of Palmer's old 1870 Log Cabin—on Tuesday afternoon, August 20, 1907. Four thousand residents headed by Major McAllister filled Antlers Park to greet them as they walked to the new Antlers Hotel which Palmer had reserved for most of them (some stayed at Colorado College). In the evening they dined in state in the Antlers ball room. On Wednesday morning they toured what they called "New Philadelphia" and in the afternoon there was a great parade led by half a dozen bands and by General Palmer in the big Steamer with Glen Martin at the wheel. Palmer wore a dazzling white uniform and his two small grandnieces sat beside him. Behind the General, the Fifteenth Pennsylvania, with its regimental banners and captured colors flying, lined up four abreast and marched smartly out Pikes Peak Avenue from the Antlers under the twirling ribbons of the decorated streets. Bouquets of flowers fell on them, thrown by the delighted sidewalk crowds. At Nevada Avenue, they turned north to Platte, west to Tejon and south to Pikes Peak and the Antlers again. It rained meanwhile, so the General ordered his regiment to fall out and take hot baths, and he had the heat in the Antlers turned on.

On Wednesday night, Palmer, the same temperance man who had put a strict liquor ban in all Colorado Springs deeds, was host at Glen Eyrie for a champagne party of epic proportions. Every carriage in the Antlers and El Paso stables was used to deliver two hundred and eighty old soldiers to the banquet in Book Hall, which was filled for the first time. In a room off the Hall, cases of Mumm's champagne and bourbon whiskey were stacked to the ceiling and the rest of the space was filled with tubs of ice from the Glen Eyrie ice machine. The General, beaming and serene in his form-fitting case, was touched when his regiment gave him a silver loving cup. He laughed when an octogenarian raised his champagne glass and called, "General, this is the best hard cider I ever tasted!" Not all the wine-bibbers were veterans. Glen Martin drank a whole bottle and weaved off to retire. At 2 a.m., Dr. Watt woke him roughly with orders from Palmer to get out the Steamer and haul some of the unsteady old soldiers to town. Martin, far from sober himself, did get the Steamer fired up and in some miraculous way made several mercy trips to the Antlers without running over anybody.

The week continued joyfully with a concert at Perkins Hall, trips up Pikes Peak, and a ride on the Short Line to Cripple Creek. On Sunday, August 25, 1907, the regiment gathered on the lawn at Glen Eyrie to say good-bye and to have its photo taken with Palmer, the girls, and the Great Dane, Yorick. A final three cheers echoed up Queen's Canyon and soon the Fifteenth Pennsylvania's special train rolled away and the General and his weary task force could relax. When the reunion bills were paid weeks later, Palmer found himself $75,000 poorer. But the celebration had been worth every penny of it to him. He had loved it all, even though he had worried over a letter to the *Gazette* by a prominent local lady who objected when some veterans hung in the Antlers lobby an original Jeff Davis reward proclamation, in memory of the regiment's effort to run down and capture the Confederate President at the end of the Civil War.

The local lady was the late Jeff Davis' only living child, Mrs. Margaret Howell Jefferson Davis Hayes. She and her husband, Joel Addison Hayes, who was president of the First National Bank, had come to the Springs from Memphis, Tennessee, in the middle 1880s, and their big house on North Cascade Avenue was a focal point of high society. Palmer had signed the offending proclamation at Athens, Georgia, on May 9, 1865, on behalf of President Andrew Johnson. It offered $360,000 for the arrest of Davis and five others who were supposed to be hurrying to Mexico to set up further resistance. Palmer's handbill described the Confederate President as the man who "incited and concerted the assassination of Mr. Lincoln and the attempt on Mr. Seward."

In her Open Parliament letter, Margaret Hayes denied politely but firmly that Davis had had anything to do with the assassination and related how her father had told her on the day of Lincoln's death that the assassin was the South's worst enemy. She concluded: "General Palmer is my highly esteemed friend, an ideal man in that he lives for others and spends his days in doing good deeds, and not long ago, in speaking of his orders to capture my father, it pleased me to have him say with his usual gentle courtesy, 'You know I was sent with my regiment to capture your father, I regret to say.' I am glad he was not successful,

but that this terrible blow came from other hands than his."
When Palmer read this August 23 letter, he phoned Billy Dunning, the Antlers manager, and had the proclamation taken down.
His *Gazette* reply to Mrs. Hayes three days later was gallant and
kindly but he stressed that he had not regretted his war's end
assignment at the time. He wrote: "While therefore I now fully
sympathize with Mrs. Hayes' gladness that 'this terrible blow
came from other hands than' those of one of her admiring friends
and neighbors, I must equally disclaim any thought that we
shrank from doing our best to capture the distinguished leader
of the Southern cause."

ELSIE PALMER married her Leopold Myers at Glen Eyrie
on January 20, 1908, and departed on an Italian honeymoon,
planning to attend Marjory's September wedding to Captain
Wellesley in England. Dorothy replaced Elsie as mistress of
Glen Eyrie and Dr. Watt tried to slow the pace of Palmer's
deterioration and to make him sleep better. In the spring, the
General announced that he might as well go to England with
the rest of the family for Marjory's wedding. There was a London
spine specialist whom he wanted to see. He instructed Glen
Martin to buy a new White Steamer and Glen sailed with it to
Liverpool where he assembled it and got it running well for the
General's use.

Dr. Watt surprised everyone, except possibly Marjory, by
giving Palmer his approval to make the trip. The big wedding
party left the Springs by Rock Island express on May 31, 1908—
Marjory and her bridesmaid, Captain Wellesley's sister; Dr.
Watt; the William Sclaters and the van Oestveens (Mrs. Sclater
and Mrs. van Oestveen were Ellen Mellen's daughters) and four
van Oestveen children; and fourteen nurses and servants and
secretaries. They all sailed from New York on the S. S. *Minneapolis* on June 6. It couldn't have been a pleasanter journey to a
wedding, save for one thing. Half way across the Atlantic, Marjory went to her father and told him that she could not marry

Captain Wellesley after all. She was hopelessly in love with Dr. Henry Watt.

And so the wedding was off, but the wedding party could not be canceled so easily. When England turned out to be damp and gloomy that summer, Palmer and Glen Martin (with extra cars and chauffeurs) carted the whole crowd all over Europe, returning in November. While sailing to New York, the General sought to go up the highest places on the ship as he had sought to go up Blair Athol. On one trip to the top deck, the stewards who were carrying him in a blanket allowed his head to roll to one side, hitting a brass rail. Thereafter, his physical decline was rapid, though back at Glen Eyrie, Glen Martin took him riding in the Steamer almost daily all winter through March 10. On March 12, he fell asleep and he died on March 13, 1909, with Elsie, Dorothy, and Marjory at his bedside. By sheer will, he had eked out more than two extra years of good life, as colorful and as exciting as any of his other seventy years.

His body was cremated in Denver and the funeral was delayed until March 17 so that Willie Bell could get there from New York. Major McAllister was a pall-bearer, of course, and Colonel D. C. Dodge and "Chumley" Thornton and Edmond Van Diest. Among others at the funeral were six hundred Colorado College students and three thousand truly grieving townspeople. There were no music and no flowers at the brief Episcopalian grave service under yellow pines at Evergreen. On the General's raised plot, there was only that single lonely grave by the big red boulder from Ute Pass which he had chosen. But a second grave appeared beside his eighteen months later without notice. On November 22, 1910, the ashes of Queen Palmer, disinterred from an English graveyard, were placed near the General's under a smaller Ute Pass stone. Today, a currant bush almost hides Queen's stone from view.[7]

CHAPTER ELEVEN

On Gold and Mr. Stratton

MANY OF US remember the magic lanterns of childhood, with prisms sliding past each other to mix and change the color of the light. When General Palmer took his last ride in the big Steamer in 1909, the light on his town had been changing for twenty years. The change began with the coming of the Colorado Midland and the cog train and the fading away of Little London. But that was a mere rehearsal. A serene blue color persisted until 1891 when the amiable Springs cowboy, Bob Womack, convinced a few people that he really had found gold in quantity on the southwest slopes of Pikes Peak. Womack had led a party of unsuccessful gold-seekers up there in 1874 and from then on he had dug holes in his spare time. After his discovery, the color of the light over Colorado Springs turned yellow, increasingly garish with the years.

Bob's news was hard to swallow. Since Colorado's first big gold rush in 1859, every inch of the Colorado Rockies had been prospected. The last ounce of gold was supposed to have been found and silver had replaced it through the 1880s as the metal of the day. It was too fantastic that gold could exist in a well-known cow pasture called Cripple Creek within eighteen miles as the crow flies of the Antlers Hotel—fourteen miles from the Colorado Midland station at the top of Ute Pass.[1] Extreme inaccessibility was part of the tradition of gold rushes. The great silver camp of Leadville, the treasure of which had made a metropolis of Denver, was one hundred and twenty-five miles away by the shortest route over the highest of Rocky Mountain crossings—Mosquito Pass, that "highway of frozen death." But

152

Cripple Creek! Why, families from Colorado Springs went up there on Sundays to picnic! Actually, the cow pasture's gold escaped early discovery for good reasons. Its characteristic dull-gray ore—a gold-silver-tellurium substance called sylvanite—was unfamiliar to prospectors and almost all of them except Bob Womack passed it by.

General Palmer and half of the Springs residents either refused to believe that a gold rush was taking place in their back yard—or looked the other way. They did not want their town to change. Its relaxed, philosophical, cultured air suited them just as it was. The Colorado Midland and its ill-mannered employees had disturbed them quite enough and they didn't care to be disturbed further. The loyalty of the Palmer crowd to its sedate past had a curious result. For eighteen years after 1891, the Springs was split into two distinctly separate communities. One was the aloof, dignified old Fountain Colony led by General Palmer. The other was the bustling, greedy center of trade for the gold camp, populated by all sorts of dubious people. The old town and the new did not mix socially. If an old-guard girl made eyes at a member of the new guard, she was apt to be lectured by her parents.

Some of the Old Guard—Irving Howbert, for instance—were apostates to the gold rush crowd and it was amazing how many consumptives found miraculous therapy in the vision of sudden wealth. Dying youngsters like Albert E. (Bert) Carlton, the future King of Cripple Creek, felt well overnight and began running around the gold camp's little hills like mountain goats at ten thousand feet of altitude. Among the restored invalids were a number of eastern playboys who discovered in Cripple Creek an outlet for unsuspected talents as promoters. They formed a curb mining exchange on Pikes Peak Avenue which rocked with the excitement of high finance as the nation learned about the gold camp's easy money. By 1894, three stock exchanges were going full blast and one of them, the Colorado Springs Mining Exchange, traded more shares than any other exchange in the world. Though the local exchanges unloaded Cripple Creek penny stocks by the bale, control of the best gold mines stayed in town. After all, Cripple Creek belonged to Colorado Springs. An alien could buy his way in but he soon found that he was strictly a guest. During the camp's quarter-century of boom, very few of the nineteen richest mines (producing $3,000,000 worth of gold or better) were owned by non-residents of the Pikes Peak area.

The extent of change in the Springs followed Cripple Creek's annual gold production, which rose from $2,000,000 worth in 1893 to $10,000,00 in 1897 to $20,000,000 in 1900, with *total* production since 1891 reaching $120,000,000 in 1902. In that year, the cow pasture on Pikes Peak led the whole world in gold production, since the mines of South Africa were closed by the Boer War. As a consequence, bank deposits in the Springs during the same stunning decade increased nine times. The Springs population tripled—from 11,000 to 35,000. The number of North End millionaires shot up from three to more than fifty. Four hundred and twenty mining companies had offices along Tejon Street. There were in the city one hundred and twelve doctors, fifty-one loan companies, and a great many men and women taking the Keeley cure for alcoholism. The water system on Pikes Peak was expanded, schools and churches went up by the dozens, Sunday school attendance soared, and Colorado City could point with pride to more than thirty saloons and gambling houses and could boast that all her Blanche Bartons worked in buildings now instead of tents.

Cripple Creek was the direct cause of other shocking events, including the election of a Bible-spouting socialist, Davis H. Waite, as Populist Governor of Colorado. In 1894, the gold camp's Irish red-neck miners had the gall to demand an eight-hour day under the auspices of one of those radical mining unions. They seized all the best mines of Bull Hill and Battle Mountain, and the Springs gasped with disbelief as Irving Howbert and James J. Hagerman and other blessed-are-the-meek Protestants brought in thugs from the East and received advice in code from the anti-Catholic American Protective Association on how to use brass knuckles in the suppression of red necks. The pro-union Adjutant General of Colorado, Thomas J. Tarsney, was kidnapped from the Alamo Hotel by the imported thugs and tarred and feathered in the barn of the distinguished millionaire, William A. Otis, at Austin's Bluffs.

Tar and feathers in Little London! The word got out that the seven hundred strikers were about to pour down the mountain from the gold camp to destroy the town. At a May mass meeting in General Palmer's Acacia Park, the enraged citizens howled for President Cleveland and the United States Army to lynch the union leaders and to impeach Governor Waite. In a passionate soap-box oration, Judge Ernest Colburn urged "every able-bodied man and boy to wrest Bull Hill from the insurrectionists before the insurrectionists despoil the Springs' fair womanhood and slit the throats of its little children." Members of the fair womanhood hurried to their homes from the meeting to make bandages and to fill canteens for the city's brave defenders. The sheriff of El Paso County swore in a Springs army of 1,200 deputies who were shipped on the Colorado Midland to battle stations below Bull Hill at Cripple Creek.

Governor Waite himself appeared in Colorado Springs on the night of June 2, 1894, and conferred with Hagerman and other Springs mine owners at today's Cutler Hall, Colorado College, while a mob milled outside muttering threats against the governor. To avoid the risk of being strung up, Waite slipped out the back door of Cutler after the fruitless meeting and walked a mile down the railroad track to his private car at the Springs depot. But the impending Battle of Cripple Creek never did come off. The governor's state militia marched in between the strikers and the sheriff's deputies and the dispute was settled in the miners' favor without bloodshed. However, the strike lasted one hundred and thirty days, the longest and bitterest of American labor struggles up to that time. It plunged the Springs mine owners—including the ex-invalids, playboys, and aesthetes—into a harsh world of spies, intrigue, blacklists, propaganda, injunctions, and terrorism. Most of the residents supported the mine owners and,

though the strikers won their eight-hour day, the gentle people
of Colorado Springs proved that they could be far from gentle
when their interests were at stake.[2]

THE CRIPPLE CREEK boom was an incontrovertible fact of life,
and even the Palmer Old Guard of Colorado Springs managed
in time at least to live with the commotion which it produced.
But neither the Old Guard nor the New Guard was able to get
used to the Springs resident who popped up from nowhere to
dominate the Pikes Peak scene for an eerie decade and brand the
city with his mark and his esoteric meaning.

Winfield Scott Stratton was born in 1848 at Jeffersonville, Indiana, the son of an Ohio River boat-builder, Myron Stratton.
Myron named him after General Winfield Scott who was at the
peak of his Mexican War fame. Young Stratton did not like his
father or his step-mother or Jeffersonville and he reached the
Springs by slow stages in 1872. He was a carpenter by trade, and
more than that soon—a contractor who built many Springs structures including Will Jackson's cottage and the Gothic gem, Grace
Church, on Pikes Peak Avenue. Though unschooled, he was in-
ventive, precise, and quick with figures. But he had unstable
impulses. Three of his early business partnerships ended in fist
fights. He seemed to live and breathe with a perpetual lack of
enthusiasm. In July of 1876, he entered into a casual marriage
with a seventeen-year-old girl named Zeurah Stewart, and
shipped her off to her Illinois home a few weeks later claiming
that the child she was about to have was not his.

Periodically, he left Colorado Springs to go on long prospecting
trips which seemed to bring him more pleasure than anything
else. He was soothed by the placidity of the mountains, the
cheery sound of rushing streams, the smell of sage after rain, the
gray-green twinkling of aspen leaves in a breeze. He plodded
across South Park with his burro and prospected Chalk Creek
below Mount Princeton. He combed the slatey gulches which
branched off from the sparkling Upper Arkansas. He curried
Baker's Park in the high San Juans and had a go at Leadville.

He tried the forested Blue River country below Hoosier Pass, swung south to Rosita in the Wet Mountain Valley and north again to the Elk Mountains and Aspen. He came to feel at home anywhere in the Colorado Rockies. And yet Stratton was not an ordinary hermit prospector. He aspired to know the nature of the mineral world. He studied gold and silver ores in the Nashold Mill at Breckenridge. He learned blowpipe analysis at Colorado College and geology at the Colorado School of Mines in Golden.

For seventeen summers seeking gold was Stratton's vice, his compulsion. He toiled and schemed and traveled—and never found a single mineral vein worth a day's time. When his Springs friend Bob Womack asked him to go up and have a look at Cripple Creek in 1891, he took a week off and did so rather than hurt Bob's feelings. If Stratton knew anything about mining, it was that Pikes Peak could not contain gold. He staked a few Battle Mountain claims just for the fun of it—one of them on July 4, 1891, which he named the Independence. For nearly two years thereafter, he divided his time between Colorado Springs and his Battle Mountain cabin where he tried to unload his holes on young greenhorns like Charley Tutt and Spencer Penrose, or on speculators like Count Pourtales and Tom Parrish. But in June of 1893, he came across a big vein in the Independence fifty feet below the surface. To his astonishment, the vein assayed $380 a ton in gold and it ran laterally for twenty-seven feet. He knew by projection that it had to be at least nine feet wide and one hundred feet deep. That meant $3,000,000 worth of gold in sight!

So there he was, Winfield Scott Stratton, a personality in monotone, moody, taciturn; aged forty-five, a lonely bachelor, tall, thin, frail, wearily stooped, prematurely white-haired. He had spent his life in a $3-a-day existence with $3-a-day friends and now the quiet of his drab days was shattered by an inconceivable wealth. From 1893 on, his tax-free income from his Independence Mine and associated properties would average one million dollars each year until 1899, when he would sell the Independence to an English group for $10,000,000. A fortune of

$16,000,000 was staggering not only to Colorado Springs. It staggered the whole wide-eyed world. Never in mining history had one man made so much so quickly—not Horace Tabor of Leadville or Tom Walsh of the Camp Bird at Ouray or any of the Comstock Lode millionaires in Nevada.

Fame is fascinating and the lure of riches is irresistible. Through those Gay Nineties, the residents of Colorado Springs were benumbed and bemused as their ex-carpenter replaced Pikes Peak and all the charms of General Palmer's town as the region's prime attraction. The burning question was: What would Stratton do now? Speculation blazed along Pikes Peak Avenue but it followed sound lines. People agreed that the point of being filthy rich was to satisfy the ego. Money was the true measure of success, the real mark of superiority. Stratton would surround himself with the best money could buy, as a reward for his achievement and to remind lesser men of his ability and character. Probably he would build a frosty palace on Million-aire's Row[3] and fancy homes at Saratoga, New York, and Paris, France. Maybe he would buy a Senatorship and a pretty young woman half his age, as Horace Tabor had done at Leadville. He might go in for a racing stable in Kentucky or a barn full of Old Masters or a sea-going yacht or a priceless collection of pornography.

The odd duck did none of these sensible, normal things. Though he could have hired the best business brains in New York to handle his fortune, he appointed his shoemaker, Bob Schwarz, to be his general manager. For many months he stayed on in his $500 Battle Mountain cabin, and then moved down to an unimposing frame house in the Springs near Will Jackson's place on Weber Street. Instead of a crew of smart servants, he hired a single housekeeper—Bob Schwarz's girl-friend. He did rent a private railroad car, the Wanderer, in 1895, but only for a short trip to California. He made no attempt to raise his social status by inviting some of the Springs' leading citizens and their wives to go with him. His companions on the trip were the friends of his prospecting days. He refused to be blackmailed about his past, which was no more tawdry than that of any other bachelor miner. A Myers Avenue prostitute named Candace Root sued him for $200,000 alleging breach of promise to marry. Candace testified in court that Stratton had lured her into his bed unfairly at Battle Mountain and had got her pregnant. Stratton denied luring her, unfairly or otherwise. He explained that it was no trick to get Candace into bed. Everyone in Cripple Creek had observed her losing her virtue profitably since 1892, and why should she blame her pregnancy on him? The case was dismissed. As Stratton left court, he gave Candace a handful of bills and asked her not to betray him again.

He had a decisiveness about him, and flashes of disconcerting nobility. During the blowy cold April of 1896, fire broke out in a Cripple Creek dance hall and burned down most of the gold camp. Before the fire could be controlled, five thousand people had no food or shelter and desperate appeals for aid were phoned to Colorado Springs. At City Hall there was a period of official buck-passing and hand-wringing and "We can't spend City funds to help Cripple Creek." Suddenly Stratton appeared. He told Mayor Plumb, "This is a catastrophe. The temperature will fall below zero by midnight. We have no time to collect money. I will pay the bills."

In half an hour, Stratton organized the citizenry into relief committees. He drove to the Colorado Midland depot and ordered a special express train. Twelve freight wagons were rushed to the wholesale grocery where volunteers loaded twenty-five cases of canned beef, six cases of beans, six cases of condensed milk, twelve crates of crackers and a thousand loaves of bread. In all, $50,000 worth of food was charged to Stratton. He called the dry goods stores and bought their blanket supply, sending five hundred pairs to the depot. Also seven hundred and fifty diapers. A shelter committee collected one hundred and sixty-five camp tents and one huge tabernacle tent.

Before dark on that cold April 28, 1896, the relief supplies were put into two box cars. Stratton's special train rattled up Ute Pass at fifteen miles an hour. At 9 p.m. it came racing around

Gold Hill, across Poverty Gulch, and into Cripple Creek. A hundred men with oil torches met the train. Two dozen four-horse freight wagons hauled food and tents all that night above the smoking camp to the reservoir where the homeless had gathered for safety. Meanwhile, Stratton sent a second relief train roaring up Ute Pass. Next morning, classes at Colorado College were cancelled and the students combed the North End for jam, vegetables, fruit, boiled eggs, hams, clothes, dishes, firewood. They carried their loot to a receiving station where Stratton had posted transfer wagons. By then, the crisis in Cripple Creek had passed and most of the residents were hard at work rebuilding their town.

As the hectic decade continued, some Springs people began to have an uncomfortable suspicion that Stratton didn't have proper respect for money—his or anybody else's. There was his unaccountable behavior during the McKinley-Bryan presidential campaign in late October of 1896. Four years earlier, he had been violently opposed to Grover Cleveland and his gold standard crowd. But then he found his mountain of gold. Surely he would come out strongly now for William McKinley, the gold Republican, and against the Democrat, William Jennings Bryan, and his vicious anti-gold heresies.

Well, the old fool didn't. Though McKinley was favored heavily, Stratton announced for Bryan. More than that, he put up $100,000 in cash as a bet on Bryan, asking odds no higher than three to one. It was said to be the largest bet ever offered by one man on an election and news of it nearly crowded both candidates off the front pages of the nation's newspapers. There were angry Republican editorials. If Bryan should be elected, he would resume silver coinage at the old silver-gold ratio of sixteen to one, which would cut Stratton's gold fortune in half, in effect. The man must be crazy! A group of New York reporters arrived at Stratton's office on Pikes Peak Avenue and asked him what ailed him. He gave each of them a slip of paper with these words:

> I do not make the offer because of any information that I have on the election but I have a feeling that Bryan is going to win. I am deeply interested in seeing Bryan elected. I realize that the maintenance of the gold standard would perhaps be best for me individually but I believe that free silver is the best thing for the working masses of this country. It is because I have a great respect for the intelligence and patriotism of the working people that I am willing to make such an offer.

The plain honesty of the statement enthralled the nation and sent chills down the spines of the Republican managers. Up to then, McKinley's election seemed certain. Now, the Republicans had serious qualms. To counteract Stratton's dramatic faith, they came out with all sorts of whistlings in the dark. And they declared over and over that McKinley's supporters were falling all over themselves in their eagerness to cover Stratton's $100,000 bet on Bryan.

Nobody did cover it. Winfield Scott Stratton, an uneducated carpenter from a remote place named Colorado Springs, had called the bluff of the whole Republican Party. The Democrats jeered and took heart. Their renewed spirit almost accomplished the impossible. William McKinley just did win the election of 1896 with 7,100,000 votes against Bryan's 6,500,000.

CHAPTER TWELVE

A Trolley Song

BY 1899, STRATTON HAD turned flamboyantly philanthropist and Colorado Springs began to see—with misgivings—what kind of animal he was. He was nothing like General Palmer, who had created a community for love of a woman and to express his own acute sense of order and dignity. He was not like the fuming James J. Hagerman, who had built the Colorado Midland to confound his enemies. He was the exact opposite of Count Pourtales, who had planned to cash in at Broadmoor by exploiting snob appeal.

In contrast to these, ex-carpenter Stratton was moved purely by compassion and he stood exclusively for plain people. He made up his mind to relieve the bleakness of their existence and to give them some taste of the happiness which he himself had never known. But his approach was not orthodox, not the patronizing tack of well-heeled do-gooders who would mold the unwashed masses into their own image. He did not want to uplift them with the blessings of culture by raising their standards of taste, personal hygiene, and morality. He admired them and believed in them the way they were.

For Christmas presents in 1899, he gave $50,000 to each of three key employees. He bought homes for half a dozen others. He dumped $85,000 on the Salvation Army. Scores of families got a winter's load of coal from him. He sent a $5,000 check to Bob Womack, Cripple Creek's penniless discoverer. He heard of the talent of a poor local teen-ager, Louis Persinger, and shipped him to Germany to study. Later Persinger became one of America's finest violin teachers at the Juilliard School in New York.

The girl who did Stratton's laundry expressed a wish to have a bicycle for deliveries. Next day he ordered a gross of bicycles to be distributed among the laundresses of the community. He gave to Colorado Springs the ground on which the present City Hall now stands. He bought the dilapidated old El Paso County courthouse so that the county could built a better one. He paid his dues far ahead as a member of Local 515, Carpenters and Joiners of America. He noticed rising unemployment at Cripple Creek and began a huge exploration program there which cost him up to $50,000 a month. When small mine owners complained of high freight rates charged by the Cripple Creek railroad company and of high milling costs, Stratton put up much of the money to build a competing railroad, the Short Line, and to construct the Portland Mill in Colorado City. Vice President Theodore Roosevelt rode the Short Line from the Springs to Cripple Creek in April, 1901, and exclaimed: "This is the trip that bankrupts the English language!"[1]

But, from Stratton's point of view, these altruisms were routine and boring. What he wanted was something new, and one day it came to him what this latest benevolence would be. Better streets cars! Most Springs people, he decided, were restricted in their work and their play by a kind of tyranny of transport. The town was not geographically compact, but extended in long narrow fingers along its vagrant streams. The old electric Colorado Springs Transit Company, the fourth electric street car system in the United States, had replaced the horse cars in 1890, but it was unwilling to grow with the town. When Stratton bought the system in 1900 for $350,000 or so, its small four-wheel cars ran only on part of Tejon Street, Spruce Street, to Broadmoor and to Manitou. The equipment was depressing and inadequate.

As the new owner, Stratton began by junking almost everything. He removed $2,000,000 from his checking account and directed it at the traction suppliers of the nation. He did not bother to ask himself if his glittering Colorado Springs and Interurban Railway might be too elaborate to earn operating ex-

penses. He had no better use for the two million dollars and he
was ready to meet any deficits.

He tore up all the old tracks and put in heavier rails. The Brill
Company in Philadelphia made the eight-wheel cars to his
special order and each car cost from $2,000 to $3,500, with air
brakes and heat and beautiful bells the sound of which made
everyone who heard them unexplainably happy and hopeful.
There were a hundred new Stratton cars, including trailers,
some wide open for summer with seats running across and
çapable of hauling mobs clustered like bees on a honeycomb. The
cars were eleven-ton monsters which could flatten to dollar size
a penny placed on the track. They were forty feet long with
five-foot enclosed vestibules where the sports could stand smoking their stogies and ogling the pretty girls inside.

The cars were painted a lovely olive green. Each one had two
throbbing forty-horse-power Corliss motors which could propel
it over the hump in the Colorado Avenue viaduct and up the hill
toward Manitou without slackening speed, or through the sage
beyond the city limits at a rocking fifty miles an hour. The interior smelled deliciously of varnish and electricity and—not a bit
unpleasant—of tobacco-juice and cuspidors. There were polished cherry doors and oakette curtains like those in Pullman cars
and a ceiling of inlaid bird's eye maple and a bell rope down the
center suspended on artistic brass hangers. After dark, the car
was lighted by eight incandescent lamps, and children who
watched it moving through the western night thought of Cinder-
ella's glowing pumpkin coach. Stratton assembled his street car
personnel with loving care. He dressed his eighty motormen and
conductors in brass-buttoned blue suits as well tailored as any
banker's. He paid them well, issued life insurance to them, arranged financing so that they could buy their homes and gave
them dignity to match their status as philosophers, advisors, and
comforters of their traveling flock.

Stratton saw to it that his tracks ran in every possible direction
—a total of forty-one miles. The joy of life in all its bright detail
and broad range and sweet romance at a nickel a ride! They

reached the very ends of the community's fringes—out Wahsatch and Institute and east to Prospect Lake and to the association race track at Roswell, of which he was president, and to the Loop at Manitou where passengers held their noses and gulped down Dr. Solly's stinky seltzers bubbling from a rock. Special theatre runs were made in late evenings to take crowds home from Irving Howbert's Opera House.

But the trip of trips was to Stratton Park on the new second line to Broadmoor along Cheyenne Creek. Stratton Park had been part of a ranch of several hundred acres running south along the slopes and base of Cheyenne Mountain. The old Pikes Peak pioneer, William F. Dixon, had bought it for a few hundred dollars in 1875 and had collected toll thereafter from Helen Hunt Jackson and all the other explorers who had used the Cheyenne Mountain stage road to reach Seven Lakes. In 1890, Count Pourtales had tried to buy the Dixon Ranch, including its orchard near Pourtales' lake. But Dixon's price was much too high for the Count, and that is why his Broadmoor City did not extend west beyond the lake.

Now, ten years later, Stratton shelled out $40,000 for twenty acres of Dixon's ranch surrounding the wooded junction of North and South Cheyenne Creeks. He spent a larger sum on landscaping, creation of ponds, a handsome band stand, and the purchase of many swings for children, picnic tables and iron benches. He pledged $5,000 a year for park maintenance, $4,000 for Colorado Midland Band concerts every summer Sunday, and $4,000 a year for dance music. Stratton Park began its immensely popular career on June 6, 1901, when it was dedicated, appropriately, by officers of Local 515, Carpenters and Joiners of America. Stratton was not among the 4,000 people who attended. The world's richest miner detested public appearances and, besides, he was glumly bed-fast in his Weber Street home being nursed through the pains of over-drinking by his household staff of one.[2]

EVER SINCE his Independence strike, Stratton had increased his consumption of whiskey to lighten his despair. He was morose by nature and, after 1893, his income of $3,000 a day made it absurd of him to go prospecting with a burro as of old and it spoiled his relationship with the only kind of people he cared anything about, uneducated men like himself. There were other penalties of wealth which depressed him. Each day brought dozens of crank letters. On the two-block walk from his Weber Street home to his Pikes Peak Avenue office he would be stopped a dozen times by strangers begging for money. If he gave them something or even spoke to them, he was apt to find himself hauled into court on some trumped-up charge. One day a young Colorado prospector asked Stratton if he should sell his promising gold claim or hang on to it as Stratton had done, hoping for millions in the end. Stratton replied:

> If you get a chance to sell your property for $100,000 do it. I once gave an option on the Independence and a thousand times I have wished that the holder had taken it up. Too much money is not good for any man. I have too much and it is not good for me. A hundred thousand dollars is as much money as the man of ordinary intelligence can take care of. Large wealth has been the ruin of many a young man.

As Stratton's spirits sank, his thin body grew weaker. By 1902, he was an invalid. His years of alcoholism had caused dietary deficiences which affected his liver. He gave himself over to his doctor in his curtained home, drinking his sad days away and staring at his four bleak walls and wondering where he was and why. He was still middle-aged and yet he felt a thousand years old. Now and then he managed to get into his plain black suit with creaseless trousers, put on his gray Stetson hat, and trudge to his Independence Building office. People saw a stooped man looking utterly spent. The cords stood out on the back of his neck. His appearance seemed to justify all the tales which had grown up around him about his bouts with the bottle, his harem of kept women, and alleged demoniac pastimes too sinful to mention.

Children of the town overheard their parents' gossip and were thrilled to conclude that they had a wonderful ogre in their midst far more frightful than Captain Kidd or Bluebeard or any old bogey man. One of these children was the daughter of Tom and Anne Parrish, old friends of Count Pourtales. Little Anne Parrish, a golden-haired girl who loved patent-leather belts, would grow up to write *The Perennial Bachelor* and other novels. She lived on Weber Street near Stratton's home, and her best friends were the neighboring children of Will Jackson. During a squabble with the young Jacksons, Anne was so goaded beyond endurance as to accept the ultimate in awful dares. She agreed to draw a picture on the clean flagstones of Colorado Springs' ogre, using burnt-out carbons which had been discarded by the man who maintained the arc light at Weber and Bijou. Almost suffocated with fear, Anne crossed the street from the Jackson yard and began scratching a face with the carbon on the flagstone near the Stratton gate. The Jackson children watched from the opposite curb. Half a century later, Miss Parrish described the incident:[3]

> I became absorbed in my drawing and did not see Mr. Stratton coming. The others ran and hid. I was caught. I hope I am never quite as frightened again. But he was kind! He asked me whose little girl I was, and said my drawing made his place look better, and that I was to draw there whenever I wanted to, and I would be very welcome. My friend Mr. Stratton! And when my father died suddenly, and my mother found that he had borrowed some money from Mr. Stratton, and went, never having met him, to try to pay it back, he told her that father had paid it the week before he died; which was a beautiful lie.

DURING THE SUMMER OF 1902, Stratton lost the desire to live, entirely. His diseased liver did not cause him much pain. He just disintegrated numbly. On Saturday, September 13, he went into a coma. On Sunday evening, Bob Schwarz, his cobbler-manager, sat with him in the still Weber Street house and Stratton

roused briefly to ask Bob how his sister was. Then he died, at
9:35 p.m., aged fifty-four.

Next day he was eulogized in mining communities throughout
the country. Nine thousand people filed by his body lying in
state at his big new Mining Exchange Building. Some of the
mourners remembered how a few months earlier, the brokers of
Colorado Springs had given a great banquet at the Antlers Hotel
honoring him for constructing this Mining Exchange Building.
One hundred and sixty town leaders had attended, including
General Palmer. Sixteen speakers had praised Stratton far into
the night and the applause had been thunderous. The only
trouble with the affair had been that the guest of honor had had
an alcoholic indispotion at the last minute and had failed to show
up.

At 2 p.m. on Tuesday, September 16, each of Stratton's olive
green trolleys stopped where it was for five minutes. On Wednesday, the gold king was buried on a wooded knoll in Evergreen
Cemetery not far from the entrance gate. The Stratton will was
read a week later while the town waited to hear about it in a
mood of high optimism. Every worthy institution expected a big
slice of that $16,000,000 fortune. But when the news came out,
it was received with angry disappointment. The will contained
nothing that it was supposed to contain. And what had happened
to all that gold? Only $6,000,000 was left. The foolish old fellow,
it seemed, had thrown away at least $7,000,000 in futile explora-
tion at Cripple Creek. His elegant trolleys had soaked up two
millions. Another million had been scattered like confetti among
a thousand panhandling bums. It was lucky, some critics said,
that Stratton died when he did. If he had lasted a bit longer he
would have died broke.

The Stratton will assigned a piddling $20,000 to Colorado
College and only $25,000 to the Deaf and Blind School. It gave
a million dollars to assorted nieces and nephews and to Isaac
Henry Stratton, the son whom Stratton had refused to accept as
his own so long ago by his ex-wife Zeurah Stewart. But it was
the main bequest which caused consternation. It consisted

mostly of Colorado Springs and Denver real estate and it was placed in trust for the establishment of a home for needy children and old people.[4] It was to be named the Myron Stratton home after the boat-building father back in Indiana whom Stratton had never liked. The will did not go into much detail but it made clear that Myron Stratton Home was not to be just another sop to a rich man's vanity. This one would express the point of view of plain people as to what, ideally, a community home should be. It would be a place of simple beauty and dignity and a large farm would surround it. Orphans would grow up there and they would have the advantages of children whose parents were well-to-do. Old people at the Home would not feel that they were charity cases. Husbands and wives would live in cottages which they would think of as their own.

The very thought of such a poor house in Colorado Springs enraged many residents. The town suddenly teemed with lawyers hired to block the project and to break Stratton's will. Even the State of Colorado had a try at grabbing the estate on the grounds that Stratton must have been out of his head when he made the will and, besides, his trustees were incompetent.[5] Suits totalling $23,000,000 were filed. Twelve women turned up in various parts of the United States asserting that they were widows or blood relatives or former mistresses of the gold king. The suits dragged on, and seven years passed before the litigious fog cleared enough so that plans could be made for Myron Stratton Home.

In late August of 1909, the trustees announced that land for it had been bought at last for $350,000. Some residents knew enough Colorado Springs history to enjoy the ironic denouement. The seller of the land was the London and New York Investment Company, the same British group which had taken over Broadmoor City, Broadmoor Casino, and Broadmoor Dairy Farm in 1893 from Count Pourtales, who had defaulted on his $250,000 loan. And so Mr. Stratton's palace for paupers wound up on the same 2,400 acres which the Count had developed for

the comfort and entertainment of the aristocrats of the Pikes
Peak region.

Myron Stratton Home opened finally in 1914. Since then it has
served as a magnificent haven against the unpreventable vicis-
situdes of life.[6] Its capacity was (and is) one hundred old people
and one hundred children whose only qualifications for ad-
mittance besides their need and good standing was that they
had to be residents of El Paso County. The handsome buildings
still stand near the banks of Spring Creek in that lower portion
of Broadmoor Dairy Farm where William Tell, Jr., Prince Tell,
and the rest of Count Pourtales' costly battery of imported Swiss
bulls once disported themselves for the greater glory of Broadmoor "Gilt Edge Crown Butter."

THE CAREER of Winfield Scott Stratton was a brief purple
passage in the Springs story which had little to do with the main
continuity. Very little remains of his trolley system or Stratton
Park. His Myron Stratton Home is a striking monument to a
tenderhearted man but it has none of the dynamic qualities for
stimulating the growth of a community which mark General
Palmer's park system and Spencer Penrose's Broadmoor Hotel
and associated enterprises. And still, Stratton taught Colorado
Springs a lesson which the overweening place needed very badly
to learn just then. Being rich or righteous or refined is not neces-
sarily a passport to happiness nor a criterion of excellence. People
of no importance are also wonderful and deserve their place in
the sun, too, especially in a land where an unschooled carpenter
can pop up from nowhere to become king for a day.

CHAPTER THIRTEEN

The Red-Blooded Blue Blood

NOTHING IS NICER than savoring today and dreaming of tomorrow. But the past, like a good play, also has its points, particularly when a leading man is about to go on stage and there we are god-like in the wings watching him get ready for his entrance.

Spencer Penrose was twenty-seven years old when he first saw Pikes Peak on a sunny afternoon of December 10, 1892. A generation had gone by since Palmer's first visit in '69. The village of shacks on the windy plain had become a city, its homes and lawns protected by tall cottonwoods and by the imported maples and elms and lindens which had begun to replace Major McAllister's pioneer trees. Colorado Springs had a little of everybody—invalids, rich and poor, people making a living out of tourists, the trade and service crowd, workers in small factories along the Midland tracks west of town. The big homes were in the North End and were supposed to be of Queen Anne and Moorish and Tudor design with stables in the rear for fine horses and carriages. Elsewhere, east, west, and south, comfortable cottages stood on neat fifty-foot lots. Their architecture was Cape Cod or Iowa Gothic or Kansas peak-roof.

The Spencer Penrose who stepped from the train at the Santa Fe depot was a man over six feet tall with a body as deep, as sturdy as that of a young bull moose. He had a square, ruddy face with a straight nose and an expression of alert composure. He was not merely good-looking. He was spectacularly handsome. And still his looks were not exactly heart-warming. His

171

manner had a certain reserve about it. He just wasn't the kind of fellow men went up to and started pounding on the back.

He had left the East four years earlier and had settled in Las' Cruces, New Mexico, to run a business called "Mesilla Valley Fruit and Produce Co., wholesale and retail dealers in fruits, vegetables, hay, grain, coal, lime, agricultural implements and stoves." His older brother, Richard A. F. Penrose, Jr., was a mining consultant who had stopped in the Springs often and had written to him about the delights of Pikes Peak, its cricket games and gay polo balls at the Antlers Hotel. When Spencer Penrose tired of selling stoves at Las Cruces, he quit the produce company and roamed the Rockies looking for a gold mine and then headed for Colorado Springs. He was met at the depot by an old Philadelphia friend, Charles Leaming Tutt, aged twenty-eight, who was even taller than Penrose and sported a reddish moustache. The fathers of both young men had studied medicine together at the University of Pennsylvania but Dr. Tutt had died when Charley was a baby and he had to go to work before finishing high school. Charley had come to Pikes Peak in '84 longing to be a cowboy. After freezing for three winters in the Black Forest, he had moved to town to sell real estate and insurance. At the Springs depot, he greeted Penrose by his nickname, "Spec," a childhood corruption of Spencer. As the two friends walked to Tutt's buggy, Spec remarked in his low pitched economical speech sprinkled with casual profanity that he was broke and needing a job. Next, he announced that he wanted a drink. That is why the buggy moved briskly through Palmer's temperance town toward the Cheyenne Mountain Country Club in Broadmoor, which had a bar.

They passed Grace Church on Pikes Peak Avenue just as Orlando Metcalf's daughter was coming out with a new husband, William Varker, of New York. On Tejon Street, they noticed an opera scene made of taffy in the display window of Thomas Gough's Chicago Bakery. Meanwhile, Charley Tutt told Spec about the mine he had located at Cripple Creek and named the C.O.D. Then he offered Spec a half interest in his real estate business for $500, if Spec would go up to Cripple Creek and run his branch there. Not having $500, Spec had nothing to lose and he accepted Charley's offer, promising to pay the $500—some time.[1] When they reached the Cheyenne Mountain Country Club in the late afternoon, Spec signed the club's guest book in a strong, forward-leaning hand. From then on for almost half a century until his death in 1939 his only home was in the shadow of Pikes Peak. But he couldn't have conceived of such a thing in December, 1892.

Like General Palmer, Penrose was a Philadelphian and he could more than hold his own with Palmer as to background even if he did arrive in Colorado Springs dead broke and thirsty. Spec was born on November 2, 1865, in an old family home with an impeccable address, 1331 Spruce Street, a few blocks from the Liberty Bell. His father, Dr. Richard A. F. Penrose, was a great-great-great-great grandson of Bartholomew Penrose. This Bartholomew was a partner of a rather important Philadelphian named William Penn who had bought Pennsylvania in 1681 for $80,000. Spec's mother, Sarah Hannah Boies, was descended from William Hubbard, Harvard College, Class of 1642, and most of the Boies men went to Harvard thereafter. Spec, however, was named for a Yale man, his great-great grandfather, the Reverend Elihu Spencer (Class of 1746), who was additionally a trustee of Princeton. The Penroses made a habit of marrying at least Drexels or Biddles or Chews. As a result, Spec, besides being a very blue-blooded Penrose, was related to practically every other blue blood that Philadelphia had turned out in two hundred years. Some of these aristocrats had managed to shake loose from the town. Spec's great-great-great-great aunt was the wife of the famous Indian fighter, Mad Anthony Wayne. His great-grandfather was Thomas Jefferson's commissioner of Louisiana Territory. His grandfather was U. S. Treasury Solicitor under President William Henry Harrison. Spec was not the first Penrose to live in Colorado. His cousin, General William Henry Penrose, established Fort Lyon on the Arkansas below Pueblo in 1867 and nursed Kit Carson during his last illness.

When Spec began his Pikes Peak career under the auspices of
Charley Tutt, his motives were clear. He wanted to get rich as
quickly as possible. He did not just have a vague idea about it.
With him, the desire to get rich—very, very rich—was burning and
fundamental, an overwhelming urge which had been accruing
in his rather complicated psyche from earliest childhood. His
father, the Doctor, was a charming, intellectual, worldly man who
had won wide distinction and some wealth in Philadelphia as a
physician and as a professor of obstetrics at the University of
Pennsylvania. His mother was a great beauty, and she had
brains, too; she passed both gifts and her large brown eyes on
to her children. She had had four sons already when Spec was
born in 1865. A first "Boies" died in infancy. Boies (the second)
was born in 1860, Charles Bingham Penrose in '62, and Dick
(Richard A. F., Jr.) in '63. After Spec came Francis in '67 and
Philip in '69.[2] Sarah Hannah Penrose was a devoted mother who
spent all her energy in the training of her sons, but she died at
forty-seven when Spec was only fifteen years old. Her totally
unexpected death occurred while he was alone with her in the
Spruce Street house. Dr. Penrose and the other boys were out
of town and it was the servant's day off. The terror and grief and
aloneness which Spec felt before his father arrived affected him
deeply. For the rest of his life he hated to be alone and he could
not mention his mother's name without tears.

The first three sons of Dr. and Mrs. Penrose developed into
men of extraordinary brilliance. In the year of Mrs. Penrose's
death, 1881, Boies and Charles ("Tal") graduated from Harvard
with highest honors—Tal standing first in his class of two hundred
(he was nineteen years old) and Boies standing second. In 1884,
Tal achieved the almost incredible feat of winning two post-
graduate degrees in different parts of the country—his Ph.D.
at Harvard and his M.D. at the University of Pennsylvania. Boies
was elected to the Pennsylvania Legislature to begin a political
career which would take him to the United States Senate and
make him one of the most autocratic political bosses in American
history.[3] Dick Penrose graduated in that same year of 1884 from

Harvard with the rating of *summa cum laude,* highest honors in chemistry *and* a Phi Beta Kappa key. In 1886, he won his M. A. degree and a Ph.D. in geology.

Such transcendental scholastic records suggested that these three Penroses were pedantic. Actually, they applied themselves with equal ardor to the study of riotous living in the Gerry Street house at Cambridge which their father had bought for them as a sort of private Harvard dormitory. Dr. Penrose was a pragmatic parent. He was a strong advocate of academic education, but he believed that young men should know about wine, women, and song, too. He was especially insistent that his offspring become versed in the wiles by which women enticed men into their nets and that they learn how to wriggle free when female enslavement threatened. For this training, he directed them to the dives along the Schuylkill River where young Philadelphians had matriculated from time immemorial.

When Spec entered Harvard, Class of 1886, he was determined to win as many honors as his brothers and it distressed him to find that he could not begin to compete with them. Even with tutoring, he barely squeaked through Harvard with an undistinguished A.B. degree and nothing else. By this time, he had acquired a conviction that Dr. Penrose had no confidence in him and, worse still, didn't really give a damn because the accomplishments of his other three sons were compensation enough. And Spec felt inferior to Boies and Tal and Dick socially and physically as well as intellectually. They seemed to him to be good dancers and at ease with these dangerous girl-creatures whereas Spec was a horrible dancer and hopelessly inept at social chitchat. Though he drank as much as he could at Harvard and rioted indefatigably, he was disheartened to learn from President Charles Eliot himself that Boies and Tal had drunk harder and had made still more clamor.[4] As a toper, Spec could almost hold his own with the more temperate Dick Penrose, but then Dick was a tremendous athlete who had been stroke on the victorious Harvard crew for two years running. When Spec tried out for the same crew, he wound up ingloriously in the infirmary after permanently damaging the retina of his left eye while trying to lift a shell from the Charles River.

Oddly, Spec did not resent his brothers because of their apparent superiority. He loved and admired them and imitated them and sought their advice. They were his favorite companions. He loved his father, too, though he was more than a little intimidated by the Doctor's cold realism and rigid standards of discipline. But Spec was quite different from the others in his attitude toward his illustrious family name. The Penroses, indubitably, were Philadelphia blue bloods, social leaders, members of the best clubs, and so on. That was fair enough, and Spec accepted the fact with pride—as long as nobody accused him of standing on his ancestors' feet. He felt that he had good feet of his own, which served his purposes. He believed in himself more than in any ancestor—his own free-wheeling, non-conformist self—and he believed in his personal liberty, too. That liberty was part of his creed and he would not allow it to be restricted by a bunch of blue-blooded ghosts. Or by live people either, for that matter.

SPEC WAS HIMSELF—for better or worse, richer or poorer. And when he arrived stony broke in Colorado Springs in 1892, he hoped with all his heart that it would be for richer. He had been getting nowhere in the West for four years now and it was time to start showing the skeptical Dr. Penrose that he could make money at least. He got off to a rather bad start the very first week by participating in a brisk brawl at the Cheyenne Mountain Country Club during which he smashed up a good deal of expensive furniture in the main lounge. But he fell instantly in love with Cripple Creek and from '93 to '96 he enjoyed a full life in "the greatest gold camp on earth"—a bewitching environment of absolute freedom where nothing that a man wished to do was barred or even frowned on. Spec became a sort of flugleman in miner's dress for a battalion of tough, shrewd, sharp, ambitious youngsters nicknamed "The Socialites." They worked hard all day mining or making deals, and they roistered through the night, playing poker or faro or twenty-one in the Bennett Avenue saloons or studying life on the next lively street south. After the collapse of Colorado silver mining in 1893, a host of unemployed professional sinners from all over invaded Cripple Creek and decorated a quarter-mile of Myers Avenue with thumping dance halls, pawnshops, drug mills, and one-room cribs where girls of every age and color offered whatever they had to sell by a technique of raising and lowering their window blinds.

Spec took a bachelor cabin on Prospect Street at the top of the roaring camp with Harry Leonard, a New York product of St. Mark's School and Columbia University. Harry, an expert horseman, drove the six-mule stage up from the Springs for a time and changed the scenery of his face monthly—from flowing moustache to Van Dyke to goatee to sideburns. The crowd's bodyguard was the Glenwood Springs polo star, Horace Devereux, a vast Princeton football hero, Class of 1881, who could lose his candle deep in a labyrinthine mine and find his way out in the dark by dead reckoning. Devereux had a sweet disposition when sober but whiskey made him as aggressive as a grizzly bear, apt to poke down a bartender or a chippy with one wave of his huge paw. Charlie MacNeill joined the group in mid-'93—a thin, high-strung Chicagoan in his twenties who had learned the chemistry of ore reduction at Aspen and set up Cripple Creek's first chemical plant.

The geologist, Dick Penrose, handsomest member of his handsome family, was in and out of town, but Dick liked dull pursuits at night such as sleeping alone or writing government mining reports, one of which (with Whitman Cross), "Geology and Mining Industries of the Cripple Creek District," is a standard reference work still. Albert E. (Bert) Carlton was there, a pale lad with ice-cold eyes and no bad habits even if he did have—all at the same time—a wife, secretly, back in Illinois, and a fiancée in Colorado Springs, and a true-love in Cripple Creek—a pretty stenographer named Ethel Frizzell.

The Cripple Creek real estate firm of Tutt and Penrose dabbled in everything. The partners erected a large office building on

Bennett Avenue, bought and leased the big Topic Dance Hall on Myers Avenue, promoted the town site of Gillett, worked placers, and ran a gold sampler. Charley Tutt sold Spec a third interest in his C.O.D. Mine which Dick Penrose and other *summa cum laude* geologists said was composed mostly of water—until some Frenchmen paid Charley $250,000 for it. The tale persists that Spec wired his oldest brother Boies for money to buy his third interest in the C.O.D. Boies wired back $150 for his rail fare home and ordered him to 1331 Spruce Street at once. But Spec (the story goes) kept the $150 and later sent Boies $10,000 as a return on his $150 "investment."

During the Cripple Creek strike of 1894, Spec and his friends banded together to form Company K of the sheriff's deputy army defending the mine owners. Spec, whose worst nightmares had to do with running out of liquor, became apprehensive that Company K might not have enough during the campaign. He hurried on horseback to the Springs to find that the drug stores had exhausted their whiskey stocks. However a Cascade Avenue mine owner donated a barrel of bourbon. Spec's horse couldn't carry a barrel, and flasks were not on hand. Inspired by necessity, Spec stopped at Glockner Hospital and bought a dozen rubber hot water bottles. He filled them with the bourbon, hung them from his saddle, and returned to Company K triumphantly by way of the Cheyenne Mountain stage road.[5]

Now and then, the Socialites took off their miners' boots and work clothes and took the train down to Little London in white tie and tails to attend gala dances with the nice North End girls at the Antlers Hotel or El Paso Club. Spec suffered painfully with these sweet young things for lack of anything to say. Once, trying to make talk, he blurted to an arch North Ender, "Do you or don't you—" and stopped, forgetting to add "play tennis?" The outraged filly denied that she did and called her fiancé to defend her honor. For a while a duel seemed the only way out until Charlie MacNeill smoothed things over.

The Socialites had plenty of females to dance with at Cripple Creek, too—and not just the short-frocked set on Myers Avenue but smart pretty girls on the prowl for husbands with paying mines attached. One of these was named Sarah Elizabeth Halthusen, a strapping big-busted, dark-eyed brunette of Spanish-Swedish extraction. Sally's gentle hobby was breaking mean horses. She had met Spec first in the Springs and, when he went to Cripple Creek, she hurried after him, living first on her father's ranch at Florissant and then moving with her corral of equine delinquents to a house on Bennett Avenue. Soon Cripple Creek residents were stirred by the sight of her as she rode her white horse astride up the steep hill toward the Leonard-Penrose shack on Prospect Street. How the affair ended is legend purely, embroidered by time's vivid imagination. In spite of the training which Dr. Penrose had given him to escape from women's wiles, Spec seems to have been captivated by Sally, even after learning that she had collected a large ransom from a Denver family to release its son from marriage to her. The legend goes that Dr. Penrose heard of the romance. At his command, Dick Penrose—or maybe it was Boies—went to Cripple Creek and had a talk with Spec about the propriety of a Philadelphia blue blood marrying a Colorado animal trainer.

Whatever happened, the white horse stopped carrying Sally up the hill to the Leonard-Penrose cabin. Very soon after, she left camp and returned to the Springs. In 1895, she married Thomas Gough, Jr., the hotel owner and taffy artist whose Chicago Bakery display window had attracted Spec's attention on his first ride through town. Sally continued to break mean horses and for years she was very touchy about her Cripple Creek affair. When she heard a chambermaid at the Gough hotel gossiping about it, she went at her with a horse whip and cut her up badly. Sally was hauled into court, pleaded guilty to assault, and was fined $10 and costs. Of course the legend has it that Spec paid the fine.[6]

BY AN ACCIDENT OF FATE, Charlie MacNeill's pioneer reduction mill in Cripple Creek burned down in December of 1895 just as Charley Tutt and Spec were wondering what to do with their profits from the sale of the C.O.D. Mine. The three thought of themselves as experienced mining men by this time. They were inclined to agree with Bert Carlton that the only sensible way to make money in a gold camp was to corner its transportation and its facilities for refining ore, and then to charge all the traffic would bear. Carlton had expanded his Colorado Trading and Transport Company and was approaching monopoly in local wagon transport. Bert, a ruthless strategist, was at the same time conniving with Harry Blackmer (of later Teapot Dome notoriety) to control the Midland Terminal Railroad, which ran from Cripple Creek to the Colorado Midland station at Divide. Tutt, Penrose, and MacNeill decided to sink their slender capital into a new mill, the Colorado-Philadelphia. Instead of building it at Cripple Creek, they put it on the mesa near Colorado City, gambling that it would be cheaper to haul gold ore down there than to haul coal for the mill forty-four miles up to the gold camp.

The Colorado-Philadelphia Mill opened in September of '96 and prospered. It did so well that Spec could afford a trip around the world in 1899 and a Cuban vacation in 1900 with his brother Tal. One year later, Tutt, Penrose, and MacNeill went to New York and organized a mill trust, the United States Reduction and Refining Company, capitalized at almost $13,000,000. With this money, they girdled the Cripple Creek district with their mills. At the same time, they cooperated with the Carlton-Blackmer transport monopoly so that the two groups could control much of the camp's business.

Sweet success! Spec Penrose, the black sheep, the dumb one, the disregarded, seemed to have within his grasp his heart's desire—a fortune at the age of thirty-six. And still, Dr. Penrose, whose approval Spec wanted above all, remained cautious and skeptical. He wrote his son Dick in 1901, underlining his doubts: "Spencer is hopeful of success, and, if they carry out their scheme, it will give us all a great deal of money on *paper*." And again, a few weeks later: "Spencer and partners have concluded their deal $13,000,000. It all *sounds* very fine."

The Tutt-Penrose-MacNeill mill trust was despised and castigated and bitterly fought on both sides of Pikes Peak because of the high price which it could squeeze out of mine owners for handling Cripple Creek ore. It was also admired and applauded by quite a few people. And so it marked the beginning of a local controversy as to whether Penrose was saint or demon which lasted most of his life. Paradoxically, the hard-boiled traits for which he was criticized were precisely those which in the end produced the most good for Colorado Springs.[7]

CHAPTER FOURTEEN

Take Me Out to the Ball Game

THE DEATH of Stratton in 1902 coincided with the fading out of problems which had kept the Pikes Peak country in an uproar ever since the rise and fall of the radical Governor Waite and Populism in the 1890s. The Spanish-American War and the free silver issue were over and done with. The stupendous growth which accompanied the Cripple Creek boom was on the wane. For the first time in its life, Colorado Springs had nothing serious on its mind. The residents—nearly 35,000 of them—were generally prosperous. Many of them were uncouth newcomers who said "ain't" and dunked bread in their coffee, causing the Palmer Old Guard to shudder and talk nostalgically of the Little London that used to be. But in 1902 Colorado Springs as a whole decided to relax and enjoy itself and the heck with being too genteel about it.

It was an era of fascinating sights and sounds and events. Pikes Peak Avenue, which General Cameron had marked with a plow only thirty years before, was a bright, bustling thoroughfare. The brand-new Antlers Hotel stood at its west end silhouetted against the Peak and big buildings rose all along, such as Stratton's Mining Exchange Building and the First National Bank. The wide street and its tree-shaded sidewalks formed a kaleidoscope of clattering street cars and every kind of horse pulling surreys and runabouts and cabs and wagons and spider phaetons. There were darting bicyclists and male pedestrians in bowlers and ladies with hour-glass figures in huge hats and trailing skirts. A proud spectacle was Hallett and Baker's white hearse, its glossy top ornamented at the corners with hand-carved urns. The hearse was

182

drawn by satiny white horses in black harness. Visiting celebrities were still common—William Jennings Bryan, the perennial candidate, and Prince von Bismarck's grandson and ex-Vice President Adlai Stevenson and President Roosevelt himself, with his Springs friends, Dr. Gerald Webb and P. B. Stewart.

The summers were filled with pleasure. Special trains on the Short Line and Midland Terminal climbed thrillingly through the forested slopes of Pikes Peak to Cripple Creek, 3,500 feet above the plain. On Sundays, hundreds of families burdened with baskets of fried chicken and potato salad took the Colorado Midland "Wildflower Excursion" up Ute Pass to South Park by way of Lake George and Eleven-Mile Canyon. The train stopped now and then so that passengers could pick armfuls of red paintbrush and purple beardtongue and blue lupine. At Florissant, some of them collected bits of petrified wood. August in the Springs was the time for Flower Parades when the Cripple Creek millionaires and their stylish wives rode past the Antlers judge's stand in gorgeous blossom-decked equipages. All these activities were covered in the daily Colorado Springs *Gazette*, which often contained thirty pages or more in contrast to J. Elsom Liller's little four-page weekly of the 1870s. The *Gazette's* four pages of "funnies" were in color, presenting the eccentric careers of Major Ozone and Sammy Small, Jocko and Jumbo, and Little Ah Sid, the Chinese Kid. Male readers pored over local Sports and the women read of Society and Fashions and the "Most Popular Lady" contests. They studied with intensity the big Lydia Pinkham and Pe-ru-na and Paine's Celery Compound testimonial ads, featuring photos of prominent ladies of Newport and Narragansett who explained how their troubles had been cured by one of these miraculous patent medicines.

Some citizens in summer hung around the Denver and Rio Grande depot for the drama of it. Since the first days of E. E. Nichols' Cliff House in Manitou, Pikes Peak tourism had continued so fiercely competitive that hotel runners boarded Springs-bound trains as far away as Kansas and Wyoming in order to make up the minds of visitors as to where they would stay. At the

depot, twenty or thirty tough drivers of fringed surreys girded
themselves for battle as the tour trains came in. Among the
drivers, none was tougher than old Ma Gaines, a volcanic Ama-
zon in coarse khaki dress and a man's hat. Ma could out-swear
and out-fight and out-smart any male in the scramble for a fare,
and if she thought that she had lost a customer unfairly she went
after her colleague with a buggy whip.[1]

The gold of Cripple Creek had caused a steady deterioration of
the moral climate of El Paso County. Every smart mine owner
had a judge or two on his pay roll in case he needed a divorce or
a favorable decision in a mine dispute. High-grading—the stealing of valuable gold ore—was a respected gold camp business. In
Colorado Springs, the thriving citizenry was too complacent to do
anything about the Duff gang of pickpockets and con men.
Members of the gang operated at Stratton Park and the Opera
House and Roswell race track and were always at the depot
hunting suckers who might want to buy lots on top of Pikes Peak.
However, in 1903, one of the gang sold a Pikes Peak lot to the
wrong sucker. This victim raised a terrible squawk and before
he left the city he proved that the gang paid protection money
regularly to Police Chief Vincent King and Detective Joel At-
kinson. Both officers were indicted and kicked off the force, to
be replaced by officials some of whom were equally corrupt.

Palmer's old liquor ban had kept saloons out of the General's
town, but the ban was more of a joke than ever and whiskey was
sold in most drug stores if the buyer made a V-sign and muttered
the medical password, "Something good for Jimmie, please."
Gambling in Cripple Creek penny stocks forced North End
servant girls occasionally to make good their losses by lapses of
virtue, but professional prostitution in the Springs was barred,
with the result that amorous males who wanted to buy love had
a long trip ahead of them—all of four blocks west of the city
limits to the red-light-and-saloon district of Colorado City. In
their book, To Colorado's Restless Ghosts, Inez Hunt and Wanetta Draper estimated that Colorado City had some twenty-
seven saloons in 1902. Its red-light district was on present

Cucharras Street from Twenty-Fourth Street west for four blocks.
The industry had upgraded itself since Blanche Barton's tenting
days. Every hustling girl owned a pure-bred French poodle and
a Cripple Creek mining claim or two. Three Colorado City
madams, Mamie Majors, Laura Bell, and Minnie Smith, were so
regal in dress and bearing that they could have been mistaken
for North End society matrons as they drove in their trim rigs
along Tejon Street.

Automobiles arrived early at Pikes Peak. Several of them were
seen in the mid-Nineties—Locomobile steamers from Denver
spouting black smoke and scaring the horses to death. However,
the *Gazette* did not report a horseless carriage in town until July
of 1899. It was a homemade affair—a heavy motorized wagon
painted red, gold, and maroon, with solid rubber tires and a
top speed of fifteen miles an hour. Two mechanics, E. J. Cabler
and Robert Temple, built it in Denver for $2,000. It spent two
days on the 77-mile Springs trip but would have made better
time if it had not been delayed by running out of a mysterious
fuel which the *Gazette* called "gasoline, the oil used to generate
motive power."

Though the Cabler-Temple wagon was no great shakes, nearly
a dozen Springs residents bought cars in 1900, including Dr. R.
H. Arnold and the Cripple Creek stock brokers William Anthony,
George Bonbright, Sherman Aldrich, and Nelson Partridge. Dr.
Joseph Wright drove a Locomobile steamer and J. K. Vanatta
bought another through Dr. William A. Bell who had finally quit
the Manitou Park hotel business in favor of making steamers in
Tarrytown, New York, as vice president of the Mobile Company
of America.[2] In 1901, Little London could boast that it had one
of the West's first two-car families. Mr. and Mrs. Charles A.
Baldwin, late of San Francisco by way of Newport, had settled
on North Cascade Avenue and had stunned the neighbors by
bringing from the East a French Panhard gas car and a high,
black, bird-cage of a tiller-steered vehicle with silver lanterns and
flower vases inside called a Columbia Electric. Charlie MacNeill
of the Tutt-Penrose-MacNeill mill trust got his Wood Electric a

few weeks later. In 1902, the broker, W. W. Price, acquired a gas
Winton, allegedly the best of American cars. The intrepid Price
accomplished the prodigious feat of driving his Winton over
Tennessee Pass to Glenwood Springs. To rival him, Spec Penrose
and Charlie MacNeill paid $12,500 for an esoteric French Rochet-
Schneider gas car to use in the Memorial Day Endurance Race of
1903 from Denver to Palmer Lake and back. Unfortunately, the
race was won easily by a Winton, the Rochet-Schneider lacking
the endurance to last 100 miles. It burst a gasket at Castle Rock
and had to be towed home by a brace of oxen.

Almost nobody as yet took cars seriously except the pioneer
garage man, C. G. Strang. Nearly all Springs residents agreed
with General Palmer that they smelled too bad and made too
much noise to appeal to civilized people. If any one divined the
revolution which these strange contraptions were about to bring
on, he closed his mind to it as too appalling for thought. The
strong tendency in the Springs—as everywhere in the United
States—was to keep cars in their place within a familiar orbit.
They were, after all, just troublesome buggies with motors that
some times worked but usually didn't and horses would always
be necessary to keep them going. Most manufacturers built
them to look like buggies and to meet buggy road conditions in
a buggy-like way. C. G. Strang's worst problem in starting his
garage was what to call it, since "garage" was an unknown
French word. He tried "automobiliary" and was criticized so
severely that he changed the name in a hurry to "Livery Stable
for Automobiles."

The fact that cars were not temperamental buggies but a new
kind of transportation which would reshape the whole planet
began to be divined in July of 1903 when a topless, twelve-horse-
power Packard car with a "cyclops" headlight in the center of its
buckboard chugged into town from San Francisco on its tri-
umphant way to New York. The welcoming crowd on Pikes
Peak Avenue learned that it had averaged seventy-five miles a
day without mechanical trouble through Reno and Salt Lake and

over Tennessee Pass. Soon after this event, a young bicyclist was almost killed by a car on North Cascade Avenue which was the only stretch of road in Colorado smooth enough for a motorist to test his top speed. Because of the accident and the racing, ordinances were passed restricting speeds to twelve miles an hour in the business district and eighteen miles an hour elsewhere. But racing on Cascade Avenue continued since no policeman could catch a car to stop it or even guess accurately how fast it was traveling.

A stark tragedy had to occur before Colorado Springs officials came to grips with the auto problem and began to regulate traffic in any sort of modern way. On September 16, 1907, the manager of a Colorado Springs auto agency spent a convivial evening with friends at the handsome new Elks Club on the corner of Bijou Street and Cascade Avenue. Around 1 a.m., the dealer was inspired to go joy-riding and brought forth from his garage across the street his fast, forty-horse power, six-cylinder Ford. It was a three-passenger job but nine Elks managed to climb aboard. One man sat on the hood and others stood on the running board. For two hours, the gay clinging riders flew about town, with honking visits to Manitou. At last, the car roared eastward down Colorado Avenue. It hit the turn at the top of the Colorado Avenue hill and went out of control, shedding men in all directions as it slithered and crashed its way to the foot of the grade. When the police arrived, three men were found dead, one was dying, and the other five were badly cut up. The driver of the car was charged with speeding and involuntary manslaughter. His case dragged through the courts for a year during which everyone came to realize that no existing law effectively covered the conduct of motorists. The driver was finally acquitted.

By 1909, 250 Springs residents had registered their cars with the city. In 1910 there were 811 cars and by 1915 the total had risen to 1,472 for El Paso County, comprising 115 different *makes* of cars. Ford led the field with 367 and then came Buick, 181. Next in order were Cadillac, Chalmers, E.M.F., Overland, Studebaker, Hudson, Maxwell, Baker Electric, Franklin, Hupmobile, Reo, and Packard. Even the diehards were beginning to admit that the horseless carriage had come to stay.

BASEBALL OF SORTS was played in the Springs from the Seventies, but it took the gold of Cripple Creek to give the town a big-time professional team. Baseball's patron was a wild Irishman named Tom Burns who had been a fireman on the Colorado Midland Railroad. Tom's wealth derived from the great Portland Mine which his shrewd brother, Jimmie Burns, the ex-plumber, had developed. In 1901, while Winfield Scott Stratton was extending his trolley system out South Tejon Street to Stratton Park, Tom Burns got his hands on a Western League franchise with Bill Hulen, the sensational Pueblo shortstop, as player-manager. Tom's business manager was Hiram Rogers, city editor of the *Gazette*—an extremely perceptive reporter but unversed in finance which bored him so much that he could forget for weeks to pick up his salary check.

It was Hiram Rogers who named the new Colorado Springs nine the Millionaires—when it was winning—or the Invalids, during losing streaks. Games that first summer were played on Washburn Field at Colorado College, attendance was poor, and even if it had been good the club would have lost money because money leaked through Hiram like water through a sieve. The only decent pitcher, "Bones" Parvin, was worked so hard that his arm nearly fell off. The Millionaires—or Invalids—ended at the very bottom of the league, winning, Rogers said, "the lobster championship."

Because of this pitiful showing, the heads of the Western League urged the Millionaires to go play baseball in some less distinguished league. But Tom Burns got his Irish dander up and refused to turn in his franchise. His first wise move of rehabilitation was to ship Hiram Rogers back to his desk at the *Gazette*. Next, he induced the ailing Stratton to build a first-class ball field, Boulevard Park, along his new trolley route near the present juncture of Tejon Street and Cheyenne Boulevard. Stratton was joined in the Boulevard Park project by Jimmie Burns and Ed Giddings, the Springs merchant and mine owner.

The park was completed for opening day, Wednesday, April 23, 1902, and 4,000 fans rode Stratton's olive green street cars out from town. The ladies with their parasols occupied the non-smoking compartments and wondered who among them worked on West Cucharras Street. The gold mill men and the Duff gang horse-played in the car vestibules and passed around their corked beer and whiskey bottles. Mr. Stratton, Ed Giddings, and the Burns brothers arrived in a gleaming landau but did not enter the field immediately. Instead they paused for refreshment at Showalter's saloon just across the street from Boulevard Park a few yards out of the city limits.

Within the park, all was joyous anticipation. The splendid Midland Band blared forth John Philip Sousa's new march, "Hail to the Spirit of Liberty," as the huge crowd filled the sixty-five cent grandstand seats and the forty-cent bleachers. Swarms of youngsters hawked peanuts and popcorn balls and the black-suited umpires tested the ball trough which ran down underground and out to the pitcher's box. Applause rocked the blue sky as the Millionaires, in maroon-trimmed cream uniforms, and the Kansas City Blues, in steel-gray uniforms, lined up bare-headed and respectful before Mayor Robinson in his place of honor. Tom Burns appeared in cutaway and silk hat and banged a big gong at the Millionaires' dugout. At this signal, a gate in the back stop swung slowly open and out on the field strode the heroes of the day, the creators of Boulevard Park—tall, thin, stooped Winfield Stratton, neat little Jimmie Burns, stalwart Ed Giddings. Judge Ira Harris followed behind them, adding a note of courtroom decorum.

Though the Millionaires' three benefactors had put away several snorts during their brief stop at Showalter's, they carried their liquor well and marched without a trace of irregularity. Stratton handed his gray Stetson to Harris, went to the pitcher's box and took a ball from the end of the pipe as a gentle breeze ruffled his white hair. Jimmie Burns moved to home plate and

squatted there, catcher's mask in place. Ed Giddings stepped
up to bat, chin jutting belligerently. The judge was plate umpire.
In a rare moment of extrovert energy, Stratton executed a long
wind-up and threw the ball in the general direction of Giddings'
bat. Judge Harris roared "Ball!" and Jimmie Burns reached to
his right to try to stop Stratton's wild pitch.

That should have ended the opening ceremony. But batter
Ed Giddings fooled every one of the 4,000 fans. He threw his
bat at the ball and somehow it connected. The ball wobbled foul
into the grandstand where it was caught by a popular Springs
maiden named Prudence Zobrist. Pandemonium reigned and the
Midland Band struck up an exultant "The Stars and Stripes
Forever." At the pitcher's box, old Stratton went limp with
fatigue and excitement and was half-carried from the happy
scene by Tom Burns.

To cap the climax, the Millionaires took the opener, 5-2. However, the Milwaukee Angels won the 1902 Western League pen-
nant with the Millionaires sixth, leading the Des Moines Pro-
hibitionists and the Peoria Booze Manufacturers. Colorado
Springs would have nosed out the St. Joe Saints for fifth place
but, as you recall, Winfield Scott Stratton died on September 14.
In his memory, Tom Burns canceled a double-header on the day
of his funeral and both games with the Saints were forfeited.

But 1902 was the Millionaires' only profitable year. Boulevard
Park lost money steadily through 1903 as Cripple Creek gold
production dipped from $18,000,000 to $12,000,000 and pro-
longed labor troubles reduced employment in Colorado City
mills and elsewhere in the Pikes Peak region. The trustees of
Stratton's estate eased out Tom Burns as the game's impressario
and then closed and tore down Boulevard Park after the 1904
Western League season. Quality baseball returned briefly in
1916 but from then on Pikes Peak saw no more of it until after
World War II when the Colorado Springs Sky Sox held forth at
Memorial Field from 1950 through 1958, winning Western
League pennants in 1954 and 1957 and placing second in 1952.

EVERY COMMUNITY needs for its well-being an equivalent of Falstaff, Shakespeare's delightful reprobate with a heart of gold. Colorado Springs was blessed with one of the finest of Falstaffs for a dozen summers. His full soubriquet was The Honorable Bathhouse John Joseph Coughlin, an Irish native of Chicago, whose brilliant career of statesmanship began modestly in a Turkish bathhouse, first as a rubber and then as owner. Bathhouse John, or simply The Bath, as his adoring constituents called him, was elected Alderman of the First Ward, nerve center of Chicago geopolitics, in 1892. Within a decade, he was the worthy recipient of a high five-figure income in pay-offs from conscientious business men and women who ran the First Ward's brothels and gambling houses, drug mills and crooked race tracks, confidence outfits, peep-shows, pimpster, tipster and pickpocket associations, tax-fixing firms, trolley men seeking franchises, and utility executives wishing to dump raw sewage into the Chicago River. Bathhouse John was personally as pure and innocent as a babe. He did not drink—much, nor swear—much, nor was he untrue to his good Catholic wife Mary, whom he addressed affectionately as "My Queen." He attended church faithfully. The Lord had ordained him to be a politician and it was not his fault if politicians in the great city of Chicago had to serve the vice industry by nature of established order and tradition.[3]

It was because of his kindliness that The Bath heard of Colorado Springs. As an important Democrat, it was his privilege to guard the health of loyal First Ward voters at the Party's expense. Loyal voting prostitutes often came down with tuberculosis and he found that they did best if he sent them out West incognito to Glockner Hospital or to one of the convalescent homes on North Nevada Avenue. In 1901, Alderman Coughlin and My Queen visited Pikes Peak in person. The Bath saw at once that it was the ideal place for expressing his goodness and nobility, untainted by ties with the First Ward's tenderloin. It occurred to him also that Colorado Springs was almost as remote as Timbuctoo. He could spend his huge pay-off income there and no

Chicagoan would be around to ask, "How'd you buy that on a salary of $100 a month?"

If the Springs was far from Chicago, Chicago was just as far from the Springs. When, in December of 1902, Bathhouse John stopped at the Antlers Hotel and revealed that he had $88,560 cash in a tin box with which to purchase the Mary E. Johnson ranch on Cheyenne Creek a few blocks beyond Boulevard Park,[4] the whole town welcomed the celebrity. All the residents knew, of course, that he was a Chicago Alderman but somehow a thousand miles of distance threw a thick haze over the exact services which he performed to be one. The bankers of Tejon Street, especially, competed avidly for the custom of a tycoon who wandered around with $88,560 in a tin box.

In his forty-second year, The Bath was big, athletic, fleshily handsome, noisy, and as full of the joy and wonder of life as a litter of new-born puppies. He admired himself with an ingenuous amazement. This was not conceit but just the working of an objective mind which could accept a wonderful reality without bias, even though the reality happened to be Bathhouse John Coughlin. His clothes expressed his contempt for the status quo. He affected purple trousers and Prince Albert tail coats of infield green and silk hats iridescently mulberry and many-hued vests. He was said to own twenty-two pairs of button shoes, all bright yellow. His bathing suit was pink polka-dotted and his double-breasted yachting costume had a vest of Cape Cod blue. His thick dark glossy hair was swept up in a smart pompadour and his moustache had sharp waxed ends. He talked volubly, mixing Chicago's racy vernacular with phrases of Puritan New England which would have suited William Dean Howells.

Whatever he was, whatever he wore, whatever he said, exactly fitted the relaxed temper of Colorado Springs in 1902. For three years, the enchanted populace watched the Cheyenne Creek farm and its small lake in transition—first a farm, then a real estate development, and then, since The Bath loved animals, a sanctuary for all the wounded coyotes, and lost bear cubs and baby deer and broken-winged eagles and retired tourist burros of the neighborhood. When an elephant named Princess Alice, an inmate of Chicago's Lincoln Park Zoo, got her trunk bent in an elevator and lost caste as a representative pachyderm, The Bath instructed the Chicago City Council to ship her to Cheyenne Creek where she won fame as a confirmed lush who drank a pint of Jim Beam every day.

The Bath had always been inspired by his own vision of what Heaven must be like—not a languid scene of soupy clouds and bare-bottomed cherubs but a sin-free honky-tonk on the order of Coney Island. When a friend told him that an amusement park had been planned at Prospect Lake until General Palmer put his foot down, The Bath went to work with evangelical fervor, and more tin boxes of pay-off cash, to create Heaven around the small lake at his home-made Zoo Park. For years in Chicago he had been storing amusement devices from the 1893 World's Fair free on city property for loyal First Ward voters. Now in 1905 he bought some of them for Zoo Park and, as word got around, bankrupt operators from all over sold him properties. Stratton's trolley company responded with a spur from the Stratton Park line to Zoo Park and continued it across Cheyenne Creek and up the creek bluff to join the Broadmoor line on Lake Avenue.

For some years after 1905, Zoo Park was Heaven indeed not only for its proud parent, The Bath, but to a great many Pikes Peak residents, children in particular. It opened early in May and closed when trade fell off in the fall. A crowd of 5,000 people was normal during week ends and lines formed for hundreds of feet at some of the attractions. The Bath, however, confined his commercial talents to Chicago. Zoo Park expressed his other, his altruistic self. He ran it carelessly, spending $20,000 or more each spring on new delights just because it pleased him to please his child customers. For one summer season he would provide hot and cold bathing pools and, the next, a lane of exotic parrots at Zoo Park entrance, or a Sacred Cow, or a troupe of Indians and cowboys for daily Wild West shows, or a few extra camels and alligators and sea lions or a big barbecue.

In 1908, Bathhouse John won national publicity by adapting menageries as a dress motif, paying $500 to a Paris designer for twelve shirts embroidered with thirty or forty of his Pikes Peak animals. By then the Cheyenne Creek enterprise was said to be the most complete amusement park west of Omaha, and it certainly did have an entrancing array of entertainments. The Roller Coaster was a monster affair yanking its shrieking customers up and down and around at sixty miles an hour. The Chute the Chutes began at the top of a sixty-five foot tower with the boat flying down the slide for 360 feet and into the lake with a tremendous splash. The Giant Circle Swing was like today's airplane rides and there was a charming Old Mill boat ride and a Miniature Railway and a Fun Factory and something called Under and Over the Sea—a series of dramatic marine dioramas with terrifying sound effects. The Buster Brown House was full of flashing lights and bobbing floors and peepholes and at the end a climactic scene in which The Devil presided over a steaming cauldron. Beyond the Roller Skating Rink was the big Merry-Go-Round, the Bowling Alley, the Penny Slots, and the Shooting Gallery.[5]

BY 1911, Zoo Park was beginning to come apart at the seams. The Bath was finding it very hard to keep it going in the old grand careless style. Successive waves of reform in Chicago had drastically reduced the pay-off cash in his tin box. As Cripple Creek sank deeper and deeper into the doldrums, few Springs residents could afford to send their children to Zoo Park for the day. Bathhouse John was deeply distressed when poor old Princess Alice, the inebriate elephant, froze to death during the Big Snow of December, 1913. He felt worse still when his fair-weather Pikes Peak banking friends refused to loan him money to refurbish his wardrobe and feed his animals through the winters of 1914 and 1915. In 1916, the comfortable home which he and My Queen had built on Cheyenne Road burned to the ground. His disillusionment with Pikes Peak was complete when El Paso County went dry.   *continued page 211*

Spencer Penrose (left) arrived broke in Colorado Springs in '92 but soon Spec and his old friend and Pikes Peak sponsor, Charley Tutt (right) were selling gold mine stocks and dreaming of making fortunes.
Broadmoor Hotel.

Cripple Creek's gold made everyone feel rich and flower parades became annual events. In 1894, first prize for four-wheel, two-horse carriages went to Mr. and Mrs. Charles L. Tutt (front seat), in a rig trimmed with smilax, geraniums, and sweet peas. Their guests on the back seat were Miss Nina Crosby (later the Marquise de Polignac) and Spencer Penrose. *Pioneer Museum.*

The flower parades had just about everything, pretty cyclists, clowns, costermongers (English apple-sellers), and exquisite equipages like Mrs. J. McK. Ferriday's five-horse group. *Pioneer Museum and Denver Public Library Western Collection, Poley photos.*

Nobody misbehaved much. Little London needed only eleven "bobbies" to keep order, headed by Police Chief L. C. Dana (left center).

The old quiet era was passing fast, but Mr. Hawkins still swept most of the chimneys along Nevada Avenue. *Denver Public Library Western Collection, H. S. Poley photo.*

By 1900, Henry Russell Wray, head of the Chamber of Commerce, was boasting that the North End had more de luxe bathrooms like this per capita than any other spot in the U.S.A. *Pioneer Museum.*

The July wildflower excursions up Ute Pass were very popular. The three Colorado Midland train-loads in the photo were pausing near Florissant. *Pioneer Museum.*

Residents laughed at this first motor tour bus at the turn of the century and predicted failure for it. *Pioneer Museum.*

But by 1905, even the ultra-conservative banker, Joel Addison Hayes, was dashing up and down North Cascade in his electric. *Gerald B. Webb Collection.*

Bathhouse John Coughlin, boss of Chicago's First Ward, and best friend of every Windy City prostitute, built Zoo Park on Cheyenne Road, an amusement center as pure as Sunday school. *Pioneer Museum.*

With tears starting, old-timers declare that they never knew greater joy than riding The Bath's roller-coaster. *Pioneer Museum.*

Another Sunday thrill was the rickety incline up Red Mountain above Manitou. *Stewart's.*

El Paso Club reading room facilities in '91 featured leather chairs, cuspidors, elk heads, and *The Police Gazette.* *Pioneer Museum.*

The Springs was, and is, a good chess town. In 1915, the U. S. champion, Frank Marshall, played the residents in this El Paso Club photo, and lost only to George W. Veditz. Ten years later, World Champion Emanuel Lasker beat thirty-five players, including Dr. Gerald Webb (first prize), and Charles A. Baldwin. In recent years, grand masters Samuel Reshevsky, Al Horowitz, and Hans Berliner have played the field in the Broadmoor Hotel ball room. *Gerald B. Webb Collection.*

In the early 1890s, the membership of the Cheyenne Mountain Country Club moved the clubhouse here and there with the abandon of ladies at the milliner's trying on hats to this final position. *Pioneer Museum.*

Broadmoor was the Rockies' great polo center before World War I. The Cheyenne Mountain Country Club team of 1903 (no hats) consisted of (left to right) Ernest Every (umpire), Gerald B. Webb, Charles A. Baldwin, Bill Ruston, and Harold Bryant. The Glenwood Springs team, partly hatted, was composed of (left to right) Umpire Ernest Every, William Devereux, Harvey Lyle, Boucher Devereux, and Horace Devereux. *Gerald B. Webb Collection.*

Rivalry between club men of Colorado Springs and Denver was especially keen. History has not recorded the winner of this contest on September 30, 1911, between the Cheyenne Mountain County Club and the Denver County Club on the Denver Country Club's diamond. *Frank Lincoln Woodward.*

The Town and Gown Golf Club was founded by serious golfers seeking escape from the frivolous sports attitude of the Cheyenne Mountain Country Club. *Gerald B. Webb Collection.*

The Cooking Club was created by Spencer Penrose and his gay companions who delighted in the art of eating and drinking. Chester Alan Arthur II served as president for the first year (1912) and thereafter Penrose presided for the rest of his life. In this rare photo, left to right, seated, were: Fred Sherwin, Clarence Hamlin, Spencer Penrose, F. Drexel Smith, and Clarence Sunderlin. Standing, left to right, were: Charlie MacNeill (Penrose's Utah Copper partner), Samuel L. Shober, Joel A. Hayes, Chaloner B. Schley, Duncan Chisolm (Count Pourtales' Broadmoor Dairy Farm manager), Eugene P. Shove, Horace Devereux, Percy Hagerman (son of James J.), and Dr. Boswell P. Anderson, who began his Pikes Peak career in 1872 in Manitou. *Gerald B. Webb Collection.*

The Charles A. Baldwins set out to astound Colorado with a show place of show places, and they succeeded when they built Claremont in 1907 at a cost of $200,000. *Gerald B. Webb Collection.*

The tale runs that young Chester II, son of the President, and a Princeton graduate, once put the entire Princeton Glee Club up for the night at the White House. When the President of the United States tried to retire, he found his bed occupied by two tenors and a baritone. *Mrs. Chester Alan Arthur II.*

Much of Charley Tutt's retirement was passed on his yacht "Anemone," shown here in San Diego Bay. Pictured from left are Mrs. Charles Tutt, Mrs. Sutherlin, Mrs. Uriel Sebree (wife of the naval officer), Mrs. Frank Baum (wife of the creator of the Oz books), Charley Tutt, and the newlyweds, Augusta Beckwith Evans and W. H. Evans. The year was 1908. *Mrs. W. H. Evans.*

In 1915, Spec and Julie Penrose, aged fifty and forty-five respectively, stopped in Philadelphia to be painted by Julian Story, the English portraitist. Story's rendition of Spec was too pretty, missing the Roman-gladiator beauty, quiet authority, and bigness which marked Spec's appearance in his prime between 1912 and the early 1920s. *Broadmoor Hotel, Bob McIntyre.*

Count Pourtales' Broadmoor was very much on Penrose's mind in 1913. From Point Sublime, above the Short Line trestle, only a dozen homes dotted the area after twenty years. The Casino still graced the lake and beyond it was the Baldwins' Claremont. *Denver Public Library Western Collection, L. C. McClure photo.*

Like General Palmer, Penrose always built ahead of public demand. In 1913, he decided that automobiles were powerful enough and roads to Colorado would soon be improved enough to create a need for an auto highway up Pikes Peak along the old abandoned carriage road. His decision was based on the arrival of a Buick Bearcat on the summit in less than four hours; the "Hospitality Tour" of Springs motorists from Pikes Peak to Galveston, Texas, undeterred by mud; and the new auto road up to Crystal Park, requiring a turntable near the top at Inspiration Point. *Pioneer Museum and Stewart's.*

Spec's Pikes Peak Highway was supposed to cost $25,000, but Penrose found himself shelling out most of the actual cost of $250,000 before it was completed in 1915. The old carriage road can be seen dimly in this modern aerial photo, and also the cog road. Cameron's Cone rises at right. Straight down the middle to Manitou and Fountain Creek is the canyon of Ruxton Creek. The Garden of the Gods can be seen upper left. *Stewart's.*

The new Broadmoor Hotel was almost finished by the winter of 1918. Note the second Broadmoor Casino, moved into place to serve as the Broadmoor Golf Club, and the untouched old Broadmoor Hotel, renamed the Colonial Club. Penrose adopted the device of raising the A in Broadmoor as a trade-mark for the name of the hotel since the word Broadmoor itself could not be copyrighted. *Stewart's.*

In a rage, Coughlin instructed his manager, Walter Colburn, to liquidate Zoo Park. The Roller Coaster and Chute the Chutes and all the other rides were dismantled and shipped away. The trolley tracks were removed. The Sacred Cow and two bears wound up as steaks at Tucker's Restaurant. The Bath deeded Zoo Park's acreage to Colburn as a reward for more than a decade of service. Colburn, a progressive young man, procured a dozen large tents, raised them on the empty spaces of the late Park, and opened for business as operator of the first motel in Colorado. Many years later, Coughlin's motel became part of the Three Eagles residential development.[6]

Back in Chicago, Bathhouse John put up with a new order of politics in which his share of the pay-off was but a tiny trickle of the once fulsome stream. He remained Alderman of the First Ward until he died broke in 1938, having managed somehow to keep from getting rubbed out during the machine-gun regimes of Al Capone, Big Bill Thompson, and Tony Cermak. But after the demise of Zoo Park at Pikes Peak he was just a shambling shadow of the dynamic Bath in dazzling attire whose best days had been spent shepherding children through the enchantments of his personal Heaven on Cheyenne Road.

CHAPTER FIFTEEN

It's a Man's World

ALWAYS, IT SEEMS, men have found it good to get away on
an organized basis from their women and other troubles. The
male club became an absolute necessity in England during the
eighteenth century and it is not surprising that, in October, 1877,
Dr. S. E. Solly and other Englishmen or copiers of Englishmen at
Little London felt the need to organize the El Paso Club. This
group claims to be the oldest men's social club west of Chicago.
Its first president was Major William Wagner, one of General
Palmer's proper Philadelphians from the Fifteenth Pennsylvania.
The club met for a time in upstairs rooms of downtown buildings
and Will Jackson became its dignified president in 1879-80. Then
Dr. Solly presided for seventeen years.

In 1890, Professor James H. Kerr, who had lost his shirt in his
Pikes Peak Tramway scheme, put up for sale his big brick home
on Tejon Street at Platte Avenue. The El Paso Club membership,
which had risen from thirty to 150, wanted the Kerr House but
hesitated because the Palmer liquor ban prevented the sale of
whiskey, the profits from which were necessary to maintain a
large building. Up to then, members had endured the inconven-
ience of keeping their own liquor supply in private lockers at the
Club. After a period of delicate negotiations with Mayor Stillman
and ten aldermen, agreement was reached that liquor at the El
Paso Club was not liquor in the liquor ban sense. And so the
Kerr House was purchased and fitted with all the facilities dear
to the hearts of clubmen, including a liquor sales bar in the Club
pantry. The opening of the new El Paso Club was celebrated

at a large ball on February 20, 1891, and from that date to this the Club has flourished in the same building.

Facilities in '91 included, naturally, leather chairs and cuspidors in the living room, and a long table for newspapers and copies of *Blackwoods* and *The Atlantic Monthly* and *The Century* and *The Police Gazette* and college alumni magazines. The dining room was next to the living room. On the second floor was the pool room with five billiard tables; also four card rooms for poker, whist, twenty-one, and piquet. Ladies were allowed within the hallowed walls at occasional balls but they were rigidly excluded otherwise until 1910 when a small ladies' dining room was provided with the opening of the men's large dining wing.[1]

All through the Nineties, full dress was usual at the Club in the evenings even if nothing special was going on. But otherwise the stiff English decorum of the 1880s was modified as more and more Cripple Creek millionaires, who had not won their fortunes by being decorous, joined the Club. Business deals involving huge sums were made over the second floor poker tables. There were squabbles now and then. Big Horace Devereux, the polo player, had a fearful billiard cue duel one night with James J. Hagerman's son, Percy, who got his muscle as a member of the Cornell crew in '89-'90, and of the Yale crew in '91. Walter Cash, a former captain of the Princeton football team, resolved a poker disagreement by dangling his opponent, Jimmie Burns, over the stair well. Spec Penrose ripped a hole in the pool table cloth and spent a tipsy hour trying to pen a legible letter of apology to the Board of Directors. He gave up at last and pitched the ink bottle through the library window in a gesture of despair.

The El Paso Club offered indoor sports only. In 1889, some of its members—Thomas J. Edsall and Godfrey Kissel among them—planned a club which would provide outdoor attractions as well, such as pigeon shooting and coursing. At first, they considered placing it on land which Will Otis was eager to donate at Austin's Bluffs to draw attention to his real estate development there. However, Count Pourtales proposed to give them better land on

his rival real estate venture at Broadmoor and so the Cheyenne
Mountain Club Association was formed in Broadmoor on February 18, 1891. Some fifty outdoor-loving members of the El Paso
Club hastened to become charter members of the Cheyenne
Mountain (Country) Club (the word "country" was added to
the incorporated title in 1901). The sportsmen chose the noble
grizzly bear as the Club's symbolic mascot, though no such beast
had been reported on Cheyenne Mountain for half a century and
the word "Cheyenne" itself was an Indian term meaning "buffalo." Some of the Club's first board of directors were the same
extravagant young men who would try to increase trade at Pourtales' Broadmoor Casino by hiring parachuting lady balloonists
and tight-rope-walking pyrotechnists. The original plans called
for a clubhouse and stable to cost no more than $4,500 at the very
most. But, between February 18 and June 25, 1891, when the
Club was opened, the directors had managed to pour more than
$14,000 into the place.

This should have been a warning to economize, except that
the turnover in house committees was rapid and each new committee had expensive inspirations for promoting the Club's welfare. In his book, *Lessons Learned From Experience*, Count
Pourtales told how the membership began moving the clubhouse
here and there with the abandon of ladies at the milliner's trying
on hats. The building, sixty feet wide and seventy-five feet long,
was put on rollers first in the fall of '91 and trundled 1,500 feet
to be near a race track which the Race Committee had decided
to construct. The move involved the costly and complicated
transplanting of trees and shrubbery, by authority of the Grounds
Committee, and it brought the total investment to $19,000, in-
cluding the expense of building the track and grandstand. Some
months later, just as the transplanted flora was taking hold nicely,
the members became unhappily aware that, to see the races from
the clubhouse, they had to stand at small windows either in the
Club kitchen or in the men's wash room. The House Committee
borrowed a few thousand dollars, movers were hired again and
the building was turned around so that the west front became the

east front and the races could be watched comfortably from the veranda. The trees and shrubbery, bewildered and discouraged by now, were transplanted a third time and the marvel was that some of them survived.

The early-day Cheyenne Mountain Country Club was primarily a health farm of congenial spirits who devoted themselves to being virile with ascetic fervor. Within a year of the Club's birth, they engaged in almost every sport under the sun—polo and tennis, shooting and cricket, baseball and archery and bowling and racing and coursing and golf and "athletics" which had to do with tossing dumbbells about in pursuit of the body beautiful. The burly Scotsman, Duncan Chisholm, laid out a nine-hole golf course which young Percy Hagerman described as "a primitive affair with sand greens about the size of dinner plates and few hazards or bunkers other than those provided by nature, and it was often said that the whole course was just one hazard from start to finish." For some time the club maintained a pack of hounds, but Dr. Bell and the Hamp family conducted better hunts in true English style and so the Country Club sold its pack.[2]

A popular activity was the shooting of live pigeons at traps across Lake Avenue from the clubhouse. Tall, lanky Charley Tutt, a crack shot, headed the Traps Committee and battled to protect the art of live pigeon shooting from the attacks, massive and continuous, of tenderhearted residents. The attacks were directed by an austere Englishman, Francis B. Hill, who had moved to Little London in the late Seventies and for a decade had protested the North End fashion of docking horses' tails and the widespread use by Springs ladies of wearing feathers, and even the skins of whole birds, in their big hats. In 1888, Hill formed the El Paso County Humane Society and by 1891 his principal aim was to put Charley Tutt and his live pigeon traps at Broadmoor out of business.

Charley was supported, of course, by most of the members of the El Paso Club and of the Cheyenne Mountain Country Club, and it was not until the summer of 1895 that Hill was able to get a suit against the pigeon traps into the courts. But from

then on a Humane Society triumph was inevitable. In June of
'97, Francis Hill won his trap suit and Charley Tutt, scapegoat
for the Cheyenne Mountain Country Club, was arrested and
briefly incarcerated on charges of cruelty to pigeons. Soon after,
live bird shooting was prohibited by Colorado law and the Club
changed its traps over to clay pigeons.[3]

Like all clubs, the Cheyenne Mountain had its internal scraps.
Gambling got out of hand for a time and roulette and baccarat
were banished. In '96, the directors levied an unpopular assess-
ment. A dozen members resigned in a huff and set up a new club
at Austin's Bluffs, which survived three years before the rebels
returned to the fold. The hardest problem involved members'
wives who insisted on intruding on the premises. Some husbands
grumbled that they had joined the Club under the impression
that it would be a sanctuary from females. But they were a
minority and had to plot by indirection toward a more masculine
environment. They observed that some wives loved to smoke
and so they slipped in a House Committee rule prohibiting such
dubious behavior except in the ladies' room. As Percy Hagerman
said, "The ladies were expected to act like small boys going out
behind the barn to smoke corn-cob pipes." The ladies, of course,
reacted by smoking everywhere except the ladies' room. All the
House Committee could do was to post larger and angrier signs
explaining the law. The signs merely encouraged members to
write witty comments on them in pencil and the rule itself died
of neglect during the early 1900s.

It has been explained that Colorado Springs was not just a
pioneer resort in the West. It was among the earliest of resorts
anywhere in the United States. The Cheyenne Mountain Country Club was similarly antecedent in the country club field. In
the 1880s such clubs included the Brookline Country Club and
the Myopia Hunt Club (both near Boston) and the Rockaway
Hunt Club (New York) and a few more. The oldest American
golf club is said to be the St. Andrews (1888) near Yonkers, New
York. When Duncan Chisholm laid out the little nine-hole
Cheyenne Mountain course in 1891, it was probably the nation's

second, or third, or fourth—at any rate, years ahead of the golf club boom of the later 1890s. Unfortunately, it existed on Broadmoor Company land and had to be relocated every time a proximate Broadmoor lot was sold. In consequence, it never improved beyond "sand greens the size of dinner plates." Its pioneer career ended in 1918 when Spec Penrose built his Broadmoor Hotel course.

The haphazard status of the Cheyenne Mountain golf course and the unpredictable deportment of its members created a demand for serious golf and a clubhouse where nobody had to duck flying champagne bottles on stag nights. The result was the sedate Town and Gown Golf Club, begun late in '97 by the tireless club-maker, Dr. Solly, his partner, Dr. P. F. Gildea, and others. They were joined by the eastern traction millionaire, W. K. Jewett, and by the young English tuberculosis specialist, Dr. Gerald Webb. By '99, the Town and Gown had 130 members, a clubhouse which still stands as a home at Columbia and El Paso Streets, and an eighteen-hole course north and east of the clubhouse. After ten years, the town's growth pushed the Town and Gown some blocks north with a new name, the Colorado Springs Golf Club. It used a rented clubhouse and 300 acres of leased land. In 1919, W. K. Jewett bought the entire property and presented it to the City of Colorado Springs as a memorial to his wife. It thrives today as the Patty Jewett Municipal Golf Course.

The Cooking Club was the creation of Penrose and his epicurean companions who enjoyed their billiards at the El Paso Club and their sports at the Cheyenne Mountain Country Club but were interested most of all in the art of gentlemanly eating and drinking. This group was patterned on the Rabbit Club in Philadelphia and it began in 1912 with twenty-one members who met each month at various North End homes. For years, the members did all the cooking, planning for days to produce exotic culinary delights—Capercailzie with Cranberry Sauce or Blackcock or Écrevisses à la Creme or Chaudfroid de Volaille washed down with Romanée '87 or Chateau Lafite-Carruades '78 or perhaps a magnum of Chateau de Beychevelle '78. In time, the wives of these amateur chefs demanded surcease from the shambles to which their kitchens were reduced periodically. To quiet them, Penrose supplied a beautiful site on the slopes of Cheyenne Mountain and a sternly functional building with nothing much in it except cooking and eating space. For a quarter of a century Penrose, in chef's white hat and apron, presided over his company of gourmets. And in 1960 his Cooking Club was meeting still each month for a few hours of devotional gastronomy.

A HIGH QUOTIENT of quality playboys has always been a feature of club life in Colorado Springs. At the turn of the century, the volume soared, many of them coming to Pikes Peak to recover from tuberculosis contracted in the Spanish-American War. Some came to gamble in Cripple Creek stocks or to play polo, a game which bloomed in Broadmoor for thirty years and more. Others came to win the heart and purse of any rich widow or any wife of social eminence who might yearn for a change of pace.

Outstanding among these glamorous males was the polo player, Charles A. Baldwin, a Navy admiral's son who had begun his rise into the upper echelons of playboyism by studying at Harrow and acquiring a sort of British gloss. In 1896, he struck it rich by marrying a San Francisco mining heiress, Miss Virginia Hobart, and thereafter he floated with ease through the rare atmosphere of high European and American society. It has been told already how Baldwin and his wife startled North Cascade Avenue in 1901 by arriving with *two* automobiles. A little later, Baldwin conceived an ambition to build a home that would stand first forever as the social show place of the Pikes Peak region. General Palmer's million-dollar Glen Eyrie had just been completed but to Springs residents Palmer was too sacred to be regarded as a social person and his sixty-seven room home was a shrine far above the show-place category.

Baldwin purchased from the Englishman, Richard Hutton, a rolling acreage on Spring Creek near the spot in Broadmoor where young Irving Howbert had feared for his scalp while binding wheat in the late 1860s. Apparently in reaction to this crude scalping background, Baldwin chose the ultimate in architectural contrasts for his version of a Rocky Mountain show place. He sent to France the local designer, Thomas McLaren, who spent a year meticulously recording the dimensions and forms of the Grand Trianon, the seventeenth-century retreat of Louis XIV at Versailles. McLaren's adaptation of this ineffable palace for Bourbons was finished in 1907 at a cost of $200,000, plus $15,000 for a garage. Baldwin named it "Claremont"—possibly after Lord Cleve's estate in England—and it materialized in a glittering magnificence of noble columns, balustrades, high French windows, oramental fencing, fountains, formal gardens, and statues of people with no clothes on.

As a show place, Claremont was an immediate sensation. Rocky Mountain visitors came from hundreds of miles away to cast incredulous eyes on its Gallic contours and on its liveried footmen and butlers in Louis Quatorze knee breeches. Even Baldwin's most worldly fellow clubmen had to admit that it was a stunner. Furthermore, it proved once again that anything, however unlikely or incongruous, could come to pass at the foot of Pikes Peak.[4]

But, for all of Claremont, Baldwin could not begin to compete as a playboy on a par with a sufferer from asthma who arrived at Pikes Peak to stay just a few weeks before Baldwin arrived.

Chester Alan Arthur II was born in New York City in 1864, the son of a New York lawyer and politician who was nominated Vice President of the United States in 1880 to placate the Grant Wing of the Republican Party. Arthur became President—and a good one—after Garfield's assassination in September, 1881. Young Alan, accent on second syllable, graduated from Princeton in '85 and spent a year at Columbia Law School to please his father. While President, Chester Alan I was too busy to pay much attention to his son though he noticed Alan's disposition to fill the White House and presidential yacht on week ends with noisy Princetonians and their squealing girls. On one Christmas holiday during an invasion of the whole Princeton Glee Club, of which Alan was a member, the President of the United States was said to have found his bed occupied by two tenors and a baritone and he had to sleep on the couch.

President Arthur was not renominated in '84 and he died two years later, prompting Alan to drop law school like a hot brick and start being an international playboy. He had chosen this career secretly some time earlier when he had observed the universal esteem in which a President's son was held by society the world over. For a dozen years he perfected his natural talent in Europe, hobnobbing with ambassadors, courting Lily Langtry and other actresses, presiding at gourmet banquets, attending soirées for famous painters and musicians, and sailing about with his good friend H. R. H. Edward VII, the Prince of Wales, on the royal yacht H.M.S. *Bacchante*. In the early '90s, the English populace knew Alan as the favorite dancing partner of Princess Mary of Teck, and there was gossip of a romance until Mary married Prince George, the future King of England. When Alan finally did take a wife in '99, nobody could complain of his taste. The bride was Mrs. Myra Fithian Andrews, a lovely and gifted Paris-American divorcée whose father, Joel Fithian, was a partner in that most socially acceptable of banking houses, Morgan, Harjes and Cie., 14 Place Vendome.

At Pikes Peak, Alan Arthur settled down with Myra at Edgeplain, Frances Wolcott's old home on Nevada Avenue facing the Colorado College campus. His elegance, his Edwardian courtesy, his wit, his sophisticated knowledge of everything from Gauguin to truffles, took the North End by storm. At the age of thirty-six he was at least as handsome as Spec Penrose—six feet four inches tall with thick black hair, dark gleaming eyes, and a waxed moustache that Napoleon Third would have envied. He was slender and graceful and poised and gallantly errant. North End males became so inspired by his example that they adopted bow ties and high collars and wine cellars. Some tried reading books on painting, and some, who had never dreamed of straying from the matrimonial straight and narrow, took to philandering behind the shrubbery at garden parties. Arthur was made a director of the Cheyenne Mountain Country Club and, in 1905, he was elected president. In sports, he proved to be an excellent trap shooter and an able honorary whipper-in at local hunts. He did not play polo well but he improved the quality of Broadmoor polo ponies by maintaining at stud the celebrated stallion, Dave Waldo.

It fell by chance to Arthur to be a link in the curious continuity of the old Maxwell and Sangre de Cristo Land Grants in Pikes Peak history. The grants, we have seen, were important factors in the financing of General Palmer's railroad and land schemes after 1870. For many years until 1907, Palmer owned the north part of the Sangre de Cristo Grant, that beautiful 250,000-acre Trinchera Estate under Blanca Peak extending from San Luis Valley to the summit of the Sangre de Cristo Mountains.

Somehow, Palmer was moved to give an option on the Trinchera to a Philadelphia promoter and part-time Broadmoor playboy named Joe Harrison, who formed a new Trinchera company with Alan Arthur and two other Springs clubmen. The third partner was Jay Lippincott, a Quaker-reared member of the Philadelphia publishing family who much preferred polo in Broadmoor to either publishing or Quakerism. The fourth was Chaloner B. Schley, a wealthy New Yorker who had come to Broadmoor for his health.

Arthur's interest in Trinchera derived from his love of the social side of big game hunting. For months he toiled at creating a 30,000-acre Trinchera game preserve modelled after the royal preserves of England where he had hunted with the Prince of Wales. He built a twenty-eight-mile game-proof fence around the Trinchera preserve and encouraged elk and deer and antelope and bear not only to domicile therein but to present easy targets for inexpert marksmen. He managed also, after great trouble and expense, to import one hundred head of buffalo from Oklahoma's famous 101 Ranch, the idea being that as a last resort anybody could hit a buffalo.

All these inducements caused Alan Arthur's friends to flock to Trinchera in droves, from Broadmoor and from everywhere else.

At the ranch's comfortable headquarters, it was Alan's pleasure to spend the day preparing for their return from the chase and then to put before them a superb feast, cooked by his French butler, Celeste, and fortified by bottles of Chateau Haut Brion or some other fine wine from his Nevada Avenue cellar.

Of course such hospitality was a heavy drain on the Trinchera income from cattle and hay and timber. To increase revenue, Joe Harrison and Jay Lippincott tried to sell bits of the ranch to small farmers in San Luis Valley. Because of cloudy land titles and other peculiarities of the Mexican land grant business, they ran into very serious legal trouble. On top of this, World War I began. It became impossible to hire labor and to buy materials to keep the huge paradise for sportsmen going. In consequence, the partners fell behind on their interest payments and finally had to give up the Trinchera entirely. Sadly, Chester Alan Arthur II saddled his hunters, packed his rifles and vintage wines, and returned to Edgeplain on Nevada Avenue.

When World War I ended in 1918, Arthur and his old friends of the El Paso Club and Cheyenne Mountain Country Club tried hard to resume the gay, carefree, sporting life which they had known before the war. But they found that their happy man's world had changed. Even at Pikes Peak things were no longer the same. In the end, they had to realize that those golden years from the turn of the century had been for everybody everywhere a time of special felicity in the course of human affairs.[5]

CHAPTER SIXTEEN

A Real Nice Clambake

THE CHAIN OF CIRCUMSTANCE which brought an eighty-million-dollar estate to Spencer Penrose and Colorado Springs began late in 1893 when a penniless Missourian, Daniel C. Jackling, arrived in Cripple Creek after a long cold hike from the Colorado Midland depot at Divide. Jackling, aged twenty-four, had served a year as assistant professor of metallurgy at the Missouri School of Mines from which he had graduated in 1892. He hardly knew for sure as yet that rock was mineral but he was an impressive fellow over six feet three inches tall and he talked about mining in slow positive phrases. He was desperately in need of work and it was his good luck that his size and his confidence made a hit with Charles Mather MacNeill.

You recall that Charlie MacNeill, the high-strung Chicago member of Spec's roistering Socialites, was putting up Cripple Creek's first reduction mill in '93. He hired Jackling, who directed metallurgy for this mill until it burned down in '95. Then Jackling disappeared from Pikes Peak for six years. While at Cripple Creek he had met Penrose and his crowd but only in a casual way. Like Spec's geologist brother Dick, Jackling was decidedly not the roistering type.

During the winter of 1902, while Dr. Penrose was still annoying his blacksheep younger son with his skepticism about the merits of the new Tutt-Penrose-MacNeill mill trust, Jackling applied to MacNeill again for a job. The big metallurgist had been mainly in Utah working on refractory gold ores. MacNeill assigned him to run the mill trust's plant at Canon City south of the Springs, but it was soon clear to Charlie that Jackling's thoughts were not on the plant. His thoughts were back in Utah where he had acquired an obsession about building a mill which could extract copper profitably from ore with a copper content no higher than two per cent. He had, as he reiterated to Charlie every time he could catch his ear, complete plans for this revolutionary mill. And he knew where the copper was—a mountain of low-grade stuff at a place called Bingham Canyon, forty miles south of Salt Lake City.

Of course MacNeill had heard all about Bingham Canyon. What mining man hadn't? Since 1850, people had been taking gold and silver and lead out of it; in fact it was Utah's principal mining property. In 1887, when it was obviously played out except for its unrecoverable copper, a deluded old promoter, Colonel Enos A. Wall, had bought most of it and had been trying ever since to get suckers to develop it. Jackling's obsession began in '99 when he examined Bingham Canyon thoroughly for his employer, the Utah gold king, Captain Joseph R. De Lamar, who refused to act on Jackling's favorable report. In 1900, the American, John Hayes Hammond, the world's most authoritative mining man (he was Cecil Rhodes' engineer in the South African gold fields), turned it down. So did the General Electric Company and Benjamin Guggenheim of the powerful Guggenheim smelting family. By this time, Bingham Canyon bore the derisive nickname, "Wall's Rocks." *The Engineering and Mining Journal,* mouthpiece of the industry, warned investors against "Jackling's Wildcat."

In his years of metallurgy after '93, Jackling had achieved a good reputation but there were many reasons why sound engineers thought he was simply foolish about Bingham Canyon. Spec Penrose, who heard of his obsession from Charlie MacNeill, agreed with the experts at first but began to veer early in 1903. Spec was thirty-seven years old then. His appearance had not changed much since '92 when Charley Tutt had spared him financial embarrassment by treating him at the bar of the Cheyenne Mountain Country Club. If anything, his striking good looks had been improved by maturity. His big body remained

strong and glowing. Like General Palmer, he was growing fond
of riding breeches and high boots and English jackets and a
moustache with waxed ends. His habit of economical talk was
still more pronounced that it had been. He preferred to listen
carefully, to ponder, to nod, to smile, to keep others guessing, to
forebear politely from committing himself. His great aim still
was to get rich but to get far richer even than the mill trust could
make him. And he wanted this wealth to win his father's approval at last and also the financial freedom which would allow
him to do exactly as he pleased.

As Penrose saw it, one trouble with Jackling's dream was the
vast capital which it required—half a million dollars at least just
to set up the preliminary pilot plant to refine the two per cent
Bingham Canyon ore. If the plant succeeded—a large question
mark—many millions more would have to be raised to finance
methods for shoveling that low-grade copper mountain into the
mill. Jackling did not play down the gamble. He stressed that
a profit depended on fantastic ore volume. He proposed to move
as much earth as would have to be moved to build the Panama
Canal—a project of such difficulty that whole nations had
foundered on it ever since the sixteenth century.

Nevertheless, Jackling's plan began to grip Penrose's imagination. He went over it with Dick Penrose, who showed a cautious
interest. Dick advised Spec not to think of copper in terms of
its standing in 1903 as a metal of minor importance but in rela-
tion to future use—in automobiles and telephones and electric
power and heating plants and household appliances and a thousand other inventions for a better life which Americans seemed
suddenly to be demanding. If these inventions were adopted
widely, they would consume copper in unheard-of quantity.

In February of 1903, Charlie MacNeill recommended that the
mill trust—Penrose, Tutt, and himself—take a chance on Jackling.
Spec discussed it with Charley Tutt, who was not enthusiastic.
Not that Charley was against Jackling's idea. It was just that his
health was indifferent, he expected to retire soon, the mill trust
was paying good dividends, and he did not care to risk a big

chunk of his fortune on wild speculation. Besides, he had a
copper scheme of his own on the fire—at Takilma, in Southern
Oregon, where ores ran from fifteen to twenty per cent copper.
However, Charley Tutt said, he certainly wouldn't let his old
friends down. If Spec and MacNeill backed Jackling, he would
go along.

The hour of decision occurred in late spring. Spec, Dick Penrose, Tutt and MacNeill accompanied Jackling to Utah where
they secured control of "Wall's Rocks"—Bingham Canyon. Then
they created the Utah Copper Company and raised the money
for Jackling's pilot mill by selling 500,000 shares of stock at one
dollar a share. Spec, MacNeill, and Tutt each bought 83,333
shares and their mill trust took 50,000 shares in exchange for
machinery. Most of the remaining 200,000 shares were purchased
by Dr. Penrose and his bright sons, Dick, Tal, and Senator Boies.
Jackling's commission was 12,500 shares.

In short, "Jackling's Wildcat"—the Utah Copper Company—was
financed almost solely by three Springs residents and their relatives, the capital deriving from Cripple Creek's gold. The ensuing year 1903-1904, was a time of terrible anxiety for everybody.
By unhappy coincidence, the Western Federation of Miners
called a strike at the Tutt-Penrose-MacNeill Standard Mill in
Colorado City. With no income and heavy overhead, the mill
trust stock took a shocking dip. The three worried partners
watched Jackling in the process of spending half a million dollars
on his mysterious copper mill in Bingham Canyon and they
suffered torments from a nagging fear that their hard-earned
Cripple Creek fortunes were flowing swiftly down a hole.

But Jackling finished the mill before they went bankrupt. And
he began running the preposterously low-grade Bingham Canyon ore through it while engineers the world over predicted
failure. The mill did not fail. Instead, it refined copper at a
profit from the very first day. The market price of Utah Copper
shares rose slowly—from next to nothing to one dollar to two dollars to three dollars and more. Jackling was hailed soon as a
genius who had revolutionized the copper industry. The relieved

promoters began to sleep better at night. Dr. Penrose's letters to Spec contained guarded phrases of admiration. Charley Tutt could congratulate himself that he had stuck with his friends. He had seen Utah Copper through and he could withdraw now with honor to enjoy his retirement at the age of forty-one. Spec bought Charley's 83,333 shares in the open market which meant that Charley tripled his investment during the year or so of his reluctant participation.[1]

Utah Copper still faced the problem of raising funds for large production. The money was raised quickly. The sons of Meyer Guggenheim—Benjamin, Murry, Solomon, Daniel—who had scorned "Wall's Rocks" in 1900, took a second look in 1905 and put their smelting resources at Penrose's disposal. As a result, the Utah Copper Company of 1906—expanded ten-fold—was soon producing enough metal to make it the most profitable of all the copper companies which the Guggenheims were financing.

In terms of copper history, it would be hard to exaggerate the importance of Bingham Canyon, which was taken up by three obscure young amateurs from Colorado Springs after all the leading professionals of the industry had pronounced it a dud. Since the opening of Jackling's pilot plant in 1903, "Wall's Rocks" to date have produced copper worth two billion dollars with earnings of nearly a billion, making it the greatest steam shovel copper mine on earth. When Spec bought Charley Tutt's interest, he became Utah Copper's dominant stockholder and he remained so until Utah Copper and its associated firms were sold to the giant Kennecott Copper Corporation in 1923. After that date, Spec was one of Kennecott's three or four leading shareholders.

It can be said that Dr. Penrose's backward boy did well for himself in 1903 when he placed a long-shot bet of $83,333 on "Jackling's Wildcat." From 1909 on, when Utah Copper began paying dividends, Spec's income averaged a million dollars a year after taxes for the rest of his life.[2]

AN UNUSUAL PARTY took place on Friday evening, January 11, 1901, when Clarence Edsall and Spencer Penrose, both bache-

lors and earnest students of advanced gastronomy, gave a clam-
bake at the Cheyenne Mountain Country Club in Broadmoor.
The clams, packed in ice, had arrived by rail from Rockland,
Maine, and they were served in fifteen different ways—steamed,
scalloped, à la marinière, batter-fried, as chowder, fritters, clam
hash, clam pie, and so on. The Charley Tutts and Charlie Mac-
Neill were among the thirty guests and so were the Arthur Con-
nells and Horace Devereux and Jim Eustis, son of the American
Ambassador to France, and Miss Lillian Solly and Miss Varina
Hayes, granddaughter of Jefferson Davis. Also present were five
young married ladies whose husbands were bed fast in the
Springs seeking cures for tuberculosis.

By far the prettiest of the five young ladies was a newcomer,
a small, blue-eyed, warmly responsive woman of thirty years with
short blond hair upswept above her ears, dazzling choker pearls
at her neck and a smart blue gown cut low at the bosom. Spec
met her for the first time at the clambake, but he had become a
confirmed bachelor like his brothers Dick and Boies and her
charms made no special impression on him.

Her name was Mrs. James H. McMillan and, as Spec learned
thoroughly during the next five years, she had been Julie Villiers
Lewis, born in 1870, the daughter of the Honorable Alexander
Lewis, Detroit's perennial mayor. Lewis' mother Jeanne was the
child of a legendary Frenchman, Louis Villiers, who had settled
in eighteenth-century Detroit when it was all French. Alexander
Lewis was mostly French himself and he behaved like a Frenchman—quick, impulsive, temperish, humorous, fond of music and
art and given to scatter-brained conduct which concealed his
basic stability. His home was a madhouse of disorganized activity, and his covey of children had the insouciant effervescence
and style of vintage champagne. Alexander Lewis was a Catholic, dutiful if not ardent. He had his offspring baptized at birth
in the Catholic Church, and then he turned their religious education over to their mother, Elizabeth—of the Detroit Ingersolls—
who brought them up as Episcopalians.

Mrs. Lewis bore thirteen children altogether, five dying in

infancy. Of the eight surviving, Ida was oldest and then came Edgar and Josie (the future Mrs. Clarence Carpenter of Colorado Springs). Next came Hattie (later Mrs. Cameron Currie), and Harry and then Julie and Marian (Mrs. W. Howie Muir), and finally Ingersoll (Inky), the youngest, who would die in his twenties from eating tainted olives. Papa Lewis adored all his brood, but Julie resembled him most and he spoiled her constantly, giving her a permanent conviction that she could always have whatever she wanted. At sixteen, she attended Miss Brown's School in Boston during which she flunked simple arithmetic. Then she spent a year fashionably taking the Grand Tour of Europe. In Vienna she heard an opera conducted by Richard Strauss and in Berlin she appeared to study piano, in between social engagements. After five months, she did manage to learn to play all sixteen bars of Chopin's Prelude, Opus 26, Number 7.

Her European visit increased her wayward charm if not her musicianship. When she returned home, she wanted and got the boy next door who happened to be Detroit's most desirable bachelor, Jim McMillan—Yale, Skull and Bones, rising lawyer, yachtsman, champion golfer, and son of the multi-millionaire James McMillan, United States Senator from Michigan. In due time, the happy couple had two children, Jimmie and Gladys, and for a decade they lived blissfully—until Jim developed tuberculosis while serving in Cuba on General Duffield's staff during the Spanish-American War. Julie brought him to Colorado Springs for treatment, setting up residence in a large handsome place off North Cascade Avenue at 30 West Dale Street on the bluff of Monument Creek facing Pikes Peak. The treatment was unsuccessful. Jim McMillan died some months after the Edsall-Penrose clambake and so did twelve-year-old Jimmie, the only son Julie would ever have, of appendicitis.

The young widow liked the Pikes Peak scene and stayed on with her daughter Gladys at West Dale Street, vowing never to remarry. For company she had a Detroit friend, Edith Field, a beautiful woman who was also tragically widowed recently. When Edith informed Julie that she didn't intend to be tragic

forever and was, in fact, in love again with one of the Detroit
Newberrys, Julie decided to stop being tragic and to fall in love
herself. It took her about five minutes to pick out her next hus-
band, though she knew him slightly. He was that handsome
Spencer Penrose who had paid no attention to her at the Country
Club clambake.

As a female suitor, Julie went after her prey with the imperious energy of a spoiled and fascinating lady who had never
been denied anything in her life. She frightened and bewildered
Spec who was trying to focus on the problems of Utah Copper.
He had reached the age of forty serene in the belief that he was
now safe from all the sly feminine strategems which Dr. Penrose
had warned him about. He thought of himself as strictly a man's
man like his brothers Dick and Boise. All three of them infinitely
preferred the thrill of filling an inside straight or shooting an
elk to any thrill a mere woman could give them. Julie McMillan
knew of Spec's attitude from town gossip and it only increased
her rugged determination to rescue him from such a colorless
and incomplete existence. She had good reason to hope, for she
heard of Spec's Cripple Creek romance with Sarah Elizabeth
Halthusen. She took the trouble to have Sally pointed out to
her at Gough's hotel, and she concluded that whatever big horsey
Sally had done to interest Spec she could do better. Julie made
a study, too, of Spec's bleak domestic environment. He lived
in ugly rented rooms around town—at the El Paso Club, or upstairs in the Everhart Building on Bijou Street or in a Boulder
Street shack or at 405 North Cascade with Horace Devereux.
He usually burned up the toast getting his own breakfast, and
he suffered chronic indigestion from the meals provided by his
part-time cook. And he had nobody even to make his bed
properly.

Gradually, Mrs. McMillan took charge of Mr. Penrose. She
did not know how to boil an egg herself, or how to make a bed,
but she was a wealthy woman who could afford an able household staff. She sent her own help to do Spec's laundry and she
invited him to breakfast regularly on West Dale Street. The

time came when she began to tell him plainly that his Utah
Copper business and his El Paso Club pool games did not excuse
him from escorting her to parties occasionally.

After two years of being coddled and courted, Spec realized
that he liked Mrs. McMillan—or worse. He was becoming dependent upon her. He was, in fact, almost trapped. More and
more often in the deep of night, he heard Dr. Penrose in his
dreams pouring scorn on him for getting into such a fix. At last,
early in February, 1906, he packed his trunk in a panic and fled
to New York where he joined Dick Penrose on the steamer
Kaiser Wilhelm der Grosse Europe-bound. He would hide out
at Nice on the Riviera long enough for this indefatigable woman
to fall in love with somebody else. But, as the ship passed Sandy
Hook, Spec saw at the ship's rail a small, svelte figure in furs de-
murely watching the pilot being dropped. It was Julie McMillan,
of course. She had trailed him from Pikes Peak and had caught
the *Kaiser Wilhelm* too with her daughter Gladys and Edith
Field.

Dick Penrose was journeying to the gold fields of South Africa.
He left the steamer at Southampton while Spec and his three
female shadows went on to Cherbourg, Paris, and Nice. Dick left
England for Cape Town on March 10, but, before he departed,
the forty-one-year-old Spec prevailed on him to compose the
following letter to Dr. Penrose. It was dated March 3, 1906, at
Paris:

> Speck has asked me to write to you about a matter, con-
> cerning which he said he was going to write to you himself.
> A couple of ladies from Colorado Springs, friends of Speck's,
> came over from New York on the same boat with us three
> weeks ago; and they have, at Speck's invitation, gone south
> with him on his automobile. One of them is a widow named
> Mrs. McMillan. Her husband was a son of ex-U. S. Senator
> McMillan of Michigan. He (her husband) enlisted in the
> U. S. Army, contracted fever in Cuba and later contracted
> consumption from which he died. Mrs. McMillan is very
> good looking and a very agreeable woman of about thirty-

five years old, a blonde of medium size. She has one child,
a girl of fourteen years old. She comes originally from Detroit,
Michigan, and Speck says that she is of one of the best
families there. He says he has known her well for several
years. She came here to put her child to school in Switzerland, and the other lady who came with her seems to have
come as a sort of companion. I understand that Mrs. Mc-
Millan is fairly well off financially and wants to educate her
daughter abroad.

Speck seems very much devoted to Mrs. McMillan, and
she equally so to him. He has talked to me about proposing
marriage to her and has asked me to write to you about it,
and pave the way for him to write to you. Mrs. McMillan
seems to understand Speck thoroughly, and the impression
I have gotten of her is that she is a thoroughly sensible
woman, whom a man ought to get along with if he can get
along with any woman whatever. The fact that she is a
widow has given her an experience with her first husband
that lets her know what men are; and her thirty-five years
of age has probably removed all the obnoxious ambitions
of many modern women, that she might have had. I doubt,
however, if she ever had any, as she seems very sensible.

Speck tells me that for two years, he has carefully considered the proposition of marrying her, and feels that he is
not now deciding on a snap judgment, but after due consid-
eration. He seems to have been with her a great deal and
to know her thoroughly. Speck is peculiarly situated. He
can't read much on account of his eye and, as he himself
says, he is not interested in any particular subject that would
lead him to seek amusement from literary or scientific sources.
He is, therefore, peculiarly dependent on social intercourse.
As he himself said to me the other day, he "cannot sit down
at eight o'clock in the evening and read until bed time,"
nor can he go on forever drinking rum at clubs. Therefore he
seems to think his only refuge is to get married.

I do not claim to have any wisdom on matrimonial subjects,
and I fully realize that I am a damned poor hand to give any
advice on such subjects, but I cannot help feeling that Speck
would be very much better off if happily married than in his

present condition, for reasons which I have just mentioned and which Speck himself gives.

Speck talked to me a good deal about this matter before he left here, though he had never mentioned it to me before we met in Paris. I could see, however, that he was very devoted to the lady coming across the ocean. I did not try to influence him one way or the other in his matrimonial desires, but I did advise him strongly, before taking any definite action, to go home in a few weeks, and see what effect a change of air and surroundings would have on his feelings in the matter. I also told him that if he was bent on getting married, it would be more dignified to go home first and to consummate the deal there, rather than to do it here in a foreign land. He said that he had tried going away from the lady for months at a time, but that separation had no effect on his affection for her. My advice to him, however, is to go home first; and if he still wanted to marry the lady, to do so there rather than here, seemed to appeal to him; and when he left here for Nice he gave me the impression that he would do so. He will then have a chance to talk to you about the matter. It seems very hard for him to get courage to write to you, because he fears you may think him foolish, but I told him you would do no such thing, and would only give him such advice as you thought best for his own happiness, and he promised me to write to you. Since he left here on his automobile, I have had a letter saying that he would write to you, and asking me again to be sure and do the same. Hence the cause of this long letter. I hope you will approve of my advice to Speck. As I have said, I am anything but a specialist on matrimony, and it seems comical for any one to consult me on it, but I have tried to give Speck the best judgment I could.

I will drop a line to you from London before sailing for Africa.

Your affectionate son
R. A. F. Penrose, jr.

While Spec was furtively sounding out his father through Dick, he made no nuptial hints at all to Mrs. McMillan for an entire month of their stay at the Hotel Ruhl in Nice. One early

April morning, as Julie sunned herself beside a beach umbrella and wondered if Spec would ever pop the question, a letter fell in her lap, tossed by someone behind the umbrella. It was, she found, addressed to Spec and it contained Dr. Penrose's cordial permission for Spec to wed Mrs. McMillan and at once, if he liked. With characteristic inarticulateness, Spec had tossed the letter to Julie as a substitute for an oral proposal.

They were married on April 26, 1906, in London at St. George's Church in Hannibal Square. Edith Field was maid of honor and Sir Northrop McMillan, the South African big game hunter and rancher who was a cousin of the Detroit McMillans, was best man. Their two-month honeymoon was a nightmarish tour of England and France by automobile during which the chauffeur kept getting sick and the Panhard car kept breaking down. Julie received as a wedding present a very expensive honeymoon diary but things were so hectic she gave up trying to record them after four days. (Keeping honeymoon dairies is notoriously hard work though Queen Palmer stuck at it for twelve weeks.) At Stratford-on-Avon, Julie took her beloved to an uplifting performance of *Richard III* at the Red Lion Inn. Spec fell asleep in the first act and snored through much of the show. The series of honeymoon disasters culminated at Vichy on July 4 when three tires on the Panhard blew up, the clutch dropped out of the gear box and Spec developed gout. The happiest moment of their tour was when Dick and Boies Penrose met their steamer in New York. Then the newlyweds spent a pleasant week with Dr. Penrose—he was almost eighty—at the old Spruce Street home in Philadelphia. In August, they arrived back at West Dale Street where Pikes Peak, in its reassuring brown summer phase, seemed to smile down upon their adventure.[3]

THE COURSE OF SMALL INCIDENT. which began with a real nice clambake at the Cheyenne Mountain Country Club in 1901 and ended with the marriage of Julie McMillan to Spec Penrose in 1906 amounted to more than a romantic interlude. As the younger member of a family of males who dominated him, Spec matured late. In a sense, he did not emerge from adolescence until he gathered his courage and tremblingly took a wife at the age of forty-one. And the process of growing up was completed two years later when Dr. Penrose died. This event permitted Spec to begin to exercise flamboyant tendencies which he had been careful to conceal as long as his father was around to remind him that the aristocratic Penroses did not make spectacles of themselves.

Furthermore, Spec's marriage to this particular woman was portentous. Penrose was primarily, almost totally, a business man whose judgment and creativity were conditioned by business aims. He was strongly imaginative in economic terms, but he was not concerned with abstractions such as beauty or religion. By contrast, the headstrong daughter of the French mayor of Detroit lived an intuitive and sensuous life of the spirit. Though Spec did not bother to try to understand why such spirituality was essential in human affairs, he was willing to follow Julie's lead in these esoteric matters because he loved her and was proud of her and wanted to make her happy. For her and for her alone he tempered his fierce egotism, his instinctive materialism, and in the end he became her plumed—if sometimes nonplussed—knight as one of America's great supporters of humanitarian and cultural causes.

CHAPTER SEVENTEEN

Builder's Itch

THE SAVORY BROTH of the Pikes Peak region has seldom been spoiled by too many cooks. Men like Dr. Solly and Hagerman and Pourtales and Stratton added spice but the body of the soup was prepared by General Palmer and enriched after his death by Spencer Penrose to suit the temper of new times. Nationally, these times had to do with agitation for Prohibition, income taxes, and government ownership of railroads, the rise of Woodrow Wilson and the threat to world peace poised by Kaiser Wilhelm of Germany.

Both Palmer and Penrose worked far ahead of public need, though in most respects they were utterly unlike. Palmer was a poetic intellectual, shy, withdrawn, motivated by love, pride, altruism, and a strong sense of order. Penrose, blue blood and Harvard notwithstanding, was a forthright extrovert, driven by a wild mixture of unruly impulses—impulses to get filthy rich, to show the world, to delight his friends, to confound his enemies, to do as he damn' pleased, and so on. He acted by hot hunches as much as by cold reasoning but his mind had a bottom layer of sense and stability. Besides, he had the shrewdness, the quickness of decision, and the courage of a first-rate poker player.

At some point after his marriage in 1906 and after his father's death in 1908, Spec became bored with merely piling up a million dollars a year. As a copper tycoon his creativity was hampered by struggles with labor unions at Bingham Canyon and by efforts to keep from being gobbled up by the wily Guggenheims, who had financed Utah Copper in exchange for a quarter interest. This is not to say that Spec worked hard all the time. In

those halcyon days before World War I it was not dignified for
successful men to stay on the job more than six months a year.
Spec did not take up yachting, as Charley Tutt had done before
his unexpected death in 1909. But he traveled with Julie everywhere—to Egypt and India, to Siam and Mexico, to Spain and
Japan and Germany and Hawaii. On these trips he took special
note of the operation of the best resort hotels and of the rapid
growth of the automobile tourist business in Europe.

He was beginning to suffer intolerably from an itch to build.
To soothe the itch, he enlarged Julie's big home at 30 West Dale
Street and added a paved courtyard and out-sized garage. He
needed the garage because he had bought four canary-colored
Lozier cars at $5,000 each, honoring the Lozier stock car which
won the 100-mile Los Angeles Motordrome race of 1911 with an
average speed of eighty miles an hour. At the same time, he
bought a ranch on Turkey Creek seventeen miles south of the
Springs down the Canon City Road and plunged into ranching
with headlong ardor. He raised exotic sheep and pure-bred Hol-
steins. He began assembling a menagerie of Colorado wild
animals—bears and coyotes and a huge elk with spreading antlers
named Prince Albert. He experimented with freezing fruits and
vegetables in an ice cave to preserve them for consumption out
of season. Once he nearly set fire to the whole country while
burning grass to improve his Turkey Creek soil. He put up a
ranch house and, in 1913, painted it a light shade of pink which
he had admired on a hotel in the island of Madeira. It seemed to
him that this transported Portuguese pinkness against Pikes
Peak and Cheyenne Mountain was even more effective than it
had been in its rocky Atlantic Ocean setting.

Both Spec and Julie were avid walkers even if they did own
$20,000 worth of Loziers. On many Sunday mornings in summer
they would set out early from Dale Street and stroll hand and
hand down the gravel path through Palmer's Monument Valley
Park toward Broadmoor. The Pikes Peak region in any season
is one of earth's favored places where vibrant air and clarity of
scene and the sun's beaming benediction combine to cheer the

soul. In 1913, as today, Monument Valley Park was a paradise for nesting birds. The Penroses strolled amid a whirring society of red-headed, lyrical house finches, blue lazuli buntings, clownish chats, and gaudy yellow Bullock's orioles and bright-blue Steller jays. The air beneath the great brown mountain and its clustering satellites had the sweet warm odor of pine and juniper. Below the path, Monument Creek burbled along in diminutive grandeur—the same brave trickle which the absent-minded General Cameron had called "the noble Cache la Poudre" at the staking of Colorado Springs forty-two years earlier.

The beautiful Park ended at Bijou Street and the Penroses would walk to the recently-asphalted Cascade Avenue past St. Mary's Church which Julie was about to join, as a returned lamb if not exactly a convert. In embracing Catholicism after her Episcopalian upbringing she was influenced by the conversion of her daughter Gladys McMillan who was marrying the Catholic Count Cornet de Ways Ruart of Belgium. Perhaps Julie hoped also, as a devout parishioner, to soften the Lord's displeasure with Spec's lack of interest in religion. She did not rejoin, however, until assured by a priest that she could be a good Catholic even though she lacked patience to memorize even five decades of the rosary and even though she might have to miss Mass now and then because of bad weather or other contingency on those Sundays when Spec wanted her to be with him at Turkey Creek.

Beyond St. Mary's the Penroses would continue south down Cascade past the front fountain and stately gardens of the Antlers Hotel which maintained its standing as a fine inn despite the fact that General Palmer was no longer around. Up Pikes Peak Avenue they saw the new four-globed street lamps and the polished white marble of Jimmie Burns' $300,000 theater, less than a year old. Next avenue south was Huerfano Street which would be renamed Colorado Avenue in 1917 with the annexation of Colorado City to the Springs. Here they could read a marker directing motorists to the new Lincoln Highway (the present U. S. 24) up Ute Pass to South Park and the Continental Divide at Tennessee Pass. South Cascade Avenue, they observed, was dotted with California-style bungalows, but the Ivywild area beyond the Tejon Street bridge was a straggle of homes. Bathhouse John's Zoo Park on Cheyenne Road was a seedy relic of better days. They would climb the street car grade to Lake Avenue and walk on past the polo field to Cheyenne Mountain Country Club where they would have a cocktail and a good dinner after their six-mile hike to Broadmoor.

BROADMOOR WAS VERY MUCH on Penrose's mind in 1913. He noticed that the ghost of Count Pourtales was everywhere—in the alluring buffalo contour of Cheyenne Mountain, in the radiating streets which the Count had furrowed out in 1889, in his bordering trees, in the central blue ribbon of Spring Creek. But after twenty years, the Count's glamorous hopes for "Broadmoor City" seemed as dead, as impossible to achieve, as during the Panic of 1893. Only a dozen people had been persuaded by real estate salesmen to build homes on Lake Avenue. A few more homes sat in lonely isolation on auxiliary streets—notably the Charles Baldwin version of Bourbon France in the Wild West, and a rambling $200,000 Spanish villa built in 1910-11 by the Ashton Potters. The newlywed Potters from New York had just shed their respective spouses (Mrs. Potter, very rich and beautiful, had been Mrs. Ganson Depew). Ashton Potter's chief distinction was his claim that on the day the Spanish-American War started he had fallen asleep as a civilian in a New York saloon and had awakened to find himself a Captain in the Twelfth U. S. Cavalry leading troops into the fray at Manila. The one-story Potter villa was placed in the center of William Dixon's apple orchard and that is why the Potters called it El Pomar— "apple orchard" in Spanish.

At the end of Count Pourtales' Lake Avenue, the small Broadmoor Hotel and the white Casino still stood—the second Casino which had replaced the Count's original in 1898. The empty Hotel was a pigeon-roost and the once-refulgent Casino was as dilapidated as Bathhouse John's Fun Factory. The Casino was used mostly now for firemen's balls and church outings. The trustees of the Stratton Estate, you recall, had bought all of Pourtales' Broadmoor in 1909, including the Casino and hundreds of unsold lots. In 1913, these trustees were fully occupied trying to get the Stratton Home started at last. Even if they had had time to promote Broadmoor, there was no market for the lots or for the Casino.

Furthermore, as Penrose was well aware, the whole Pikes Peak region was in a state of economic paralysis worse than that of the early 1880s when General Palmer had had to foreclose on the first Antlers Hotel. The main trouble, as we perceived in Zoo Park's demise, was the fall in Cripple Creek gold production —from $20,000,000 in 1900 to $11,000,000 in 1912. Most of Cripple Creek's four hundred and seventy-five mining companies had folded and their worthless stocks were papering Springs privies and drying to dust in Springs attics—sad symbols of the destruction of local capital.[1] Only one mill still ran in Colorado City. The Colorado Midland and Short Line Railroads were bankrupt and the old dream of expanding local industry had vanished as hordes of unemployed workers left town. While the nation's population zoomed in ten years from 76,000,000 to 92,000,000, Colorado Springs proper lost hundreds of residents and its population became stationary by 1913 at 30,000.

As Penrose mulled over the deflation of Pikes Peak values, the town's leaders whistled in the dark. Some insisted that Cripple Creek would revive. Others talked wistfully of a return to the idyllic quietude of Little London. This last, Spec knew, would be fatal. The national level of wages and costs had shot up since 1900. The Springs was having a hard time already paying for its streets, water supply, parks, lighting, schools, fire and police protection. There is nothing idyllic about a community too poor to bury its own garbage. Some citizens, remembering the gay Flower Parades of the Nineties, sought a more profitable tourist trade by staging historical pageants, called Shan Kive, about Indians and the sixteenth century-doings of the Conquistadores in New Mexico and Old King Tartarax of Quivera. Shan Kive culminated in amateur rodeos at the Garden of the Gods and in masked balls on Kiowa Street with Bo Peeps and Roosevelt Rough Riders and Friar Tucks and Skeletons and Frogs cakewalking through the Pikes Peak night. The pageants were great fun but they did not increase the Springs' income or its population. Paradoxically, the region's one thriving industry—the care and treatment of tuberculosis—was not discussed out loud for fear of losing tourists who were afraid of the disease. Nevada Avenue was lined with convalescent homes and Glockner Hospital was almost hidden by the invalid tents around it. Cragmor Sanatorium, nestled in yellow bluffs northeast of town, was being enlarged and was jammed with lungers drawn to Pikes Peak by the fame of specialists like Dr. Gerald Webb. But too many of these visiting invalids were poor. The rich ones took their large incomes to more luxurious health resorts—to Asheville and Pinehurst and Lake Placid.

AFTER MONTHS OF THOUGHT on local deflation Penrose decided to do something about it. As a starter, he announced his support in 1913 of Charles Noble, a retired Colorado Midland official, who had been recommending an auto road to the top of Pikes Peak as a tourist attraction. Noble went to Washington to talk with Department of Agriculture men who controlled Pike National Forest. They were not encouraging. They reminded Noble that the seventeen-mile carriage road which John Hundley had built from Cascade in Ute Pass to the summit in 1889 had had no traffic since 1905 because of the popularity of Zalmon G. Simmons' Cog Train. The Department had never issued an auto road permit in any National Forest due to the paucity of touring autos. Department records showed that, because of Colorado's poor roads, only 1,300 tourist autos had made it to Colorado Springs in 1912. Few of those cars had enough power to crawl up such a steeple as Pikes Peak. And anyhow a Pikes Peak Highway might cost as much as $25,000. Where, the Department asked Noble, was that kind of money coming from?

While Noble jousted with politicians, Penrose bided his time and worked behind the scenes. As he expected, auto traffic up

Ute Pass on the new Lincoln Highway increased markedly in June, 1913. On July 17, two motorists from Denver, H. Brown and J. F. Bradley, drove through the Springs in a twenty horsepower Buick Bear Cat and ran up Hundley's carriage road to Pikes Peak Summit in four hours—the first car to go all the way. The old nine-mile Crystal Park road which had scared Lincoln's biographer, John George Nicolay, so badly in '81, was opened for cars and was well patronized even though turntables had to be installed to negotiate two of its seventy-five hairpin turns.[2]

As Noble's Peak road became more feasible, Spec hit on two promotion devices which he would use to gain his ends for the rest of his life. The first was financial. To avoid having to offer from his own pocket the entire $25,000 for the Pikes Peak Highway, he put the bite for some of it on business associates whom he knew could afford it—friends like Charlie MacNeill of Utah Copper, and Bert Carlton, who had succeeded Stratton as king of Cripple Creek. The second device was the exploitation of celebrities to focus attention on Pikes Peak. Penrose's first celebrity was Berner Eli (Barney) Oldfield, the cigar-chewing racer who was the first man to drive a car at sixty miles an hour on a circular track. Even in 1914, Oldfield's fame was such that traffic policemen greeted speedsters with "Whoja think y'are—Barney Oldfield?" Barney promised to appear in the first Pikes Peak Hill Climb and Spec saw to it also that the proposed event was approved by the American Automobile Association. Some months later, the Pikes Peak Highway Association was formed and Lincoln Highway was marked through Colorado with tin stencils depicting Pikes Peak. And then Charles Noble suddenly received from David Houston, Secretary of Agriculture, a permit allowing Penrose and associates to build the Pikes Peak Highway along the Hundley carriage road and to charge toll on it for twenty years. Houston, Penrose heard later, admired Barney Oldfield and felt that anything Barney was mixed up in deserved U. S. Government sanction.

The Pikes Peak Highway was constructed during the summer and fall of 1915. It was a twenty-foot-wide tawny ribbon which

curled through the evergreens up the first steep ridge above
Cascade and unrolled across the long high valley on the north
side of the Peak to Glen Cove. From there it zigzagged above
timberline to the top of the sky and the stone Signal Station
where in '76 the bereaved Sergeant John and Nora O'Keefe had
mourned the death of their little Erin and had cursed the pack
rats who had eaten her. The seventeen-mile road (twenty miles
today) began at 7,415 feet above sea level and climbed 6,746
vertical feet on an average six per cent grade with a ten per
cent maximum. Spec was mildly disturbed when the first mile
above Cascade cost $5,956.10 instead of the estimated $1,470.
He was unhappier still when he had to pay $12,057.17 for the
second mile. His associates refused to kick in more than their
agreed share of the original $25,000, so Spec gritted his teeth and
decided to meet the excess alone. Above the ninth mile at 10,000
feet of altitude the workmen had to rest half the time to keep
their noses from bleeding and Spec found himself shelling out a
monstrous $21,454.20 for Mile Fourteen. When the road was
finished in October, 1915, its total cost was more than a quarter-
million dollars.

But it did what Spec had hoped it would do. The Springs
tourist business for 1916 was very good indeed. And Spec found
himself enjoying the feeling of having built the highest auto
road in the world even if it cost him a fortune. He was especially
pleased when the whole nation took an interest in the first Pikes
Peak Hill Climb over a twelve-mile stretch of the highway on
August 11 and 12. Newspapers everywhere ran pictures of the
great Oldfield passing out his usual "You know me, Barney Oldfield" autograph. Other pictures showed the excruciatingly elaborate Penrose Cup for the winner which Spec had had made up
by Bailey, Banks and Biddle in Philadelphia at a cost of $1,200.

Though Barney brought publicity to Pikes Peak, he could not
do better than place twelfth in the Penrose Hill Climb with his
big French Delage. Ralph Mulford won the time trials in a
Hudson Super Six. Fred Junk was first-day winner in a wire-
wheeled Chalmers and Rea Lentz won on the second day in a

little eight-cylinder Romano. Lentz had the best time for both races—twenty minutes and fifty-five seconds. He was a small man and he left town bent almost double under the sixty-pound weight of Spec's solid silver Penrose Cup.[3]

WHILE THE PIKES PEAK HIGHWAY was emerging, Spec bought the one-and-a-quarter-mile Manitou Incline which had been built in 1907 to carry pipeline materials from Manitou to the top of Mount Manitou's first rise and then had been converted into a tourist cable car by Dr. N. N. Brumbach. But Highway and Incline absorbed only a small part of Spec's energy in 1915-16. His chief preoccupation was a project of far greater scope and import which resulted when he came to terms with the Stratton Estate to buy the Broadmoor Casino and 450 acres of lots around it.

The idea of picking up the pieces of Broadmoor where Count Pourtales had dropped them in 1893 had been hatching in Spec's mind for years. During those pleasant Sunday morning walks with Julie, he had become almost foolishly fond of the place. Perhaps he found in the red-and-green Cheyenne Mountain and soft silver mesa below it the component parts of a pastoral divan where a man of his proportions could spread himself, and express himself. Plan upon plan for developing the Count's "sunny place for shady people" crystallized in his imagination—some of them grandiose extensions of his experiments in decoration and zoology at Turkey Creek Ranch. These large schemes promised to satisfy most of his raging impulses—his builder's itch, his towering egotism, his love of bigness, his exhibitionist urge, his swashbuckling yen to do what nobody else had the gall to do. The plans appealed to him also because they would bring into play his total experience as business man, traveler, promoter, expert on resorts, gourmet, sportsman, auto enthusiast and militant disciple of progress and the American spirit of free enterprise. With his huge Utah Copper income, he could afford heavy and sustained investment. And he was sure that the new Broadmoor of his dream would return his capital to him in the end. And then some.

The keystone of Spec's rainbow arching over Cheyenne Mountain was the Broadmoor Hotel, to be finer and more complete than the sum of all the hotels which he had admired with Julie during a decade of global wandering. Early in 1916, Spec came out publicly with some details. The structure would cost $1,100,-000. The cuisine would be splendid; the bars so numerous that no guest would ever be far from refreshment. Charlie MacNeill and Spec would put in $350,000 each. Other "business associates" would be pleased (more or less) to contribute a total of $400,000 —friends like Bert Carlton, Eugene Shove, Clarence Carpenter (Julie's brother-in-law), and the late Charley Tutt's son, young Charley.

The Broadmoor Hotel's first architect was the same Frederic J. Sterner who had run himself lean enlarging General Palmer's Glen Eyrie. Sterner had built the second Antlers and the Greenbriar Hotel at White Sulphur Springs and he set out bravely to squeeze all of Spec's notions under one roof. The outside terra cotta had to be Madeira pink, as at Turkey Creek Ranch. The bedrooms would have touches of Honolulu and Aix-les-Bains and, to please Julie, Lausanne. The ballroom would suggest a salon in the Royal Palace at Peking. The card room would be Brothers Adam. Charlie MacNeill and Bert Carlton had to have suites after Louis Quinze. Horace Devereux, Spec's old friend, wanted something Pompeian to live in. The general layout should take into account that the Turkey Creek Ranch menagerie might be moved to the hotel grounds, including the big elk, Prince Albert, whose mating shriek was as piercing as a locomotive whistle.

Sterner lasted briefly on the Broadmoor job and resigned a nervous wreck. To avoid further loss of time, Spec hired the redoubtable New York firm of Warren and Wetmore. These men had proved their stamina by surviving the erection of New York's Grand Central Station, the Biltmore, the Vanderbilt, the Ritz, the Commodore, and many other construction nightmares.

Charles Wetmore, a hardy and resourceful spirit, prepared plans quickly which Spec could and did approve. Wisely, Wetmore was vague as to his chosen style of architecture for the Broadmoor. "Italian Renaissance," he would say, or "Massive Alpine" or "Moorish Mediterranean" or "American Riviera." Actually, he spoke the exact truth when he told a *Gazette* reporter: "I have tried to combine the best features of many famous European hotel resorts, blended to conform with the landscape of the Pikes Peak region."

WHATEVER THE STYLE, a very handsome building rose above Pourtales' lake on the site of the second Broadmoor Casino during 1917 and part of 1918. Though World War I raged in Europe, the work was pushed along steadily by James Stewart Company of Salt Lake City, builders of Jimmie Burns' theater. The central portion had nine stories and a tower. There were 350 rooms, including those in the four-story wings. Spec moved the Casino a few hundred feet south to use as clubhouse for the eighteen-hole golf course being laid out by Donald Ross, the Pinehurst designer. The old Broadmoor Hotel was left where it was and renamed the Colonial Club, to serve for offices and annex. Landscaping was assigned to the Olmsted Company of Brookline, Massachusetts, the founder of which had created New York's Central Park. As his first hotel manager, Spec hired William Dunning away from the Antlers where Dunning had been employed since 1906.

Residents of the Springs watched the Broadmoor scene with mixed skepticism and admiration. As far as they could see, the Pikes Peak region needed another hotel about as much as it needed another mountain. Business at the Antlers Hotel was poor and what tourist was going to ride a street car five miles out into the wilds to get a room?

And still Penrose poured money into the place. When the $1,100,000 was spent he put up a second million dollars, and then a third. While the minority stockholders fretted and sweated, he added things as blithely as a child decorating a Christmas tree—Turkish baths, an indoor swimming pool, a second dining room, a billiard room, a fleet of lake boats, sixty-five sleeping porches with Venetian blinds, a squash court. To be closer to operations, he moved out of 30 West Dale Street with Julie and into the Ashton Potter villa, El Pomar, which he bought for $70,000.[4] Since the villa had only thirty rooms, he added a second and third story to one wing, and a bathroom of Italian tile for Julie at a cost of $15,000 for tile alone.

The private hotel opening and ball was scheduled for June 1, 1918. Because of the War, celebrities for publicity purposes were scarce and Spec had to settle for a mere tycoon, John D. Rockefeller, Jr., to be the Broadmoor's first guest of honor. The oil king arrived from Pueblo in the afternoon of June 1 just as Spec's army of carpenters and painters were departing. He retired to rest a bit in the sixth floor suite which Spec had prepared for him.

The evening opening was a brilliant triumph. Many of those who congratulated Spec and Julie in the gleaming lobby were the same community leaders who had toasted Count Pourtales at the Broadmoor Casino in 1891. Spec was in the happiest of moods as he led the crowd through his great kitchens, his power plant, his ballroom, and the other attractions which he had produced in this magnificent effort to supplant the Antlers as the greatest hostelry in the West.

When midnight approached, it occurred to Spec that he had not noticed his guest of honor among those present. There was no answer when he went to the front desk and phoned the sixth floor suite. But the bell captain came by just then with a note for Mr. Penrose. It was from the guest of honor explaining with deep regret that he had had to leave the suite and go to the Antlers because the smell of fresh paint had given him a severe headache.

Spec was downcast for only a minute or two and then he had to laugh. After all, though he had spent $3,000,000 trying to put John D. Rockefeller Jr., up for the night, it was the bare beginning of what his builder's itch was going to do to Colorado Springs.

CHAPTER EIGHTEEN

Penrose Orchard

WITH THE BROADMOOR COMPLETED, Spec built on and on, incessantly, relentlessly, irresistibly. Now and then he built for the same uninspired reasons which activate ordinary men, but most of the time he went at it simply because he wanted to, in response to a confused bundle of emotions defying analysis. He yanked a young jack-of-all-trades, Milton Strong, off the Manitou Incline, appointed him building superintendent, and put him to work on the new sidewalk around the lake with a crew of five. After a bit, the crew numbered 100, then 300, and Milt found himself installing everything from septic tanks to swimming pool chlorinators.

Milt's hardest job was rising early enough to meet Penrose at El Pomar for the day's orders. No matter how late the party had lasted the night before, Spec rose habitually at dawn and was ready to see Strong at 6 a.m., clad as usual in boots or puttees, riding breeches, sports jacket, checked vest, and Stetson hat. He breakfasted at seven and rode his horse around Broadmoor until nine, inspecting projects. Then he went reluctantly to the Mining Exchange building offices to be a Utah Copper magnate until one. He would nap for an hour after lunch and ride his horse from El Pomar to the hotel hitching rack where he would dismount and enter the building to catch up on correspondence. Next he would ride over the golf course from end to end, stop briefly at the Country Club for a drink, and arrive back home at 6:30 p.m. to take a shower before dinner with Julie.

Rapidly, the faded Broadmoor of Count Pourtales was transformed and revitalized. During the next decade, Spec would splatter the lovely mesa with everything under the deep blue Colorado sky—the Broadmoor Greenhouse, miles of bridle-paths and hiking trails, the Cooking Club on Cheyenne Mountain, the hotel's spectacular front fountain and hitching racks, the Broadmoor Stables for 400 mounts, tennis courts, rustic bridges and shelters for the golf course, the Broadmoor Garage, embellishments at El Pomar, an improved tournament polo field at Cheyenne Mountain Country Club and three practice fields. In 1921, Spec demanded and got a new public road to Lake Avenue and the hotel. In June, he and his Stetson led a joyous cavalcade of champagne-fired motorists, polo players, and hunt people up the wide, curving highway which had been laid from Nevada Avenue at a cost of $125,000. Penrose himself had supplied most of the money.

As Spec had anticipated, news of the expanded polo program at Broadmoor, of the horse shows and drag hunts and tennis and squash, spread among the Newport strain of Easterners who could indulge in such expensive pastimes. Soon most of Pourtales' "Broadmoor City" was filled with the homes of rich sportsmen and invalids. Between the gushing hotel fountain and the plethora of private swimming pools, a water shortage plagued Broadmoor. Penrose produced a million dollars so that Milt Strong could buy water at Rosemont eighteen miles up in the hills toward Pikes Peak and pipe it down to a reservoir below the Cooking Club. When the water arrived, Spec revealed that he had bought what was left of the old Dixon Ranch and two other parcels for residential development—2,000 more acres of Broadmoor mesa sweeping east and south of the hotel for miles. The Dixon Ranch enclosed much of the east face of Cheyenne Mountain. Spec named its mesa portion Broadmoor Heights. He called the 160-acre Ferguson Tract Pourtales Addition. On the third tract, Polo Park, Spec built a second tournament polo field and a $25,000 covered grandstand of Moorish design so that Julie and her friends would not get rained on during tournaments of the Broadmoor Polo Association. The polo players remarked

that they didn't like to get rained on either. Partly to please
them, Spec built in 1928 a big indoor arena, the Broadmoor
Riding Academy, on the lake opposite the hotel so that they could
play polo during a snowstorm if they liked.

In his Broadmoor schemes—the hotel, the sale of residence lots,
the polo fields—Penrose was countering the deflation of Cripple
Creek and creating local capital by luring the rich to the region.
But all the while he kept a weather eye on his plebeian Pikes Peak
Highway venture and watched for other opportunities to attract
the people of the flat, hot, and dusty plains to his part of
the Rockies.

He was especially intrigued with the Cog Train, and so was
Julie, perhaps because the neat, perky, steaming, stylish little
engine reminded her of herself—the same Cog Train which Simmons the Bed Man had pushed to the summit in '91, the tails of
his cutaway flapping gaily. Zalmon G. had died in 1910 and the
Cog Train passed to Zalmon G. Junior who added to it the Crystal
Park Auto Road. Thereafter, young Simmons and his Simmons
Bed Company became involved in bringing about one of the
historic revolutions of American life—the putting of American
couples into twin beds instead of letting them sleep—unhygieni-
cally, according to Simmons—together. In the meantime, the
neglected Cog Train fell into disrepair. By 1925, while absorbed
in his sensational Beautyrest Mattress advertising campaign,
Simmons was glad to unload the Cog Train on Spec for $50,000,
and also the Crystal Park Road. In ensuing years, with Julie
breathing spirited encouragement, Spec rebuilt the line, improved the rolling stock, and restored the morale of Cog Train
personnel. The rejuvenation cost him around half a million
dollars.

THE BUILDING OF THE CHEYENNE MOUNTAIN HIGH-
WAY brought more vitriolic criticism on Penrose than anything
else he ever did. The story of it began in 1922 when the Short
Line Railroad was put up for auction at El Paso County Courthouse. The Short Line, you recall, had failed after 1901 to break

the monopoly of Penrose, Bert Carlton, and others on Cripple Creek milling and transport. Spec recognized the strategic value of the Short Line's thrilling right-of-way above Broadmoor as it wound up the drainage of Cheyenne Creek toward Rosemont and beyond. He attended the auction in 1922 entirely sure that nobody would or could top the generous $200,000 bid which he intended to make.

The only other bidder was a fellow named W. D. Corley, who, Spec understood, had settled in the Springs in 1914 and was earning a modest living as a small-time coal operator. Spec made the first bid. Corley upped it. Spec upped that and Corley upped *that*. For the hitherto-almighty Penrose, it was an irritating situation, to say the least. The duel continued. When the price reached the absurd figure of $370,000 on Corley's bid, Spec, in a quiet rage, let his opponent have it. He was sure that Corley could never meet such a commitment and the Short Line would revert to Spec at a sensible price. However, instead of welching on his bid, Corley gave the auctioneer a check for $370,000 cash. The check did not bounce and, as a consequence, Spec acquired a permanent bête noir. He discovered too late that Corley had put one over on him. The coal operator had only pretended to be small-time, having made a fortune earlier as a Mississippi cotton king.

Corley scrapped the Short Line, widened the roadbed, and opened the superb Corley Toll Highway in 1924 from the Springs to Cripple Creek (today's free Gold Camp Road). This toll road was a constant headache to Spec who had to trespass on it to reach his mountain lodge, Camp Vigil. It was the best route also to his Rosemont water sources. At last he lost his temper up there, struck a toll road employee with his riding quirt, and landed in court at Cripple Creek. The incident cost him $2,500 in an out-of-court settlement, to the delight of Gold Campers who had disliked him ever since '94 when he had brought aid and comfort to the enemy in the form of twelve hot water bottles full of bourbon for his strike-breaking Company K.

Soon afterward, Corley asked the Forest Service to let him build a fourteen-mile road from the Corley Highway at Rosemont to the top of Pikes Peak, following the old Seven Steps to "Minnetonka" and "Minnehaha" and the other Seven Lakes which Helen Hunt Jackson had raved about. That, to Spec, was the last straw. He wasn't going to let his bête noir use the top of his mountain even if he had to blow it up. Spec's roar of protest boomed from the state capitol in Denver to the halls of Congress as he told the world that he hadn't built the Pikes Peak Highway and bought the Cog Train just to provide business for W. G. Corley's toll road.

The Forest Service saw Spec's point and felt besides that Corley's proposed Pikes Peak spur would not be used enough to justify issuing a road permit. Meanwhile, Spec was seeking something to draw sightseers to Broadmoor and he suddenly saw how to kill two birds with one stone. He would build a toll road himself—from the Cooking Club to the top of his own Cheyenne Mountain. It would bring swarms of motoring tourists to Broadmoor, some of whom would otherwise be paying toll to drive the Corley Highway. If traffic on the Corley could thus be held down, Spec's rival was not apt ever to get a Pikes Peak road building permit.

The dramatic Cheyenne Mountain Highway, completed in 1925, cost Spec a million dollars. It was seven miles long and the ragged yellow switchback scars which it left on the face of the mountain were sickening eyesores to residents who had loved those unmarred slopes. Spec, who believed that the road would benefit the whole region, was bewildered and hurt by the public outcry which included the disapproval of his own friends. Possibly in reaction, he decided to give the ingrate community something really to complain about by decorating the top of Cheyenne Mountain at the end of the road with a giant searchlight. It would be the largest in the West and it would rake the sky with flashings of 7,500,000 candlepower as it rotated six times a minute all night long, reminding the country from the Continental Divide to Kansas that Colorado Springs was on the map.

Fortunately for Spec, and for the town, government officials advised that the searchlight might confuse airplane pilots and the idea was dropped.

AS WE OBSERVED far back in these pages, General Palmer had no sense of publicity values. He never realized in the 1870s how much he owed to General Cameron and to Dr. Bell for making his village known. And we saw how he dismissed W. E. Pabor when the latter drew tourists to the Garden of the Gods by naming a rock formation "Seal Making Love to a Nun." Penrose, on the other hand, was a natural press agent whose merits included the belief that no expense was too great if his message got on the AP wire.

After his early experiments with Barney Oldfield and the paint-allergic John D. Rockefeller, Jr., Spec's touch improved steadily. Before he was through, the tourist attractions of the Pikes Peak region—his own and everybody else's—became almost as well known as Coca Cola and Ivory Soap. His indifference to the culture that Julie was always promoting did not apply when his pretty wife brought great artists like Chaliapin or Paderewski or Rosa Ponselle or Lily Pons to El Pomar. By hook or crook, he always managed to get such people up on a horse or into bathing suits to pose for publicity pictures. Spec was an admirer of Will Rogers and was overjoyed when the celebrated humorist and political commentator succumbed to his frequent invitations and spent a week end at Pikes Peak. In 1925, Spec nearly persuaded President Coolidge to pass the summer at Broadmoor, and then settled gladly for Vice President Charles G. Dawes and his upside-down pipe. Dawes was an interested spectator at the opening of the hotel's bathing beach. The first of Spec's annual bathing beauty contests was held that summer, with the girls shockingly attired in nothing but skimpy black suits with brief skirts and black silk stockings rolled at the knees.

Though Will Rogers and Dawes and the bathing beauties were good AP wire service material, the best Spec ever had was Jack Dempsey, heavyweight boxing champion of the world, who spent July of 1926 at Broadmoor. Dempsey, thirty-one years old, was at the peak of his fame. Everyone on earth wanted to read about his beauty-and-the-beast marriage to the movie star, Estelle Taylor, about his forthcoming title defense against Gene Tunney, about his failure to fight the colored giant, Harry Wills, about his relations with the promoter Tex Rickard and the New York boxing official, Jim Farley. Spec had become part-owner of the Colorado *Gazette-Telegraph* in 1923, and he assigned his star reporter, Stuart P. Dodge, to shadow Dempsey around the clock for the AP so that a billion readers would know what Jack was doing during every minute of his Broadmoor sojourn.

The world champion, somewhat dazed but anxious to please Spec, punched bags for the public all morning in an improvised gym in the Broadmoor Golf Club and boxed exhibition rounds in green silk tights at 4 p.m. in the Broadmoor Hotel ballroom. The rest of the time, Spec had him photographed in every kind of Broadmoor setting for the delectation of the nation—riding a horse on a bridle-path, soaking in a Turkish bath, plunging in the pool, trout fishing at Rosemont, hunting deer at Camp Vigil, patting the elk, Prince Albert, at Turkey Creek, retiring in the honeymooner's bed at Spec's new Lodge on top of Cheyenne Mountain. Late in July, Jack was supposed to gallop up the seven steep miles of Cheyenne Mountain Highway to beat the fifty-seven minute record of a Hopi Indian named Amesoli Patazoni. Jack tried, but after dashing up hill a hundred yards or so he collapsed and decided that he would have to pull out of Spec's Broadmoor and get some rest. He completed his training for the first Dempsey-Tunney fight at White Sulphur Springs.

Most of Spec's promotions were cold business affairs but his developing zoo came straight from his heart. He had always loved animals, whether hunting them on some maharajah's preserve in India or making pets of them at Turkey Creek. He took pride in the fact that his brilliant brother Tal (Dr. Charles Bingham Penrose) was a director of the Philadelphia Zoo and had founded there in 1903 the Penrose Research Laboratory, the first zoo lab in America. When Spec visited European capitals, he might not go with Julie to the current art show but he was sure to stop at the zoo—in Paris or Amsterdam or London or Hamburg or wherever—and to take notes on its exhibits and arrangement. In 1922, he installed a few cages of animals between the Broadmoor Hotel and the Golf Club. Some guests complained of their smell and noise but Spec did nothing about it until a monkey bit a child. The child's parents sued and Spec had to fork over $8,000. As a result, he moved his animals to a site half a mile up the new Cheyenne Mountain Highway where he had fenced forty acres and built four concrete bear pits, three coyote runs, lion and bird cages, and a glass tank for a boa constrictor. This permanent zoo was augmented by the denizens of Spec's Turkey Creek menagerie, including Prince Albert, a tottering old monarch of the forest by this time, as tame as a venerable family horse.

Meanwhile, Spec had become friends with the great circus press agent, Courtney Riley Cooper, and had decided to emulate Cooper's use of the ultimate superlative. For publicity purposes, Broadmoor became "The Golf, Tennis and Polo Capital of the World" and the zoo became "The Highest Zoo in the World" and Prince Albert was "The Largest Elk in the World." But Spec was unhappy because "The Highest Zoo in the World" had no elephant and he hated to buy one at the outrageous prices which prevailed in the open pachyderm market. Just then, a circus-owning friend of his was having psychiatric trouble with a four-ton elephant named Tessie who detested her winters quarters at French Lick, Indiana. The circus man offered Tessie to Spec free if he would haul her away. And so it was that, amid tremendous fanfare, "The Largest Elephant in the World" came to Broadmoor, complete with howdah. Penrose saw to it that she was no longer plain Tessie but "The Empress of India, Gift of the Rajah of Nagapur to Spencer Penrose."

Spec derived endless pleasure from his zoo and usually ended his day's ride there, besides turning up often in the middle of the night with guests whom he and Julie had been entertaining at El Pomar. There was sadness, too. A friend met him one early

evening striding zoo-ward in pith helmet and high-powered rifle
looking like a South African on safari. Spec had tears in his eyes
as he told the friend, "Got to shoot an old elk."

The old elk, of course, was Prince Albert.[1]

LATE IN 1931 Spec was threatened briefly by cancer. He was
still a fine physical specimen but he was sixty-six years old, the
last of the Penroses, Senator Boies having died in 1921, Tal in
1925, and Dick in July, 1931—all of them leaving large estates
because they had invested in the copper companies of their dumb
younger brother.

After four decades of happiness at Pikes Peak, Spec did not
care to wind up in the Penrose burial ground with all those stuffy
blue bloods back in Philadelphia. Instead, he planned a simple
plot along Cheyenne Mountain Highway above the zoo. Since
he and Julie had not managed to have children, the plot would
be just for the two of them and for two bachelor friends of his
Cripple Creek days, Harry Leonard of Denver and big Horace
Devereux, a helpless and impoverished invalid now whom Spec
looked after at the Broadmoor Hotel.

Architect Charles Thomas made a few modest designs for the
proposed Penrose Cemetery, but the more Spec thought about
it the more he hated to devote so much valuable sightseeing
space to non-commercial use. Though the volume of traffic up
the Highway was fair, it could be increased, particularly if there
were something large and interesting and expensive for tourists
to visit between the zoo and the honeymoon lodge on top. The
upshot was that Thomas discarded his modest designs and drew
plans instead for a large tower several hundred feet high which
would be equipped with "the most complete amplification system
in the world" to boom chime notes twenty miles out over the
surrounding prairie. The tower would be made of blocks carved
from a single granite shaft on the side of Cheyenne Mountain
and it would cost $250,000.

For some months, Spec was determined to call his musical
tower Penrose Memorial but was dissuaded by friends who

argued that some of his fellow citizens were mad enough at him already for building Cheyenne Mountain Highway. And besides, they said, why would tourists from Oklahoma pay toll to visit the memorial of a Colorado man they had never heard of?

One of Spec's most disarming traits was his abiilty to listen to reason and to take good advice. He shelved the name Penrose Memorial. Just as construction work was about to start, he received the sad news that his idol, Will Rogers, had died in a plane crash in Alaska. Soon afterwards, announcement was made that the granite tower on Cheyenne Mountain would be called the Will Rogers Shrine of the Sun.

BENEATH THE FROTHY TALES—some true, some mythical—about Penrose lay the reality of a shrewd, able, tenacious, and far-sighted personality, equal in these respects to General Palmer himself. Penrose more than held his own in the brutal competition of the copper industry, in contrast to his partner, Charlie MacNeill, who frittered away his fortune in Wall Street before dying in 1923. Instead of spending his wealth on ephemeral pleasures or on some static accumulation of rarities, Spec spent it on dynamic projects to promote the charms and the prosperity of the Pikes Peak region. Doubtless he expected to cash in some day on his $10,000,000 total investment, but he never did, and he didn't seem to care.

Penrose believed that creating business, jobs, opportunity, growth, was the best gift which he could make to his community. But he practiced orthodox giving, too. In 1914, the Penroses built the $12,000 Monument Valley Municipal Swimming Pool. Three years later, Spec directed the war fund drive of the American Red Cross, staging a week of city-wide patriotic frenzy that exhausted everybody and brought in $217,000 as against the Springs' previous record of $10,000. In 1919, Julie Penrose built the lovely small Catholic church in Broadmoor and named it Pauline Chapel after her young granddaughter. No Catholic church, it appears, should be named after a living person, but Julie usually got her way even with the good fathers who made

haste to discover a deceased Saint Pauline in Rome to justify the
naming of Pauline Chapel.

A number of events seem to have led Spec by slow stages to
set up his final and most opulent structure. He called it El Pomar
Foundation. He had been much impressed when his brother
Dick willed his entire fortune of $10,000,000 to be divided equally
between the Geological Society of America and the American
Philosophical Society. Spec's poor health in 1931 moved him to
study the problems of disposing of his own property. He realized
from the beginning of the Depression of 1932-33—and the start
of Franklin D. Roosevelt's first term as President—that all kinds
of tax rates were bound to shoot up. Julie, and her daughter
Gladys in Belgium, had large estates of their own and needed
nothing from him. His concern, therefore, was not for the welfare of survivors but for the continuance of all the Colorado
Springs projects which he had devised and wet-nursed along for
fifteen years and more, since the construction of his Pikes Peak
Highway. He was sure that every one of them would stand on
its own feet just as soon as the Depression ended and tourism
revived. But in the meantime their losses had to be met or they
might fold up as completely as had Count Pourtales' "Broadmoor
City." The Broadmoor Hotel, for example, had cost Spec from
$75,000 to $150,000 annually in operating losses since 1918.[2]

The big problem was high estate taxes. If Spec died, these
taxes could reduce his copper holdings and income below the sum
needed to meet the deficits of the hotel, Cog Train, Zoo, and so
on. It was not his problem alone. Rich men everywhere faced
it. The Henry Ford family, for instance, had pledged themselves
to the perpetual support of certain hospitals and now wondered
if they would have to go back on their word when Henry Ford
died. The solution was the tax-free Ford Foundation, which
Edsel Ford erected in 1936 as a small family trust and which
became the largest of all charitable institutions.

This sort of private, tax-free foundation had been around for
a long time, evolving from the Carnegie Institution (1902) and
the Rockefeller Foundation (1913). While Spec studied the

possibilities of its operation, two of his business associates were studying also. One was the New York banker, Charles Hayden, who would create the great Hayden Foundation for helping needy young men. The other was Claude Boettcher, the Denver financier, who would set up the general purpose Boettcher Foundation.

El Pomar Foundation, comprising Spec's entire copper assets and Pikes Peak properties (except a fraction for personal expenses and bequests), was incorporated under the laws of Colorado in December, 1937. Its articles stated that it was "exclusively for charitable uses and purposes (including public, educational, scientific and benevolent uses and purposes), as will in the absolute and uncontrollable discretion of the trustees of the corporation most effectively assist, encourage and promote the general well-being of the inhabitants of the State of Colorado, and that the principal and income of and from its funds and property shall be limited for use within the State of Colorado." El Pomar's first gifts were the sums of $8,900 to bring the Springs Community Chest Drive of 1938 up to quota, and $10,000 for an addition to the Colorado Springs Boys Club.

The historical continuity and strong Philadelphia tinge in the whole El Pomar idea were striking. The foundation was named, of course, for the apple orchard below Cheyenne Mountain which William Dixon had homesteaded in 1875. The first board of trustees included, besides Spec, Charley Tutt, the son of Spec's Cripple Creek partner—a Philadelphian like Spec himself; William Howbert, son of Irving Howbert who had bought for General Palmer of Philadelphia much of the Springs townsite; and Henry McAllister (Spec's lawyer), son of Major Henry McAllister, late of Phialdelphia and the Fifteenth Pennsylvania Cavalry, and former secretary of Fountain Colony![3]

CHAPTER NINETEEN

Portrait of a Small College

BUT LET US briefly drop the subject of Philadephia at Pikes Peak to examine an outpost of Boston, Colorado College, the growth of which paralleled the growth of Colorado Springs. New England professors and New England benefactors have domi- nated the institution since it opened its doors in 1874.[1] And yet it is New England with a difference. These austere westering Yankees seemed to shed their inhibitions in the bright sunlight and high tonic air. They caught fire in the Rocky Mountain wild- erness and that is why Colorado College looks like something not very far north of Boston while at the same time behaving like New England on the loose.

General Palmer donated the land, naturally—some twenty acres of Spanish bayonet and sage and bunch grass out North Cascade Avenue on the windy bluff above Monument Creek. Will Jackson and Henry McAllister and the Reverend Thomas Haskell and a few others got things started in a groping sort of way but the first real president was Edward P. Tenney, a New Hampshire Congregationalist, who took hold of the place in 1876—all three rooms of it.

This Tenney, aged forty-one, was not an educator at all, but a tough frontiersman who had mined gold in California and in Central City. His main claims to the presidency of Colorado Col- lege were his reverence for Harvard, and his close friendship with a rich man, Henry Cutler, who lived near Boston. Henry Cutler was not rich enough to build a Rocky Mountain Harvard on General Palmer's prairie dog tract, but he did give his friend Tenney the money to build Cutler Hall in 1880—the same jaunty, focal Cutler Hall which brightens today's campus. Tenney also built a stone home for himself near Cutler, and those two structures constituted Pikes Peak's pioneer "college of liberal arts and sciences" for quite a while.

Tenney's New England puritanism underwent the usual barometric softening. Though he refused to install a billiard table in Cutler Hall, he was constrained to let his boy and girl students dance together, provided they prayed afterwards. He was as luxuriant an optimist as Palmer or Hagerman, Pourtales or Bathhouse John or Penrose. In those days there were no high schools to supply students to the college, so he set up Cutler Academy as a prep school in the college building, and launched other prep schools in New Mexico and Utah as feeders. (From the one in Sante Fe came William E. Strieby, the long-time chemistry professor who made candy in class for his students, to compensate for the lab smells.)

In Boston, with Henry Cutler's help, Tenney borrowed $100,000 at twelve per cent interest with himself as security and he bought 800 acres of land north of the campus as a speculation for the college. In a nostalgic moment, he named the purchase New Massachusetts. He planted trees and windmills and raised hay and grazed cows which he hoped would get milked in time by eager students of his projected Agriculture School. As you can guess, the twelve per cent interest ruined his real estate career. He had to resign and depart from Pikes Peak in 1884, leaving Cutler Hall, New Massachusetts, and $100,000 in debts. Springs residents said harsh things about him. And yet Tenney was a good president who saw Colorado College through its feeble infancy until it was too strong to die of malnutrition.

In 1888, William Frederick Slocum took charge. He was a Congregational minister, Massachusetts-born, and he reached Pikes Peak at the age of thirty-seven. Thereafter for twenty-nine years he and his Boston supporters were mainly responsible for everything progressive that happened to Colorado College. On the surface, Slocum was the stock stage president—ponderous, absent-minded, and remembered by students for "a kind of apostolic rumble in his Friday morning ethicals."² But he loved every inch of the campus and he knew exactly what was good for it. He worked well with General Palmer and Hagerman and W. S. Stratton and other Springs people with money to give away. He was fearless, as he proved in 1894 when he went through the picket lines at Cripple Creek to try to arrange peace with the armed mob of angry strikers.

Slocum found fine teachers and somehow got them to come to Pikes Peak for peanuts and promises. They stayed. For one thing, they liked the climate and the scenery. For another, they found quality in each other and enjoyed the mutual stimulation.³ Colorado College was an intimate little place and it inspired affection. Alumni of the time can recall football games when the famous Professor Florian Cajori would toss his hat half a block to celebrate a touchdown—Cajori, known to every mathematician in the world. Others remember E. C. Schneider, the first air age physiologist, and Elijah Mills, the linguist whom King Alfonso invited to Spain, and Homer Woodbridge in English and Moses Gile in classics.

The Slocum story had an unhappy end. As the president grew older he became more militant. He collided at last with the independent spirit which he himself had encouraged in his faculty. The battle between the prexy and his faculty got far out of hand and wound up with most of the contestants retreating from the field, leaving the college as the principal casualty. Slocum returned to Massachusetts in 1917. Fifty out of the sixty professors whom he had lured to the Springs resigned or retired in the next few years.

It is a wonder that the college was able to move from under such a black cloud and to survive the depressed Thirties and the problems of World War II. It was saved by the reconstruction of Professor Charles Mierow (president, 1923-34); the fundraising and renovation of President Thurston Davies (1934-48); and the steadying post-war regime of General William H. Gill (1948-55).

THE CAMPUS HAS changed a lot in recent years. Modernism is on the march in structures like the men's residence (Slocum Hall, 1954), the women's residence (Loomis, 1956), the cheerful Rastall Student Center (1959), and the germinating new library, science hall, and gym. And yet most of the dear old buildings of Slocum's era and before are still in business. The hodgepodge of architecture is a bit confusing, but the variety gives the scene its charm and atmosphere and brooding sense of past time and toil.

The hodgepodge is New England with a Rockies twist. In 1880, Henry Cutler of Massachusetts specified pure Boston Gothic for Cutler Hall and got it except for the bell tower, which came out vaguely Venetian. President Slocum wangled a men's dormitory out of James J. Hagerman just when he was finishing his Colorado Midland Railroad to Aspen. Slocum planned to build the dorm of gray stone from nearby Castle Rock to match the limestone of Cutler Hall. But Hagerman remembered that he owned a quarry called Canon Diablo served by his railroad on the Frying Pan River 170 miles away. And so, in 1889, Hagerman Hall came out in pink "peachblow" sandstone from Canon Diablo. Of course the style had to fit the color—Richardson Romanesque rather than Gothic. And still Boston was at the bottom of it all since Henry Richardson was a famous Boston architect.

Dear old Hagerman Hall had to be torn down in the 1950s and hauled off to the dump to make room for Rastall Center but its New England spirit and design lives on. Because of it, President Slocum fell in love with peachblow stone and with Romanesque architecture, too. When his boyhood friend from near Boston, Nathaniel P. Coburn, gave him $50,000, he ordered both stone and style—plus a roof of red Spanish tile—for Coburn Library (1894). The building seemed too long at first but Slocum was glad of it later when Winifield Scott Stratton sent him an unsolicited eighty-two foot skelton of a whale from a defunct "museum of curiosities" in California. The $30,000 whale just fitted Coburn Library's basement, running almost the full length of the ceiling.

Slocum's duet of peachblow and Romanesque contined in the new music and art building, Perkins Hall (1899), given by Willard B. Perkins of Lawrence, Massachusetts It achieved a crowning harmony in Palmer Hall, the $280,000 science building which the General erected in 1904. Palmer was too much of an anglophile to accept Slocum's Latin-American preferences in toto. Peachblow? Yes. Romanesque? Yes. Roof of red Spanish tile? Certainly not, Dr. Slocum! That is why Palmer Hall has a roof of green English tile. Its construction brought many problems, the most ticklish of which was the job of moving Stratton's whale from Coburn's basement. Fifty students toiled a week and you can see the skeleton today right where they hung it in the Colorado College Museum upstairs in Palmer Hall.[4] ,

For all of Slocum, his strong-minded wife, born Mary Montgomery, was no admirer of Romanesque. When the local Women's Educational Society, which Mary Slocum founded, raised money for a women's residence, the result was Montgomery Hall (1891), roughly Elizabethan in design and made, sensibly, of stone from adjacent Castle Rock. Her views prevailed again when Ticknor Hall, also for females, was built of green Ute Pass stone in 1898. The donor was Miss Elizabeth Cheney, a Boston heiress barely out of her teens, who named it for a Boston friend. The third residence, McGregor Hall (1903), was Elizabethan too, constructed of red Manitou sandstone from the Red Rock Canyon quarry which Palmer's English backer, William Blackmore, had owned in the early 1870s. Finally, Bemis Hall was built in 1908, completing the Women's Quadrangle. Bemis was the gift of the Boston-born paper bag king, Judson M. Bemis, who had come to Colorado Springs to live in the 1880s.

The architect Maurice Biscoe designed Bemis but he abandoned English styles six years later when he built the big gym, Cossitt Hall, which could be Greek, or at least classical. One of President Slocum's relatives, Mrs. A. D. Juilliard, put up the money for Cossitt, naming it for her father. And so Colorado College accrued over those struggling years, reflecting the dreams and tastes of mainly New England people—a touch of Gothic, lots of Richardson Romanesque, Queen Elizabeth for the girls, and an athletic splash of Greek-and-Roman. And then, in 1931, Romanesque once more—but the Norman kind this time. The result was Shove Memorial Chapel, the gift of the Cripple Creek broker, Eugene P. Shove. Shove Chapel was not built of peach-blow from the Western Slope, the cost of which had become prohibitive. Some $20,000 was saved by hauling Bedford stone for it all the way from Indiana.

SINCE THE LATE NINETIES, Colorado College, being of eastern paternity, has called its teams the Tigers, as at Princeton—eschewing western nicknames such as the Longhorns or Buffalos or Mountaineers. In the early days, when student man power was limited, the faculty played on the football team, and so did local blacksmiths, plumbers, and bartenders. The cheering section was mostly feminine, producing such shrill encouragement to great deeds as:

> With a Vevo! With a Vevo!
> With a Vevo, *Vivo*, Vum Vum!
> Johnny get a Rat Trap
> Bigger than a Cat Trap!
> CANNIBALS! CANNIBALS!
> Siss! Boom! Ah
> COLORADO COLLEGE, Rah, Rah, Rah!

For forty years these Vum Vum-inspired teams, often sumptuously subsidized by local alumni, more than held their own in Rocky Mountain competition, winning countless trophies and producing three All Americans—the immortal "Dutch" Clark (1928), and the basketball stars, Earl "Dutch" Mueller (1925) and Ernie Simpson (1927). Earl Harry Clark was the modest halfback who for three years wafted himself like a wraith through every team those vastly bigger schools up north could field. He won a permanent place in the hierarchy of football history when he was elected a charter member of the National Football Hall of Fame. But that was that. With the coming of bigtime football, little Colorado College has sought less elevated status and the

students back their Tigers with the restrained passion of ivy-
leaguers instead of the complex razzmatazz of the state uni-
versities.[5]

The story of ice hockey at Pikes Peak is still being written.
Colorado College won the national intercollegiate championship
in 1950 and 1957 and was runner-up in 1952 and 1955. This
astonishing record by a school with a total enrollment not much
over a thousand, half of whom are co-eds, derives from the purest
accident. You recall that Spencer Penrose built the Broadmoor
Riding Academy in 1928 to meet the needs of the equitation and
polo crowd. During the Depression, support of the Riding Academy fell away and Penrose began seeking a profitable use for his
indoor arena.

The Penrose solution, typically, was to convert the Riding
Academy into the year-around Ice Palace and to make Broadmoor
"the Figure Skating Capital of the World." In addition to figure
skating, people took up ice hockey and then several Colorado
Springs firms formed a hockey league. One team of the league
was composed of Colorado College students who could barely
stand up on skates. In the late 1930s, a few expert Canadian
hockey players drifted in for exhibition matches at the Ice
Palace. The town went wild over the skill of these imported
youngsters and the first thing they knew they were enrolled as
Colorado College students and members of the Colorado College
hockey team. Their brand of hockey has prevailed ever since.

IN 1955, LOUIS T. BENEZET, a New Englander, of course,
arrived at Pikes Peak to become the eighth president of Colorado
College. He was a tall, young, lean scholarly man and it was
clear from the hour of his inauguration at Shove Chapel that a
new day had dawned. The pioneer, President Tenney, and the
builder, President Slocum, would have been delighted with
Benezet, his educational ideas rooted in liberal arts tradition
and sparked with imagination. Benezet's regime was hardly out
of swaddling clothes when two large chunks of money appeared—
a Ford Foundation grant and funds from Ben Rastall, Class of

1901. Benezet resumed large-scale building where Slocum had left off—more faculty, a stronger student body, educational innovations. A modern heating system moled its way under the campus and the Annual Alumni Fund moved up 300 per cent in four years, and gifts poured in for vital expansion.

In 1963, Benezet moved on to greater achievement as head of Claremont Graduate School in California and then to the presidency of The State University of New York at Albany. His Dean of the College, Lloyd E. Worner, who graduated from Colorado College in 1942, replaced him and continued his good works so ably that hardly a ripple of change was felt. By 1970, President Worner was coping well with the problems of that changing era in education. Some of the parents of his students in '68-69 raised the roof when he and his trustees gave permission for beer to be served in Rastall Student Center, and for boys to visit girls' bedrooms in Loomis Hall during certain hours—and to lock the door if they felt like it. After the college's Annual Symposium in January of 1969, the town was rocked with debate for months over three of the Symposium's programs on the subject "Violence"— Dick Gregory's bitter talk on "Violence and the Civil Rights Movements"; "Violence on the Campus"; and, especially, the theater performance, "Dionysus in '69" directed by Richard Schechner, during which the cast of boys and girls performed with no clothes on.

Many townspeople denounced all this odd behavior, but the students remained calm. By spring some adult detractors were praising the controversial Symposium. They saw that students at Colorado College were not much different than they themselves had been—love and youth being fixed attributes like the sun and stars. Though these young intellectuals of 1969 thought of themselves as no-nonsense realists, they would go strolling romantically as their parents before them in the moonlight past Rastall and the campus flagpole,[6] and down into General Palmer's Monument Park where the finches trilled and the creek burbled by this touch of New England at the foot of Pikes Peak.

CHAPTER TWENTY

C Stands for Culture

THE GREAT TEMPLE OF TASTE, the citadel to the finer things of life, the things that really matter—whatever you would call art—in Colorado Springs is a somewhat awesome block of monolithic concrete near Colorado College called the Colorado Springs Fine Arts Center. It cost a million dollars to build and another million to endow and the purpose here is to trace the series of events which led to this rather expensive climax.

As we have seen, culture of sorts reared its pretty head at Pikes Peak with the beginning of Palmer's dusty village. Rose Kingsley ran a benefit in 1872 at which Queen Palmer and Maurice Kingsley sang their hearts out. When the Hayden Survey party left the region in 1873, one of its members, a water colorist named Walter Paris, stayed behind to become the Springs' first artist. Tom Parrish, Pourtales' painting friend, arrived soon after Paris, and so did the landscapist, Harvey Young, to whom General Palmer loaned his private railway car so that Young could be creative in comfort anywhere along the tracks of the Denver and Rio Grande. Charles Craig, an Ohioan, opened a studio in Howbert's opera house building in 1881 and started his long and successful career depicting cowboys and Indians at work and play. His works were as much a feature of the lobby of the old Antlers Hotel as the antlers on which guests hung their hats.

During the Nineties there were art exhibitions from Knoedler Galleries in the Consolidated Book Store on Pikes Peak Avenue. The wealthy New Yorker Louis Ehrich often displayed his collections of Dutch and Flemish old masters at his North Cascade Avenue home. There were frequent shows in Perkins Hall at

Colorado College after 1900, and in 1913 the Colorado Springs
Art Society was formed. The event was celebrated with the display of twenty-five oils by Philip Little.

Among the directors and patrons of the Colorado Springs Art
Society was Mrs. Spencer Penrose, and another was Mrs. Alice
Bemis Taylor, the quiet, reserved daughter of Judson M. Bemis
whom we last saw giving Bemis Hall to Colorado College. For
Julie Penrose, the study of art was not so much an exercise in
aesthetics as a sensuous joy in the same category as gay parties,
vintage champagne, clothes with flair, and French poodles. In
this spirit, she gave in 1919 the big Penrose house at 30 West
Dale Street with its swimming pool, greenhouse, and gymnasium,
to be used for the establishment of an art school and exhibition
center. Though the school was seven miles distant from the
new Broadmoor Hotel and Broadmoor residential real estate,
Spec Penrose was pleased to have it called the Broadmoor Art
Academy for the publicity value. After all, Spec felt entitled to
something more than the plaudits of art lovers in return for a
$250,000 gift.[1]

Colorado Springs was far from being a haven for Bohemians
after World War I. To get the feel of a real art atmosphere, the
Penroses and other Pikes Peak residents often drove south along
the smoky-blue Sangre de Cristos past Trinchera Ranch to visit
Santa Fe, the ancient capital of Spanish New Mexico. Here, in
1920, Julie met an attractive young portraitist, Randall Davey,
who took his art and his life as gaily as did Julie herself. Mrs.
Penrose's first major art purchase was a full-length picture of a
gypsy girl by Davey, and, in 1924, she brought the artist to the
Broadmoor Art Academy to teach at the summer session for $800
a month. That sum was more than twice the salary of Robert
Reid, the winter instructor. Spec questioned such a wage for
merely being able to paint until Davey told him that he was also
a first-class polo player and needed a high stipend to maintain
his ponies if he were to help promote Broadmoor polo.

For eleven years, the Broadmoor Art Academy flourished with
its school and regular shows in the old Penrose gymnasium. The

deficits were as regular as the shows and they were met by the
Penroses, by Alexander Smith Cochrane, the carpet man who
owned Glen Eyrie, and by many others. They were met cheer-
fully for the most part because the Art Academy was a cultural
plum for the town and, besides, it added much color to its social
life. People who had learned how much fun parties could be
during Chester Alan Arthur's heyday, found the old spirit revived
at Art Academy balls. Costumes at these Beaux Arts affairs were
stimulating and imaginative, such as those worn by the three
beautiful Holt sisters. They attended in the blue vestments of a
religious order, the cloth in back of which turned out to be sheer
in any light at all, revealing from the rear three of the town's
prettiest figures.

WHILE MRS. PENROSE and her circle ran the Broadmoor Art
Academy, Alice Bemis Taylor, Julie's friend of the old Colorado
Springs Art Association, was engaged in a different kind of cultural project. Mrs. Taylor's father, Judson Bemis, died in 1921,
leaving his children a fortune at least as large then as the Spencer
Penrose fortune. His daughter Alice decided to continue in her
father's philanthropic footsteps. Her first gift to Colorado Springs,
completed in 1923, was the Day Nursery on Rio Grande Street.

If Mrs. Penrose could be described as a generous hedonist,
Mrs. Taylor was an example of the New England conscience at
work—serious, dedicated to the common good, self-effacing, and
with a Yankee love of precision and thrift where money was
concerned. Her bearing was regal, even authoritative, but beneath this exterior was a rather shy person who, having everything in the world, suffered still from a feeling of insecurity.
Socially she was restrained, sensible, and correct, and she never
appeared at Broadmoor Art Academy balls in anything but the
most sedate of costumes. She was known generally as "Aunt
Alice," though not to her face.

Intellectually, she specialized through the 1920s in collecting
rare books, and Southwestern folk art—Navajo blankets and silver-
ware, Indian pottery, religious objects, and so on. She scattered

her collection around her house on Wood Avenue, and when it
overflowed the place she began to think of buying a small house
for it. Her husband, Fred Taylor, had died in 1926, creating an
estate tax problem which could be eased by a charitable project.
Aunt Alice knew that the Coburn Library at Colorado College
was becoming inadequate, and unemployment was increasing
after the stock market crash of 1929. If the college had a bigger
library it could help her storage problem by housing her rare
books. For these reasons, Mrs. Taylor decided to spend $400,000
for a new college library. She bought James J. Hagerman's old
peachblow quarry on the Frying Pan that had supplied stone for
Coburn Library in the first place, and soon new cut stone began
to pile up on the Colorado College campus.

Alice Bemis Taylor did not build solely for humanity in general. She built for herself at times, including a beautiful home in
Black Forest. She wanted a chapel for this home and called in a
Santa Fe architect, John Gaw Meem, who was the husband of
her niece, Faith. This Meem was far from being an impecunious
relative-in-law who needed a job. He was even then one of the
most original of Southwestern architects, the inventor of a practical modern adaptation of the old Spanish adobe style. While
Meem was in and out of Colorado Springs designing a Black
Forest chapel, Mrs. Taylor began wondering if she could buy a
portion of the Broadmoor Art Academy property (the old Penrose
home) to house her Southwestern collection. At her request,
Mrs. Penrose and the Art Academy board discussed the matter
in February, 1930, but no action was taken.

AND SO, leaving Mrs. Penrose for the moment with the Art
Academy, and Mrs. Taylor in need of space for her folk art, we
take up a third heroine, a Mrs. Meredith Hare, who was variously
described, during the period of this complicated narrative, as a
cyclone, a tempest, a celestial disturbance, a cosmic cataclysm.
Betty Hare was born Elizabeth Sage in Albany, New York, married a Hartford millionaire whom she divorced out of boredom,
married a second time one of New York's most brilliant corpora-

tion lawyers, and came to Broadmoor around 1928 because of Meredith Hare's poor health.

She was rich, she was witty, she was smart, she was imperious, she was dominating, she was tremendously energetic, and she numbered among her close friends absolutely everybody worth knowing in New York and Europe. She knew also, as members of the Springs' ultra-conservative, Republican society soon were telling one another in shocked tones, just about all the crackpot liberals, socialists, communists, and avant-garde intellectuals in the land from John Dewey to Lincoln Steffens to Amos Pinchot to Eleanor Roosevelt to Boardman Robinson, head of the New York Art Students League. She had a summer place in Santa Fe where one of her good friends was Mrs. Taylor's nephew-in-law, John Gaw Meem.

Two of Betty Hare's sons attended Avon Prep School in Connecticut. When most of the Avon faculty resigned in revolt against a dictatorial owner, Mrs. Hare bought Jack Bradley's ranch south of Colorado Springs and founded Fountain Valley School for Boys, using seven Avon masters as a faculty under Francis Froelicher. The Spencer Penroses were drawn to Mrs. Hare and came in heavily on the Fountain Valley financing. So did the eminent heiress and Congresswoman, Mrs. Ruth Hanna McCormick who became involved in Pikes Peak history by purchasing General Palmer's old Trinchera Ranch a decade or so after Chester Alan Arthur and his friends had given it up.

Any school founded by Betty Hare had to have an exceptional art teacher. Her choice for the job at Fountain Valley School—the New York Socialist, Boardman Robinson—should have been enough to bring the conservatives out with fiery crosses on Cheyenne Mountain. Robinson had covered the Kerensky revolution in Russia for *Metropolitan Magazine* with his friend John Reed, who wound up a Soviet hero, buried in the Kremlin. But by now, the driving Mrs. Hare, backed in depth by the powerful Ruth Hanna McCormick, had overawed and buffaloed the unsophisticated natives of Colorado Springs from Julie Penrose and Aunt Alice Taylor on down. Socialist Robinson was taken to the local

Republican bosom like a prodigal son and was even made an instructor at the Broadmoor Art Academy. Soon after, the Art Academy found itself without a head. The board considered both Robinson and Randall Davey, but Davey withdrew from the running because of the decline of polo at Broadmoor and returned to Santa Fe with his ponies. Thereupon, Robinson was named director.

Mrs. Hare went on the Art Academy board in 1929 and began hearing all about Mrs. Taylor's folk art and about her housing problem and the $400,000 which she meant to give to Colorado College for a new library. The thought of the $400,000 was specially tantalizing to Mrs. Hare and she discussed the possibilities of such a sum often with Boardman Robinson and with John Gaw Meem whom she had hired to put up a dormitory—Sage House—at Fountain Valley School. In time, these three agreed that there were more interesting ways to spend Mrs. Taylor's money than building a library. First, they suggested to Aunt Alice that her folk art collection deserved its own structure—a simple little Spanish adobe affair, perhaps. But Robinson kept tossing in broader aims and Betty Hare kept adding wings and before long Mrs. Taylor found herself committed to ideas concerning something entirely new in the cultural field—a vast center where all the community could practice all the arts in democratic bliss.

During October of 1931, Mrs. Hare and Mrs. Taylor described the arts center scheme in detail to Julie Penrose, who became eager to go ahead. At the next meeting of the board of the Broadmoor Art Academy, approval was given to tear down the big Penrose home on its bluff above Monument Creek so that Mrs. Taylor could erect thereon John Gaw Meem's revolutionary concrete building, incorporating something for everybody—the Taylor folk art collection, a theater for the Drama Club, a music room for the Music Club, assorted avant-garde notions of Betty Hare's, four exhibition galleries, studios galore, and the beautiful patio which was Mrs. Penrose's particular delight. Mrs. Taylor told Colorado College regretfully that the new library would not be

built just yet but that she would provide for it in her will.[2] Her
$400,000 was thus deflected to 30 West Dale Street—plus several
hundred thousand dollars more before John Gaw Meem built
all he wanted to build, plus a big block of Bemis Bag Company
stock for future maintenance. Mrs. Penrose was elected Honorary
President of the building committee and, on January 4, 1935, the
name of her pioneer Broadmoor Art Academy was changed to
the Colorado Springs Fine Arts Center, with Mrs. Hare as first
president. Construction of Meem's building was completed in
April, 1936.

During the course of this book, we have recorded quite a few
periods of excitement at Pikes Peak, but the greatest of all was
the week of theater entertainment and general hoopla which
Betty Hare organized to mark the opening of Mrs. Taylor's re-
splendent Fine Arts Center. Mrs. Hare was the kind of intellectual who felt that if you weren't familiar with the advanced views
of Orage of England or the mysteries of the French composer
Satie or who had what at the Armory Show of 1913, you just
didn't know much. She was sure that Springs residents knew
even less than that, and she was determined to give them a lesson
in what modern culture was all about.

The thrifty Mrs. Taylor, who footed the bill of tens of thousands
of dollars for that April week of what Mrs. Hare called "divertissements," did induce her to schedule a plain Monday concert
by the Colorado Springs Symphony Orchestra and a plain Tuesday piano recital by James Sykes, head of the Colorado College
music department. But the rest—prepared and rehearsed in
New York—was pure avant-guarde, most of it so expensive and
so bewildering that Mrs. Taylor took to her bed and just did
recuperate enough to attend some of the performances. What
Boardman Robinson, the man of the masses, thought of it all
he never revealed but he must have wondered what had happened to his art-for-everybody ideal.

There was the supreme question of who would be allowed to
see the "divertissements." Mrs. Hare decreed that admission was
by invitation only. The Fine Arts Center theater seated only 400

continued page 291

The building of the Broadmoor Hotel and the rejuvenation of Broadmoor by Penrose were boons to the doctors of the region who were carrying on the traditions of skill and personal charm established by Dr. Anderson and Dr. Solly in the 1870s. Led by Dr. Gerald B. Webb, the Colorado School for Tuberculosis was begun in 1920. Physicians from everywhere flocked to its summer sessions taught by Springs men. Teachers and their students in this mid-1920s photo, left to right, at the El Paso Club were: Front row (three) standing: Dr. G. Burton Gilbert and two students. Second row (five) standing, all students. Third row (four) standing: Dr. J. A. Sevier; student, Dr. Gerald B. Webb, president; and a student. Top rows (five): Dr. John B. Crouch; Dr. J. F. McConnell; Dr. W. V. Mullin; Dr. H. C. Goodson; and Dr. Peter Oliver Hanford. Seated, left to right: Dr. Charles Fox Gardiner (General Palmer's old physician); Dr. A. M. Forster of Cragmor; Dr. C. T. Ryder; and Dr. Frank T. Stevens (far right). *Mrs. G. Burton Gilbert.*

Showman Penrose never missed a chance to photograph celebrities to boost the Broadmoor. The trio (left to right) were: Clarence Hamlin, of the *Gazette and Telegraph;* Vice-President Charles G. Dawes; and Penrose (1925). The Penroses greeted their old friend Jack Dempsey and trainer, arriving by plane (late 1920s). Spec shook hands with Shirley Temple (late 1930s). *Broadmoor Hotel and Denver Public Library Western Collection.*

Penrose revived polo at Broadmoor in the 1920s by building Polo Park with its Moorish grandstand. Note in back how his Cheyenne Mountain Highway scarred the landscape. *Denver Public Library Western Collection.*

It was Spec's nature to make a paying proposition out of everything he did. His idea of laying out a simple Penrose Cemetery evolved into the Will Rogers Shrine of the Sun, a prime tourist attraction which cost $250,000. *State of Colorado.*

In those days, the Faculty baseball team played the undergraduate nine and often won, as on June 11, 1896, when the game ended 20 to 12. In the photo, the Faculty team was photographed leaving Montgomery Hall for the field, carrying along their own fair rooting section. Top, left to right, were: Professor Lewis A. E. Ahlers, German, right field; Dean E. S. Parsons, English, pitcher; Rev. Philip Washburn, first base; Florian Cajori, physics, left field; Arthur F. Stearns, elocution, catcher; F. W. Cragin, geology, second base; Manly D. Ormes, librarian, center field; Charles Sprague, *Telegraph* editor, third base; and President W. F. Slocum, shortstop. The visible rooting section within the coach were (left to right): Nina Lunt, Mrs. Mabel Stearns (behind bar), Faith Gregg, Regina Lunt (mugging camera); Sarah Jackson (Mrs. P. A. Loomis), Mary Noble, Foster Dickerman, and Mrs. W. F. Slocum. *Colorado College Library.*

An all-New England menu was probably served around 1919 at this wedding anniversary dinner for Colorado College's Boston benefactors, Mr. and Mrs. Judson M. Bemis. At the table, left to right, were: Miss Ellen T. Brinley, Dr. and Mrs. Florian Cajori, Mrs. Irving Howbert, Joel A. Hayes, Irving Howbert, Mrs. John G. Shields, Mrs. George Taylor (daughter of Major McAllister), Judson Bemis, Miss May Howbert, Mrs. Alice Bemis Taylor (who built the Fine Arts Center); and her mother, Mrs. Judson Bemis. *Gerald B. Webb Collection.*

Colorado College, Boston's outpost at Pikes Peak, was slow to mature on
General Palmer's prairie dog tract. In its twentieth year (1894), it consisted of
these four buildings (left to right): Coburn Library, Hagerman Hall, Palmer
Hall (called Cutler today), and Montgomery Hall. *Colorado College Library,
Hook photo.*

But the place had quality. These co-eds of '91 called themselves "The Girls
Broom Brigade" or "Plantagenets," honoring the Twelfth Century Count of
Anjou, Geoffrey the Handsome, who wore a sprig of broom, or plantagenet, in
his helmet when jousting to win a girl's favor. The Broom Brigade drilled
mysteriously behind closed doors to achieve what the *Gazette* hoped would be
"a sweeping success." Front row officers (left to right) were Marguerite Lamb,
first lieutenant (Mrs. Clarence W. Bowers later); Virginia Currier, captain; and
Sylvia S. Brigham, second lieutenant. Privates (left to right) have been tenta-
tively identified as: Alice Bacon, Ida Fursman, May Howbert (daughter of
Irving), Marguerite Upton (she married Professor Ernest Brehaut), Elsie Rowell,
Nellie Kellogg, Grace Loper, Della Candy, Clara Sweet, Henrietta Cheney,
Florence Hastings, Emeroy Stevens, Mabel Spicer, Leah Ehrich, and one un-
known Plantagenet at the far end. *Colorado College Library.*

Sir Hubert von Herkomer's portrait of General Palmer. The equestrian statue of the General was by Nathan D. Potter of New York. It was erected in 1929 at Platte and Nevada Avenues at a cost of $33,000 which was raised by subscription. *Pioneer Museum.*

In 1943, Boardman Robinson painted the late Spencer Penrose from memory and the portrait was hung at the Cooking Club. The Penrose statue at the Broadmoor Hotel was created by Dr. Avard Fairbanks, who did also the statue of Daniel C. Jackling, Spec's Utah Copper engineer, in the Utah State Capitol.

Present at the 1958 Penrose statue unveiling were Mrs. Albert E. Carlton, widow of the Cripple Creek leader and Charles L. Tutt, president of El Pomar Foundation and son of Spec's original Pikes Peak sponsor. *Broadmoor Hotel.*

At the time of this 1953 photo, Julie Penrose was eighty-three years old, still a bewitching, headstrong and vital woman. To her other cultural projects, she had added sponsorship of the Central City summer opera festival. *Denver Public Library Western Collection.*

Randall Davey, the Santa Fe artist-poloist, completed the Shrine of the Sun murals in 1937. He was photographed touching up the figures of Spec, Julie Penrose (left) and Milt Strong (right). *Broadmoor Hotel, Bob McIntyre.*

The El Paso Club in downtown Colorado Springs began in 1877. It is the oldest men's social club (women are allowed in) in the Rockies. *Stewart's Commercial Photographers.*

Alice Bemis Taylor had planned a small museum for her collection of southwestern folk art. But she ended up in 1936 building a million dollar Fine Arts Center as a gift to Colorado Springs. *Bill Bowers photo*(top)

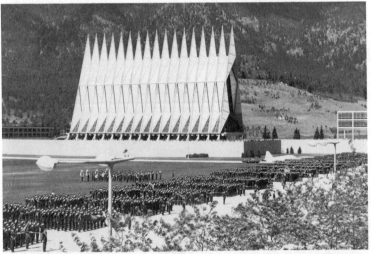

In September 1958, the first cadets moved into the $200,000,000 U. S. Air Force Academy a few miles north of Pikes Peak. By 1987 the enrollment had reached 4,500 (10 percent women). Cadets are shown on the parade ground before the all-faith chapel. Its unusual design is admired by 18 million visitors annually. *Academy photo.*

Former Mayors of Colorado Springs continue to work for the community: William C. Henderson (1958-1963), promoting Pioneers' Museum; Harry W. Hoth (1963-1967), new airport plans; T. Eugene McCleary (1967-1973), president Cheyenne Mountain Zoo; Andrew Marshall (1973-1975), chairman advisory committee planning and building the Pikes Peak Center; Larry Ochs (1975-1979), Olympic Training Center. *Photo View Newspaper.*

In 1987, this Colorado Springs City Council (unpaid) had their hands full into the 1990s coping with the city's growth. In the photo, left to right, Mary Vieth, Frank Parisi, Wilton Cogswell, Bill Snyder, Mayor Robert Isaac, Vice Mayor Leon Young, Bruce Shepard, Mary Ellen McNally, Mary Lou Makepeace. (*Photo, courtesy Susan Watkins, C. S. Public Relations*).

Of executives in the Pikes Peak region none has greater responsibilities than Sister Myra James Bradley, president of Penrose Hospital and its many health-care affiliates (3). She is a major employer (2,800) in Colorado Springs. She participated in the 1987 merger of Penrose Hospital and St. Frances Hospital with combined assets of nearly $1 billion. *Photo courtesy of Sister Ruth Anne, Penrose Hospital.*

For many years Kenneth D. Dowlin has been the creative force in the expansion of the Pikes Peak Library District, its eight branch libraries and three bookmobiles serving rural communities. Photo courtesy of *Nancy De Lury.*

James D. Phillips, Director of C. S. Department of Public Utilities, has met the city's insatiable need for water as projected into the 1990s. He is admired also as a fly fisherman. (*Photo C. S. Water Division*).

Amateur theater of professional quality has been an important feature of living in Colorado Springs. Photo shows the Star Bars Players in the Lon Chaney Theater playing "Who's Afraid of Virginia Woolf?" with Bob Pinney (George), Cecile Wood-Gort (Martha), Eve Tilley (Honey), Chris Schutz (Nick). *Photo kindness of Eve Tilley.*

Frank Aries gave the 150 acres of land on which to build the Olympics Hall of Fame, the U. S. O. C. head-quarters and the U. S. Space Foundation. *Photo from Paul Burke.*

Some Colorado Springs residents find it exciting to drink a glass of water because it comes from one of these beautiful high lakes on the Continental Divide 160 miles from the city at altitudes of 11,000 feet above sea level. This is Homestake Lake. The water at left flows through the divide in the 5.5 mile Homestake Tunnel to Turquoise Lake above Leadville and into the Arkansas River. *Howard Arnberg photo, kindness of Jack A. McCullough.*

The $10-million dollar East Library and Information Center at 5500 N. Union Blvd. opened January 10-16, 1987, in George Fellows Park facing Pikes Peak. *Photo courtesy of Pikes Peak Library District.*

The enormous popularity of the five or six free summer concerts given by the Colorado Springs Symphony Orchestra in conjunction with the Parks and Recreation Department is suggested by this Memorial Park crowd and their picnic baskets. The tower beyond the bandstand in the far left is the Veterans' Memorial.

Charles Ansbacher, conductor of the Colorado Springs Symphony Orchestra and his young clowns add to the gaiety of the free children's concerts sponsored by the Parks and Recreation Department in Antlers Park. *John Morgan photo.*

Some 12,000 hungry people fill Pikes Peak Avenue at 7 a.m. in late July for the annual Street Breakfast of scrambled eggs, coffee, pancakes with syrup. They are there to cheer the Range Riders off on their horseback ride around Pikes Peak and to kick off the annual Pikes Peak or Bust Rodeo. *Darrell Porter photo*.

The Library Building on the 400-acre campus of the University of Colorado at Colorado Springs, founded in 1965 on the site of Dr. Solly's Cragmor Sanatorium. The new university includes seven colleges and schools at the undergraduate and graduate levels. A $4.1 million student center and gym is under construction.

people and, though several amateur sleuths tried later to find how these priceless invitations were distributed, they always ran into the same blind alley—"I guess you had to know Betty Hare to get in." A rumor spread that a mere invitation to the various performances was not enough. Men had to wear white tie and tails. There was a wild scramble in the stores for full dress suits, many of which were worn during that week and then were never worn again.

Everyone loved Albert Spalding's violin recital and some enjoyed Manuel de Falla's puppet show opera. But Martha Graham —well, honestly! Miss Graham's unique dancing was utterly new west of New York, and when she began gallumphing barefoot around the stage interpreting "Frontier" and "Quest" and "Sportive Tragedy" most of the audience slumped into a stunned and uncomprehending stupor. The *Gazette* reviewer, Elizabeth Hylbom, was on the spot because she didn't feel qualified to pan a world celebrity like Miss Graham. So she straddled the issue, concluding her review with a small sour pickle—"But does her art contain within itself the germ of universality? One wonders."

What really got people down was the Satie evening. It was a recitative sung principally by Eva Gauthier and it had something to do with Socrates—or so the audience inferred from the title. The action was obscure and the music eccentric and it droned on and on to no apparent purpose. It was pretty soporific, but the audience was kept awake by the assortment of objects suspended on wires over Miss Gauthier. These included a huge red sun that wobbled here and there and appeared about to fall smack on the great singer's head. In her *Gazette* review, Mrs. Hylbom called the Satie act "of purely antiquarian interest," and added cryptically: "You may be thrilled to the heights by Miss Gauthier, and you may be left untouched. But in any case you will be forced to think—if you can."

IN TIME'S SOFTENING PERSPECTIVE, that week-long opening of the Fine Arts Center has come to be remembered with pride and affection, and Mrs. Hare's memory is revered because of it. She is revered also because the remarkable institution which she encouraged Mrs. Taylor to create on Mrs. Penrose's land has been of great value as a means of community self-expression and as a point of reference for local art standards.[3]

An immediate result was Spencer Penrose's decision during the summer of 1936 to decorate the interior of the Will Rogers Shrine of the Sun with historical murals. Randall Davey, the polo-playing artist, happened to be visiting in Broadmoor and Spec explained his plan to him. Davey denied knowing any history, except a little polo history, but Spec asked him to look at the Shrine anyhow and to report to him first thing in the morning. The artist agreed, discovering too late that Spec's "first thing in the morning" meant 6 a.m., which was earlier than Davey had ever been up before.

The partly-built Shrine was a mere shell then with high cat-walks, and Davey had a scary time crawling around them. That evening, in his host's library, he found a copy of Irving How-bert's book, *Memories of a Lifetime in the Pikes Peak Region,* which the old pioneer had written in 1925. By 3 a.m., Davey had roughed out a series of mural subjects based on material from the book. After a brief nap, he hauled himself out of bed and ap-peared hollow-eyed but on time at El Pomar. Spec took to his idea at once of depicting the evolution of the Pikes Peak region from "an Indian playground to a white man's playground." And Spec was willing to pay the muralist $10,000 for the work.

Randall Davey made his twenty-five-foot-high designs in Santa Fe on great sheets of paper and transferred them in paint to the walls of the completed Shrine during four months of 1937. Most of the murals presented Irving Howbert's story in dramatic vignettes—Indians hunting, Pike staring at his Peak, General Palmer building the Denver and Rio Grande, Palmer laying out Colorado Springs, Stratton and Penrose and Charley Tutt and Bert Carlton at Cripple Creek. The concluding panels were based on Penrose's Broadmoor career—the building of the hotel, people playing golf and polo, and all the rest. Though Spec was pleased with Davey's version of his personal history, what delighted him most was the presence—with Julie and himself—of his closest friends—Horace Devereux, both Charley Tutts, Dr. Jack Sevier, the Arthur Connells, Charlie MacNeill, the lawyer Fred Sherwin, Milton Strong, and other hotel employees.

The Will Rogers Shrine of the Sun was dedicated on September 5, 1937, with Spec pulling out all the stops on his perfected organ of publicity. The new chimes and vibra-harp blared out "Empty Saddles" over a nation-wide radio hook-up as a saddleless horse was led slowly up Cheyenne Mountain Highway to the Shrine and its distinguished audience, which included relatives of Will Rogers, Senator Ed Johnson, Edna Ferber, the novelist, and Randall Davey. A bust of Rogers by the sculptor Jo Davidson was unveiled, the tower was christened by a full-blooded Osage Indian, a cowboy quartet sang "Old Faithful" and "Home on the Range," and a squad of soldiers sent a nineteen-gun salute rumbling o'er the prairie toward Rogers' native Oklahoma.

At the conclusion of the ceremony, the Penroses gathered friends and celebrities inside the Shrine to honor Randall Davey and to drink toasts in champagne to his historical murals. It was a happy and memorable occasion for everyone except Davey himself who somehow got locked outside. By the time he was admitted, the toasting was over and all the champagne was gone.[4]

CHAPTER TWENTY-ONE

Harvest Time

FOR SEVERAL YEARS before the dedication of the Shrine, Spencer Penrose had endured the threat of cancer. In 1938, he went to Philadelphia for an updated diagnosis. While lunching there with his wife Julie and Dr. Gerald Webb and his daughter Marka of Colorado Springs, a note of diagnosis was brought to the table which Spec read aloud, "Inoperable cancer of the larnyx." There was a moment of silence. Then as tears appeared in Julie's eyes, Spec rose to his feet and said, "Let's all go to the Zoo." And they did.[1]

Thereafter, Penrose mentioned his illness only once. In September 1939, he said to Dr. W. P. McCrossin, "Dixie, how about setting up a cancer clinic?" Two weeks later plans were released for the Penrose Tumor Clinic (today's Penrose Cancer Hospital).

In the last fortnight of his life, Penrose suffered much pain without complaint. He made himself as comfortable as possible in his third floor bedroom at El Pomar the picture window of which faced his Cheyenne Mountain. Through the window he watched the patch of world which he had fashioned—his cog train for children wending from his Ice Palace along the golf course toward his Zoo and his Shrine of the Sun. One day he put on his bath robe and spent two hours with his chauffeur touring the streets and alleys of Colorado Springs with a pause at Cheyenne Mountain Country Club to look at his signature in the club's guest book dated December 10, 1892.

He died on December 7, 1939, aged seventy-four. The secular funeral service was held at the Will Rogers Shrine with the playing of Dvorak's "Going Home" and a reading of Tennyson's "Crossing the Bar."

The preface of this book outlines the succession of decades that brought Colorado Springs through the years to the 1990s and that fourth (and largest) decade of explosive growth.

Much of the century of growth should be credited to the city's farsighted leadership. But it owes a great deal to the work of less publicized people—the men who brought to the city its water, that most essential element of life in the Pikes Peak region where the annual rainfall is only 14 inches. The city's water story is one of constant hardship and danger as the crews probed the mountain wilds to find water and coped with disintegrated granite, cliffs and deep canyons, sub-zero temperatures and 12,000-foot altitudes. And there were endless financial and legal problems to solve before water reached the faucets of the residents.

Back in the 1870s, the pioneers of Little London depended for domestic water on shallow wells which they dug in their backyards. When their wells went dry in the 1890s, the city obtained from Congress water rights to 5,500 acres on the south slope of the Pikes Peak watershed. (In 1913 water rights on the north slope were acquired). This major source of snow and rain water met the demand until the 1950s when the Air Force Academy was under construction. The city did not have enough water to supply the Academy's annual need of a minimum of 5,000 acre feet of water.

To meet this water crisis, the city council asked the help of a water wizard from Pueblo named Raymond D. Nixon. The Nixon plan at first was regarded as wildly impractical and hideously expensive. Water rights were bought on the Blue River which was on the west side of the Continental Divide at Hoosier Pass (11,541 alt.) 150 miles from Colorado Springs.

Three tunnels under Hoosier Pass brought the Blue River water to Montgomery Reservoir near Fairplay. From that reservoir a 150-mile gravity pipeline pushed the water over Wilkerson Pass to Catamount Reservoir on Pikes Peak. While Nixon's crews struggled to get the pipeline across South Park, Nixon found time to expand the city-owned utility system from two to three electric power plants. The Raymond D. Nixon plant went into service in 1980.

But in 1966, the City Council told Nixon that the city was almost out of water again. The new shortage was caused by the arrival of a swarm of manufacturers of electronic equipment—Hewlett-Packard, Honeywell, Ampex, NCR and TRW among others. People talked of changing the name of Pikes Peak to "Silicon Mountain." As Howard J. Arnsberg has written in his history of the city's public utilities, Ray Nixon "zeroed in to meet the new demand with the greatest single financial-construction program in Colorado Springs history."[2] Water rights for the Nixon plan were found on Homestake Creek under Homestake Peak (alt. 13,227 feet) across the Continental Divide 15 miles northwest of Leadville. Because of the size of the project the 60 million dollar cost was divided between Colorado Springs and Aurora near Denver. The access road to Homestake Creek up the rock cliff face of the mountain cost $100,000 per mile.

In June, 1967, Ray Nixon and his water superintendent Jack A. McCullough experienced the thrill of watching Homestake water start its 160-mile trip down Homestake Mountain to Turquoise Lake and the Arkansas River and on to a point near Buena Vista where it was pumped over Trout Creek Pass to the South Platte River and so on to Pikes Peak. The city of Aurora received its half share of the water at Eleven Mile Reservoir in South Park, picking it up out of the South Platte downstream. Water from this joint Homestake system equalled the amount used annually by Colorado Springs and Aurora.

Ray Nixon retired from the Utilities Department just as the population explosion of the 1980s was beginning to create a new water shortage. It was the city's good luck that Nixon's successor was James D. Phillips, an engineer who had been involved locally and nationally with water problems and pollution control since his graduation from Colorado College in the 1950s. Phillips had an unsurpassed knowledge of the Pikes Peak region as a resident of Cripple Creek where he was born in 1932.

During the construction of the Homestake Project, the Bureau of Reclamation was working on the Frying Pan-Arkansas Project on behalf of Colorado Springs, Pueblo and agricultural users in the Arkansas River drainage area. By the late 1970s, waters in tributaries of the Fryingpan River (a famous trout stream) were diverted beneath the Continental Divide north of Independence and Aspen to Turquoise Lake (already storing Homestake water) near Leadville. Re-

In the Fall of 1987, President Gresham Riley of Colorado College opens this $7 million Lloyd Edson Worner Campus Center, named for "Lew" Worner who was president of Colorado College from 1963 to 1981. Other buildings planned include a $9.3 million science building and the renovated Dern House for the Southwest Studies Program. *Artist's rendering of the Center by the architects John James Wallace and Associates.*

In mid-June each year the city of Colorado Springs takes the week-end off for a city-wide festival—free concerts, a beer bust in the fine Arts Center Patio, races for children and adults on Pikes Peak Avenue. Photo shows an ice cream social under the benign authority of the beloved El Paso County Courthouse (Pioneers' Museum) surrounded by the administrative buildings of the Civic Center. *Photo kindness of Carol Shannon.*

Now in its 69th year, Spencer Penrose's ever-growing Broadmoor Hotel prepared in 1987 for the 1990s with a $10 million complete renovation of all its 560 rooms including its English Pub (Golden Bee). The hotel maintains a 54-hole golf course and a mountain trout pond for its guests. The background is Cheyenne Mountain. Photo shows center original hotel (1918), Broadmoor South (1961) at left, Broadmoor West (1976) across lake next to the World Arena (for figure skaters and ice hockey games). *Robert McIntyre photo.*

Into the 1990s the children of Colorado Springs know no joy like spending the day with the lion cubs, monkeys and penguins at Cheyenne Mountain Zoo. *Robert McIntyre photo.*

This Sports Center is among the 17 buildings of the main U. S. Olympic Training Complex at 1750 East Boulder Street in Colorado Springs. The Sports Center contains five gymnasia and weight training quarters. It provides on-site training for eleven Olympic sports. *Photo courtesy of Michael Moran of U.S.O.C.*

These three Colorado Springs residents worked for ten years to bring the Olympic Training Center and then the Olympic Hall of Fame and Olympic National Headquarters to Pikes Peak. Left to right, Ryer Hitchcock, fund raising chairman, Harlan Ochs, William B. Tutt, vice president of U. S. O. C. *Photo kindness of Phyllis Cook, View Newspaper.*

Nothing demonstrates the historical continuity of Colorado Springs better than these two men at the start of the 1980s, Russell Tutt (left) and his brother, Thayer. Their grandfather, Charles Leaming Tutt, arrived in Colorado Springs in 1884. Their father was Spencer Penrose's associate from 1909 on. The statue of Orpheus by Edgar Britton is at Penrose Public Library which was dedicated July 5, 1968, with the Tutts officiating as board members of the donor, El Pomar Foundation. *Robert McIntyre photo.*

leased to the Arkansas River after generating electricity at Twin Lakes Reservoir, the crystal clear Frying Pan water ends its journey 140 miles downstream in Pueblo Reservoir near the City of Pueblo.

From Pueblo Reservoir, four pumping stations move the water (20,000 acre feet annually) via the Fountain Valley Conduit to residents in Colorado Springs, Fountain, Widefield, Security and Stratmoor Hills. Work on the Fountain Valley Conduit was done by the Bureau of Reclamation at a cost of around $63,000,000.

While Frying Pan water moved to Colorado Springs to meet the needs of the 1980s, Harold E. Miskel, head of Resources and Planning for the Colorado Springs Utilities Department, prepared for the 1990s and beyond. He managed the complicated environmental permitting processes for the second phase of the Homestake Project, while Phillips saw to the purchase of controlling interest in Lakes Henry and Meredith and the Colorado Canal Company, all east of Pueblo. Together, they fashioned a complicated exchange of agricultural water for municipal treated wastewater to significantly increase the water supply for Colorado Springs.

This foresight in water planning by the likes of Phillips and Miskel, with support from the City Council, was key to meeting increased population needs and to the bringing of several major facilities to the City, including the Olympic Training Center.

ALL HAPPENINGS in Colorado Springs seem to have some sort of historical continuity. Such was the case in 1977 when the Olympic Training Center came to Pikes Peak to serve America's amateur athletes. That event was initiated by Thayer Tutt, one of the numerous Tutt family who have pushed growth in Colorado Springs since 1892 when Thayer's grandfather, Charles L. Tutt (the first) shared a miners' cabin in Cripple Creek with Spencer Penrose.[3]

Since the 1940s, Thayer Tutt had been involved in international amateur sports—figure skating, ice hockey and golf. When he heard that the U. S. Olympic Committee (U.S.O.C.) planned to locate an Olympic Training Center at the Keystone ski resort west of Denver, he asked his nephew, William B. Tutt, and Larry Ochs, the mayor of Colorado Springs, to go into very secret action to divert the training center from Keystone and bring it to Colorado Springs.

Bill Tutt was a member of the U. S. O. C. He knew that an Olympic executive session would be held on February 12, 1977, in Oconomoc, Wisconsin. He assembled a glowing presentation and borrowed a prop airplane from NORAD. He loaded it with conspirators—Mayor Ochs, his brother Harlan, Ryer Hitchcock, Shelby Dill and Gordon Culver and headed east at 5 A.M. in a raging blizzard. The delegation reached Oconomoc in spite of terrifying flying weather. Tutt gave his presentation to the Olympic officials and ran a movie showing all the fine things that Colorado Springs could do for Olympic athletes.

In less than ten minutes, the Olympic executives voted to give the Olympic Training Center to Colorado Springs. They stipulated that the center would need at least 250 acres and $250,000,000 to pay for administrative buildings and training facilities. It was a jubilant homecoming for the Springs conspirators. They refused to be bothered by the fact that they had no site and no money to meet their commitment to build an Olympic Training Center.

It was Col. Bill Depew of Fort Carson who proposed the use for the training center of the 36-acres of Ent Air Force Base on East Bijou Street which was abandoned when NORAD moved to its cave under Cheyenne Mountain.

Several months were spent unravelling the complicated ownership of Ent Air Force Base so that it could be given to the U. S. O. C. The various owners of Ent cooperated in what Bill Tutt called "an extraordinary spirit of friendship and good will"—NORAD, Fort Carson, the Colorado Springs City Council, Peterson Air Force Base, the Air Force Academy, the Pentagon, the Colorado delegation in Washington, and local banks which dropped plans to put a shopping center at Ent.

Late in 1977, General James E. Hill of NORAD and Mayor Ochs turned over the Ent Property to the U. S. O. C. for the Olympic Training Center at an annual rental of one dollar. Meanwhile, El Pomar (the Spencer Penrose foundation) donated a million dollars to renovate and clean up the dilapidated Ent buildings.

Two surprises came with the happy ending. The U. S. O. C. voted to set up its national headquarters at the Olympic Training Center. And one day a mysterious fleet of trucks rolled up East Boulder

Street and delivered to the training center tons of kitchen equipment and used furniture. Months later, the U. S. Air Force divulged that it had removed the furnishings from discontinued radar installations in California and sent them to Colorado Springs.

The first Olympic Sports Festival took place in 1978, followed by the World Speed Skating Championships in '84 and the Cycling World Championships in 1986. The training center complex by then contained dozens of administrative buildings, dormitories for 600 athletes, a 400-meter track, a velodrome, five gymnasia, and other facilities to accommodate eleven of the sports on the program of the Olympic Games. The center had 230 full time employees.

In 1985, the first water of the Pan-Ark system began to be pumped from Pueblo Reservoir to Colorado Springs. The 20,000 acre feet of water reached the Pikes Peak region at a strategic time—just as news of two new projects was attracting thousands of thirsty newcomers to the city. Preliminary work had begun on the billion-dollar Consolidated Space Operations Center to control all military satellite systems through a ground-to-space communication system. It is linked to a world-wide network of tracking stations and to NORAD Command inside Cheyenne Mountain. *The Denver Post* described this project in 1985 as making Colorado Springs "the nerve center of America's space defenses."

The Space Center had been lured to Pikes Peak by General James E. Hill who had retired as commander of NORAD to become president of the Colorado Springs Chamber of Commerce. He had observed that the Pentagon had dropped a plan to locate such a space center in California because earthquakes there disturbed electronic systems. General Hill had enjoyed his part in bringing the Olympic Training Center to Pikes Peak. He felt that Colorado Springs should have the Space Center as well. The case to this end that he made to the Pentagon was traditional, the same that had brought Camp Carson in 1941 and the Air Force Academy in 1954—the Pikes Peak climate and environment would be as beneficial to Space Center personnel as it had been to General Palmer's health seekers in the 1870s.

The Consolidated Space Operations Center was to be built on 640 acres of rolling prairie at Falcon Station ten miles east of Peterson Air Force Base. It was planned to be in full operation by the 1990s. It would have part in the Strategic Defense Initiative as that program develops. A Shuttle Operations Complex was given up by the Pentagon after the Challenger shuttle tragedy of January 28, 1986, for evaluation later.

Before the bedazzled residents of Colorado Springs had recovered from the shock of winning both the Olympic Training Center and the Consolidated Space Operations Center still another rich plum fell in their lap. At a large meeting in Reno, Nevada, on November 23, 1986, the U. S. Olympic Committee and 36 Olympic sports federation voted to locate an Olympic Hall of Fame and museum and a new U. S. O. C. headquarters on a 150-acre tract near the Consolidated Space Operations Center.

The U.S.O.C. vote followed the announcement by the Colorado Springs delegation under Ryer Hitchcock, Harlan Ochs and Bill Tutt that $20,000,000 had been pledged to build the Hall of Fame. The largest contributor to the fund was a newcomer to Colorado Springs, Frank Aries, who pledged at Reno gifts totalling $12,000,000 including 150 acres of land as a site for the Hall of Fame, the U. S. O. C. headquarters, the U. S. Space Foundation and an IMAX wide-screen theater for space-related films.

In 1985, Frank Aries had bought a home in Colorado Springs and moved his wife Judy and son Jonathan here. Frank Aries, aged 52, was born in Chicago, graduated from Tulane University, became a real estate developer in Tucson, Arizona, and in the San Francisco Bay area. In 1982, he bought in Tucson the 12,328 acres of the Howard Hughes estate for $75,000,000 and sold it later for $200,000,000. Hearing that the 21,000 acres of the Banning-Lewis Hereford Ranch[5] was up for sale he flew over the ranch in his helicopter, liked the location of it between the Consolidated Space Operations Center and Peterson Air Force Base and bought the ranch for $96,000,000 a purchase that made Frank Aries the largest land owner in El Paso County.

GENERAL PALMER enjoyed being outdoors which was where he had spent most of his life as cavalry leader, explorer of the far west and railroad builder and he wanted the people of his Colorado Springs to enjoy the outdoors too. That is why he gave the city its extraordinary system of public parks. His gift of parks are listed on pages 150-151.

This large system is the basis of the outdoor recreation of residents in Colorado Springs today. During the 1980s, the facilities for enjoying the city's parks was enormously expanded by Laurence A. Schenk who became director of the Colorado Springs Park and Recreation Department in 1978.

Laurence Schenk, a graduate of Michigan State University, has spent his entire life in public park management. He carries one of the heaviest work loads of any city executive. It involves the direction of 111 Colorado Springs parks (7,132 acres in all) including the world-renowned Garden of the Gods, Austin Bluffs Park, that favorite of family picnickers, Monument Valley Park for the joggers, and Memorial Park where 50,000 people gather with tons of fried chicken for the Fourth of July fireworks and concerts by the Colorado Springs Symphony Orchestra.

In spare moments, Schenk keeps an eye on two city golf courses, a soccer field, four baseball fields, soft ball tournaments, tennis and shuffleboard courts, swimming pools, 14 hiking trails, and the job of keeping water in Prospect Lake for the sail boaters and anglers. In 1986, the city added to his duties the running of Ski Broadmoor for novices to his duties.

Director Schenk developed the unusual Otis Park to assist the handicapped to achieve meaningful lives through leisure activities. He promoted White House Ranch in 1983 on property once owned by General Palmer. Children at White House Ranch learned how ranchers in the past built log cabins, shod horses, raised cattle and grew their own food. A White House museum displayed artifacts of the region. An arboretum showed the species of trees suitable for the climate at Pikes Peak.

Just as Laurence Schenk brought Colorado Springs more varied uses of the outdoors, so in the 1980s, Kenneth E. Dowlin, director of the Pikes Peak Library District brought residents the wonderful world of books in larger measure. In 1975, Dowlin became director of the District's eight branches (plus a mini-branch in the county jail), after the retirement of Margaret Reid who had served as director for 27 years. Dowlin circulated books to many rural communities by means of three bookmobiles. In 1981, his "Past as Prologue" lecture series was attended by overflow crowds.

The Pikes Peak Library became because of Dowlin's leadership one of the first libraries in the U. S. to provide access by computer to the District's 425,000 books. A second computer center was named "Maggie's Place" in honor of Margaret Reid. By dialing in "Maggie's Place" users could find answers to a host of questions. A clearing house called "Springspace" was established in the new East Library by Deputy Director Lynn Magrath as a repository of all documents relating to community activity in the city.

Early in the 1980s Kenneth Dowlin realized that the District's libraries were not meeting the demands of the city's huge increase in population. His solution was the construction over a three-year period of the $10,000,000 East Library and Information Center at 5550 North Union Boulevard. This beautiful building with a sweeping view of Pikes Peak was placed in a ten-acre park named in honor of George Fellows who served Colorado Springs for many years as city manager.

Noting that the new Georges Pompidou Library (1977) in Paris was acclaimed as the most modern in the world, Dowlin brought its computer expert Jacques Foule to Colorado Springs to see that the East Library system was as good as the Paris system. He sent his public relations director, Nancy DeLury to Paris to study the operation of the Georges Pompidou Library.

The grand opening of Dowlin's East Library took place on January 10, 1987, with more than 12,000 people attending the three days of celebration. The guest speaker for the dedication was David McCullough, who wrote the best-selling history of the Panama Canal, "The Path Between the Seas."

The pursuit of culture has been practiced with religious zeal in Colorado Springs since Little London days when Cara Bell set a high standard by paying the unheard of sum of $16,000 in 1880 for Thomas Moran's landscape, "The Mount of the Holy Cross" to decorate her Manitou living room.

The same standard was maintained in 1936 by Alice Bemis Taylor when she built the Colorado Springs Fine Arts Center and gave it to the city. On the fiftieth anniversary in 1986 of the Center's opening the residents turned out in force to applaud its library, the expansion of the Taylor Museum and its renowned collection of New Mexican art, innovations at the Bemis Art School for children, and the renovation of the 450-seat theater. During the opening, the Center's galleries were filled with paintings from its permanent collection by Georgia O'Keefe, Walt Kuhn, Bernard Arnest, Boardman Robinson, bronzes by Charles M. Russell, and John Singer Sargent's portrait of General Palmer's daughter, Elsie.

As a rule, people in Colorado Springs take their culture calmly. But on October 15, 1982, they responded with an orgy of enthusiasm at the opening of their Pikes Peak Center for the performing arts. For years, Beatrice Vradenberg, manager of the Colorado Springs Symphony Orchestra, its conductor, Charles Ansbacher, and Phillip Kendall of the symphony board had struggled to win voter approval of funds for a modern concert hall to replace the old Palmer High School auditorium.

Three times the voters turned them down until 1978 when a resolution was approved by the voters to build the center with county, federal and private funds, including a grant of $1.5 million by El Pomar Foundation. The ultra-modern Pikes Peak Center was designed by James Wallace and Clifford Nakata. Its effect on the cultural life of the Pikes Peak region was immediate and electrifying. It has a seating capacity of 2,143, and back stage equipment which made possible the staging of every kind of theatre entertainment including the popular "Shakespeare in the Park" series of the University of Colorado. Among guest stars who have performed at the Center with the symphony were Isaac Stern and Leontyne Price.

In contrast to the modern Pikes Peak Center, the stately El Paso County Courthouse (1901) is the city's most striking landmark. Its interior houses the spacious Pioneers' Museum which presents a visual history of the Pikes Peak region starting with the founding of Colorado City in 1860. Here visitors find many exhibits of how people lived in the long ago. A covey of docents in blue smocks have been trained to give accurate background on all the exhibits. The Pioneers' Museum also presents the Starsmore Research Center which was funded by private donations and dedicated to the memory of James W. Starsmore who died in 1978. It houses a vast collection of documents pertaining to local history, including records from General Palmer's estate and the authoritative Cragin Collection.

It is of course thrilling to live in a city with its population increasing in fifty years from 30,000 to nearly 400,000. But plenty of residents found the explosion not thrilling but horrifying. These people mourned the demise of the old Antlers Hotel (1901) and the demolition of the elegant Chief Theater. However, sentimental residents find solace in the splendid survival of General Palmer's Glen Eyrie and the presence of Major Henry McCallister's home (1874) now a museum. They find still more reassurance in Bob Hibbard's store on South Tejon which his father founded in 1892. Hibbard's thrives in the same ornate building with its hand-operated elevator and pneumatic tubes whizzing money from the customer to the cashier.

And so we will stop at the threshold of the 1990s in this happy continuing story, even though we hate to say good-bye to the quiet Little London that used to be, with a nod to the busy city that it has become.

Times have changed, but the continuity has remained, in leadership, in standards of taste, in reverence for yesterday and hope for tomorrow, in a community still fond of comfort, gentility and peace.

Perhaps this continuity derives from a force stronger than the city's. Life and progress at Pikes Peak may derive from the grand old pile itself. That is why people, past and present, bow to the mountain's ageless authority, adapting their ambitions to what the setting requires of them—vigilant protection of its beauty, enjoyment of its climate, and acceptance of its limitations as well as its unique advantages.

THE END

Notes

CHAPTER ONE

MOUNTAIN FEVER

1. Ellen Clarke Mellen was Queen Mellen's aunt as well as her step-mother, according to John S. Fisher on page 237 of his family-approved biography of General Palmer, *A Builder of the West*. Queen's real mother, born Isabel Clarke, was a daughter of Charlotte Seymour Clarke and Major Nathan Clarke who were married in Hartford, Connecticut, in 1816. Major Clarke, according to his pension file in the National Archives, fought in the War of 1812 and spent his career at Indian frontier posts of Wisconsin-Minnesota.

Between 1817 and 1830, one son, Malcolm, and at least two daughters, Charlotte Ouisconsin and Isabel, were born to the Major Clarkes at these posts. In the latter year, Major Clarke established his famliy in Cincinnati, Ohio. The major died at Fort Winnebago, Minnesota, in 1836, the same year that his youngest daughter, Ellen Seymour Clarke, was born in Cincinnati. In 1855, his eldest daughter, Charlotte Ouisconsin, was among the founders of Minneapolis, Minnesota. His son Malcolm married a Sioux Indian and became a member of a Sioux band. He roamed widely as an Indian trader, even visiting the soda springs at Pikes Peak. In his later years he moved to a ranch in Montana where he was killed by Indians in the late 1860s. His career is sketched by his sister Ellen Clarke Mellen in Eliza Greatorex's *Summer Etchings in Colorado* (G. P. Putnam's Sons, 1873).

Isabel Clarke married William Proctor Mellen in Cincinnati after his arrival there in 1843 to study and practice law. Mellen was born in Pelham, Massachusetts, in 1814. The only child of the couple, Queen, is said to have been born on March 26, 1850, in Prestonburg, Kentucky, where Mellen had coal interests. According to Chase Mellen, son of William Proctor Mellen, Queen's given name was Mary Lincoln Mellen. The "Lincoln" may have derived from the fact that W. P. Mellen's brother-in-law in Cincinnati was named T. D. Lincoln.

During the Civil War, William P. Mellen supervised such commerce as was necessary between the Union and the Confederacy. In 1866, he moved to Flushing, Long Island, where he was a partner in the law firm of Jordan, Hinsdale and Mellen.

William P. Mellen married three times, according to his obituary in the *Cincinnati Commercial* of November 18, 1873. His third marriage in 1856 was to Isabel Clarke's sister, Ellen Seymour Clarke, who was twenty-two years his junior. What happened to Isabel and the other wife is not reported in the obituary or in Chase Mellen's book about his family in Colorado, *Sketches of Pioneer Life and Settlement of the Great West*. By 1869, when Mellen and Palmer met on the train, Mellen and his third wife Ellen had produced six children. He had no other children except Queen.

CHAPTER TWO

LOTS OF LOTS FOR SALE

1. Irving Howbert was born in Columbus, Indiana, in 1846, the son of a Methodist Episcopal minister. He came to Denver with his father in 1860 and to Colorado City in 1862, in the meantime crossing the plains a dozen times between the Missouri and the mountains. From 1870 on, he had an important part in the growth of Colorado Springs until his death in 1934.

2. General Cameron's town site blocks in Colorado Springs were— and are—400 feet square, the same as many blocks in Meeker's town of Greeley. Residential lots in the Springs are 190 feet deep, a figure reportedly decided on by Cameron because he believed that flies from the stable could not migrate to the house if the distance between stable and house was more than forty feet. Cameron made the streets of the Springs unusually wide—from 100 to 140 feet, including space for sidewalks. Today, Palmer is the one who gets the praise for his foresight in making the streets so wide, but it was all Cameron's doing, and Palmer criticized him for it later.

3. Cameron's original platted area (about 1,000 acres out of the 2,000-acre total town site) ran roughly from Moreno Street on the south to Willamette Street (named for Oregon's Columbia River tributary) on the north. Monument Creek was the west boundary, Shook's Run the east. Later street names north of Willamette followed the general scheme. Dale and Cache la Poudre referred to branches

of the South Platte. Yampa, San Rafael, and Uintah were streams which Palmer had investigated during his 1867-68 railroad survey. San Miguel is a Western Slope river in the San Juan Mountains. The next street north of San Miguel (today's Columbia) used to be called Astoria, honoring John Jacob Astor's trading post at the mouth of the Columbia.

The Spanish street names south of Pikes Peak Avenue could lead visitors to think that Colorado Springs itself had a rich Spanish colonial past. It did not. Very few Spaniards came as far north in the mountains as Pikes Peak during the eighteenth century and up to the time of the Mexican Revolution in 1821. Only one official Spanish expedition approached the Pikes Peak town site—that of Governor Juan Bautista de Anza while trailing Comanche Indians in 1779. And yet Colorado Springs is entitled to its Spanish street names, being the offspring of those indubitably Spanish parents, the Maxwell and Sangre de Cristo grants.

French influence as well as Spanish could be inferred from the street names Cache la Poudre and St. Vrain. Actually, Frenchmen had nothing to do with Pikes Peak, though French trappers in 1836 did apply the charming Cache la Poudre name to the northern Colorado stream where they had cached their powder to hide it from Indians. St. Vrain Creek—near Cache la Poudre River—was named for the trader Ceran St. Vrain. He was a Frenchman right enough, born in Spanish Missouri, but he became an American at age one after the Louisiana Purchase in 1803.

4. To this day, Colorado Springs warranty deeds open with the proviso that "intoxicating liquors shall never be manufactured, sold or otherwise disposed of, as a beverage, in any place of public resort in or upon the premises hereby granted, or any part thereof; and it is herein and hereby expressly reserved by the said parties of the first part, that in case any of the above conditions concerning intoxicating liquors are broken by said parties of the second part, then this deed shall become null and void, and all right, title, and interest of, in and to the premises hereby conveyed shall revert to the parties of the first part"—etc. Today purchasers of Spring property who plan to sell liquor often take steps to protect themselves against threat of forfeiture under the above clause.

As we shall see, General Palmer's liquor ban never did work in spite of desperate temperance efforts by some people. One reason

for failure was the fact that most Fountain Colony members (including Palmer) and later residents had no moral objections to drinking plenty themselves. They just didn't want saloons which would
bring in rowdies and lower property values. With the liquor ban still
in the deeds, Colorado Springs today has sixty liquor stores and countless bars. By contrast, Greeley, Colorado—founded and sustained by
moral teetotalers—remains a fairly strict temperance city.

CHAPTER THREE

THE EARLIEST EARLY BIRDS

1. Charles Kingsley's title baffled many Pikes Peak pioneers. For
them Rose composed a set explanation: "A Canon is one who governs
the clergy of an English Cathedral. My father is Canon of Westminster
Abbey."

The quoted passages are from a delightful book, *South by West:
Or Winter in the Rocky Mountains and Spring in Mexico,* by Rose
Kingsley (edited by Charles Kingsley), which was published in 1874
in London by W. Ibister & Co. The book is a rare item but it exists in
good western collections such as Tutt Library at Colorado College in
Colorado Springs.

2. In 1949, Mrs. Kittie Paster Fryhofer, a Pikes Peak pioneer, explained that this ominous County Cemetery stood between present
Sierra Madre Street and the Denver and Rio Grande tracks. During
1872 most of those graves were moved to a new Colorado Springs
Company cemetery plot east of town near Mount Washington,
and some to the old Colorado City Cemetery on the Mesa near
General Palmer's road to Glen Eyrie. It was in this Mesa Cemetery
that Charley Everhart and the Robbins boys, Franklin and George,
were buried after being murdered by Arapaho Indians on September
11, 1869, at the present site of Cascade Avenue and Boulder Crescent.
In 1949, the El Paso County Pioneer Association placed a pink
granite marker at Mesa Cemetery, which is westward from Mesa Road
in the Friendship Lane area. By 1900, Mesa Cemetery was virtually
abandoned. Colorado City people were buried in Fairview Cemetery,
near Twenty-Sixth Street. In his volume *The Book of Colorado
Springs,* Manly D. Ormes reported that Palmer's Colorado Springs
Company cemetery came to be called Evergreen by city council

action in 1877. It is a beautiful place and well worth any tourist's visit. The remnant mesa, Mount Washington, was so called because its altitude above sea level was about the same as that of New England's Mount Washington (6,288 feet).

3. The yellow cliffed hills (today's municipal picnic heaven, Palmer Park) would be known as Austin's Bluffs, for Henry W. Austin, a Chicago hardware merchant who bought the area in 1873 from Matt France for sheep-raising purposes. Templeton Gap was named for a pioneer of many talents, "Uncle Jack" (Andrew J.) Templeton who began ranching in the Gap in 1860. Uncle Jack was a skilled veterinarian who soon found himself delivering babies as well as calves and colts. He came to be so highly regarded that it was a mark of high distinction to have been brought into the world by him.

4. Gerald and Marcellin De Coursey, both Springs pioneers, were typical examples of the sort of "proper Philadelphians" whom Captain Palmer had recruited for his Fifteenth Pennsylvania during the Civil War.

5. This pastime, invented by a New Yorker in 1863, had caught on in the East about 1870 and it didn't take long for roller skates to get out to Denver.

6. Elsom Liller edited *Out West* from March 23 to December 26, 1872. On January 4, 1873, he began publishing Palmer's *Colorado Springs Weekly Gazette*. The *Daily Gazette* edited by Benjamin F. Steele was added in 1878. Palmer sold the newspaper in November, 1896, to Thomas C. Parrish, Henry Russell Wray, and C. V. Barton for $30,000.

7. Lt. John Charles Frémont and his party of Army engineers visited Pikes Peak twice in July, 1843, en route to California. George Frederick Ruxton, the young English adventurer, was entranced by the scenery of Ute Pass in 1847.

8. It certainly did. Comparative populations in 1980 were: White Sulphur Springs, West Virginia, 4,000; Saratoga Springs, New York, 20,000; Newport, Rhode Island, 36,000; Colorado Springs, Colo., 250,000.

9. The eggnog incident was typical of the attitude of many members of Fountain Colony toward the liquor ban.

10. Maurice Kingsley resigned in March, 1872, as a Fountain Colony officer and Palmer gave him a job on his surveying crew in Mexico. Maurice quit that, too, returned to England, and then became an American citizen in the East.

11. *Heritage of Years,* by Frances M. Wolcott (Minton, Balch & Company, New York, 1932). The Colorado Springs chapter of Mrs. Wolcott's book are delicious but the author never permitted historical accuracy to spoil a good story. Her first husband was Lyman Bass, a Denver and Rio Grande lawyer, and they built and christened with champagne the noble stone house "Edgeplain," on the northwest corner of Nevada Avenue and San Rafael Street. Chester Alan Arthur, son of the President, lived in "Edgeplain" later. Bass died and his widow married Senator Edward O. Wolcott of Colorado in 1890 and became mistress of Wolhurst near Denver, then the most elaborate country place in the Rockies.

12. Palmer brought the jovial John Blair, a ruddy Scot, out from Chicago and named the 160-acre canyon tract just north of Glen Eyrie in his honor, Blair Athol (Blair was from Athol, Perthshire, Scotland). The name was partly a joke since Blair Athol was an English race horse which won the English Derby in 1864. John Blair built the road from Manitou to Glen Eyrie and landscaped the two parks in Colorado Springs which are still called Acacia and Alamo. In 1888, Captain Marcellin De Coursey bought Blair Athol from Palmer but Palmer bought it back soon. The upper part of the Blair Athol area became a part of Pike National Forest and mineral rights for building stone thereon were acquired by the Castle Concrete Company. The result was the hideous scars on the ridge just north of the Garden of the Gods and adjacent to Queen's Canyon. No amount of legal action availed to stop this quarrying.

CHAPTER FOUR

POTPOURRI: THE FIRST DECADE

1. Perhaps these two tub-thumpers had served their purpose but their equal in ballyhoo would not appear at Pikes Peak again until Spencer Penrose built the Broadmoor Hotel forty years later. After General Cameron founded, in 1873, Fort Collins, Colorado, he went with Pabor to San Francisco to start an avant-garde literary magazine which went bust in about two issues. Pabor wrote a history of Greeley, Colorado, and wound up as editor of the *Grand Valley Star* on the Western

Slope. General Cameron served (1885-87) as warden of Colorado State Penitentiary at Canon City and then became promotion director of the Denver and Fort Worth Railroad.

2. After William P. Mellen's death, his family moved into the Springs from Glen Eyrie, but General Palmer looked out for their welfare as long as he lived. The Mellen boys worked now and then on the Denver and Rio Grande Railroad. One of the Mellen girls, Charlotte, married Professor William L. Sclater, whom Palmer put in as head of the Colorado College Museum in 1906 (Palmer built the big white house on Camp Creek below Glen Eyrie for Mrs. Sclater). At the turn of the century, Clark Mellen joined the Colorado Springs Company and the General loaned him $50,000 for investment in a real estate venture in the Wood Avenue section of Colorado Springs.

3. William Sharpless Jackson, like Palmer and McAllister, was born in 1836 (and a Quaker) at Kennett Square, Pennsylvania, thirty miles southwest of Philadelphia, and not much farther from Palmer's birthplace in Delaware. In the 1860s, Jackson went to St. Paul, Minnesota, as treasurer of the Lake Superior and Mississippi Railroad and then to Denver in 1871 to join the Denver and Rio Grande.

4. You should be aware by now of the importance of Fifteenth Pennsylvania alumni in Colorado Springs affairs since the day in January, 1870, when Captain William F. Colton picked the town site for Palmer. The Fifteenth Pennsylvania had only three majors and Fountain Colony got two of them, McAllister and Wagner. Altogether, sixteen men from the General's beloved regiment helped him build the Springs at one time or another.

5. The Supreme Court upheld the liquor clause in 1879, but the Colorado Springs Company remained unaggressive.

6. Blackmore owned, among other things, 320 acres of land between Colorado Springs and Manitou in what is known as Red Rock Canon, the quarry of which produced the brilliant red stone for many Springs buildings.

7. Robert M. Ormes' remarkable *Pikes Peak Atlas* (privately printed, 1959), is packed with geographical and historical detail on the Peak, including the route of the original Bear Creek trail. The atlas shows the progression of foothills which are interposed between Colorado Springs and the summit and which block off the summit from the view of many residents in Broadmoor. The highest foothills from Ute

Pass southward are: Mt. Manitou, 9,450; Cameron's Cone, 10,709; Mt.
Arthur, 10,807 and Mount Garfield, 10,925—twins; Mount Rosa, 11,499;
Mount Big Chief, 11,200; and Almagre Mountain, 12,367. Mount Rosa
was probably named for Rose Kingsley, though she did not report
ever having climbed up there with her trusty pickax.

Dr. Hayden's beautiful *Atlas of Colorado* was published in 1877
and is a bibliographic joy. Hayden's Sectional Maps Seven and
Thirteen—Central Colorado—present the topographical and geological
finds of Hayden's men during their 1873 visit to the Pikes Peak region.
Hayden's gratitude for his warm reception at Fountain Colony is
shown by his care in labeling the resort's main attractions—Cheyenne
Mountain, Garden of the Gods, Glen Eyrie, Austin's Bluffs, Cameron's
Cone, and even Willie Bell's Manitou Park Hotel. The region around
present Divide, at the top of Ute Pass, is named Hayden Park on
the maps (Divide used to be called Hayden Divide).

8. The Ormes *Atlas* shows Sackett Mountain (12,590) two miles south
of Pikes Peak summit, with Boehmer Creek two miles below that.

9. Fred McKown, long-time City Forester in Colorado Springs, has
said that McAllister's original cottonwoods were probably brought up
from the Arkansas Valley. Round-leaf cottonwoods instead of the
narrow-leaf variety were bought because they gave more shade and
shaped up better. Cottonwoods are short-lived—about fifty years—and
none of the originals is know to be alive. Early-day doctors hated them,
saying that the cotton pollen of the male trees gave their patients hay
fever. The late Springs millionaire, William Lennox, used to boast
that his first Pikes Peak job was planting McAllister's cottonwoods at
fifty cents a tree for the first five blocks of North Cascade Avenue.

10. This was Grant's first visit and he was greeted with wild enthusiasm. He came again in August of 1880 after his world tour and spent
a month at the Beebee House in Manitou but local Republicans were
cool then. They were Garfield supporters and were displeased because
Grant had opposed Garfield's July nomination for the Presidency.

11. The charm and good looks of Drs. Anderson and Solly set standards
which have been adhered to ever since by Pikes Peak medical men.
Most beautiful and charming of them all was the Englishman, Dr.
Gerald Bertram Webb, who arrived at the turn of the century and
married Jefferson Davis' grandaughter, Varina Hayes. Besides play-

ing polo, golf, tennis, poker, chess, cricket, bridge, and rugby, Dr. Webb (bright carnation always in the buttonhole of his Bond Street suit) inspired thousands of invalids to think themselves back to health. He died in 1948.

12. Manly Ormes' *The Book of Colorado Springs* states that Glockner began in 1890 in memory of Albert Glockner of Pittsburgh with Dr. Anderson as house physician. The Sisters of Charity of Cincinnati, Ohio, took it over soon from Mrs. Glockner. It was torn down in 1959 and replaced by the $10,000,000 Penrose Hospital. In 1887, Dr. Anderson started an infirmary to care for injured workmen of the Colorado Midland Railroad. The sisterhood of St. Francis of Perpetual Adoration in Denver supplied the nurses and then built their own St. Francis Hospital in 1888 on its present eminence, moving in the sick railroaders. Cragmor Sanatorium was the result of thirty years of planning by Dr. Solly and was built up by degrees between 1905 and 1914, partly with funds supplied by General Palmer. Cragmor had a gay career during the 1920s as a haven for well-heeled young men and women chasing the T.B. cure—and each other—and is now a very popular extension center of the University of Colorado.

13. Helen Hunt Jackson's grave, a raised, vault-length slab of dark stone, is beneath an old sycamore in the big Jackson plot, Block 17, in the old part of Evergreen Cemetery. It is labelled simply "Helen, wife of Wm. S. Jackson, died August 12, 1885." The foot of the slab bears the single word "Engravit." Will Jackson had no children by Helen Hunt.

CHAPTER FIVE

LITTLE LONDON

1. Kingsley's letters to Fanny and the Mr. Bug tale can be found in *Charles Kingsley—His Letters and Memories of His Life,* edited by His Wife (Scribner, Armstrong & Co., New York, 1877).

2. These impressions of Dr. and Mrs. Bell are based on a paper by Elma Jane Reilly of Manitou Springs which she read before the Historical Society of the Pikes Peak Region on November 18, 1952. Dr. Bell's American interests included the Denver and Rio Grande Railroad; the Colorado Springs Company; other Colorado town sites at Pueblo, Durango and Westcliffe—the last named for his home town in England; land at Woodland Park, Colorado, which he named "Bel-

mont" at first and then Manitou Park Junction; the Colorado Coal and Iron Company (today's huge Colorado Fuel and Iron Corporation); coal lands at Crested Butte and elsewhere; two hotels in Manitou; and, for good measure, a street car line in Missouri.

3. *The Heritage of Years,* page 87.

4. A paper by Raymond G. Colwell states that after the log hotel burned down in 1886, Bell built on the site a larger frame hotel which burned down in 1899. Willie built his narrow-gauge logging railroad out of old pieces of Denver and Rio Grande stock which nobody wanted and hauled an old locomotive up Ute Pass to the railhead near present Woodland Park. Bell laid out his line by eye like a happy child playing with his toy train. When the logging ended around 1896, the Denver and Rio Grande took back its rails and its tired old engine. This was the year in which Bell dammed Trout Creek to make the present lake at Manitou Park.

General Palmer, an ardent conservationist, was worried about Willie's logging business and he was glad to buy his partner out and to transfer the entire 10,000 acres of Manitou Park to Colorado College in 1906 as the foundation for a School of Forestry. The school was never a success. In 1912, Colorado College sold off 3,237 acres of Palmer's gift. The School of Forestry was discontinued in 1931. Soon thereafter, Manitou Park began to be managed by the U. S. Forest Service for Colorado College. In 1949 or 1950, title to the entire 10,000 original acres passed to the U.S. Forest Service.

5. Mrs. Patrick Frederick Gildea, the widow of Dr. Solly's partner, grew up in Colorado Springs and spent many hours listening to "Chumley's" bellow as a captive audience.

6. All these Little London matters are taken from an excellent paper, "English Influence in the Early Life of Colorado Springs," by Dr. Paul V. West which is on file at the Pioneer Museum in the Springs.

CHAPTER SIX

THE TOURISTS, BLESS 'EM

1. The history of tourism in the West has been developed well by Earl Pomeroy in his *In Search of the Golden West* (Alfred A. Knopf, New York, 1959).

2. It seems a little late to be mentioning that Pikes Peak was climbed first by Edwin James, a member of Stephen Long's Expedition, in 1820. While James and his men were on this trip they started a nice forest fire in the Englemann Canyon area. Pikes Peak's first careless campers! Lt. Zebulon Pike and three of his men tried to climb it in November, 1806, but their approach was from the south where a series of deep canyons blocked them off from the summit. Besides, they wore summer clothes and it was already winter with snow above 10,000 feet on the mountain.

3. Lake Moraine was called Mystic Lake in the 1870s. After 1890, it was enlarged by a dam and became a part of the Colorado Springs water system along with Seven Lakes and most of the north slope drainage of the mountain. In the 1950s, the Pikes Peak system was vastly augmented by water piped by gravity from source waters of the Blue River across the Continental Divide near Hoosier Pass more than a hundred miles away and from Homestake Creek and its tributaries beyond Hagerman Pass, some hundred and sixty miles away. Robert Ormes' *Pikes Peak Atlas* contains a masterly account of all Pikes Peak region water development.

The "steep slope" mentioned in the text was the first stage of what was called the Frémont Trail, a west-running route to timberline. From there hardy souls picked their own way to the top. (John Charles Frémont never saw Frémont trail.) The Manitou Incline occupies the lower Frémont Trail today.

4. They do actually drain away when somebody in the City Water Department pulls the plug in St. John Tunnel which takes Seven Lakes water to Lake Moraine.

5. Many parts of Pikes Peak are in Pike National Forest today and are explored by hikers on week ends—Jones Park, for instance, by trail from the Municipal High Drive (see Ormes' *Pikes Peak Atlas* for complete trail list). But the old-style mountain hotel tourism is long dead. No trace remains of Dr. Huntington's Lake House. The Seven Lakes Hotel burned down in the 1880s and the lakes themselves have been fenced off by the City Water Department, though much of the Seven Steps road from Rosemont toward Seven Lakes can be traveled in a jeep. Tom Palsgrove's Half Way House kept open into the 1900s and was bought and dismantled by the City Water Department in 1925.

6. John Hay's cabin is still up there, albeit flat on the ground, a pile of rotting timbers. But its memorial, the Nicolay-Hay *Life of Lincoln*, dominates the Lincoln shelf in every library in the world. Crystal Park today is a small cottage community.

7. It still does. Until 1955, pumping water up to the Garden was such a problem that the Colorado Springs Water Department flinched every time anyone flushed a toilet at Hidden Inn.

8. The Garden's "mystic confections" are mainly seen to the left after tourists pass westward through the main gateways. For tourists staying in Colorado Springs, the carriage drive to Manitou was very popular and out of it grew a fable. The carriage horses were rested in Colorado City and when tourists complained of having nothing to do there, a pioneer, Anthony Bott, made them happy by showing them a two-room log cabin which he said had been the Territorial Capitol of Colorado for four days in 1862. The log cabin had been no such thing, but the fable became gospel truth a generation or two later and the cabin, labelled COLORADO'S FIRST CAPITOL, was bought by Spencer Penrose and moved to the Broadmoor Golf Course as a glorious relic of the past. During the 1959 Rush to the Rockies Centennial, it was moved to the Denver Capitol grounds where it kept historians busy arguing over its authenticity.

9. The Howbert-Crowell-Humphrey Opera House brightened the lives of Colorado Springs residents for a quarter of a century. Most of the world's great artists appeared there, including Maude Adams, three Barrymores, George M. Cohan, John Drew, Dustin Farnum, Trixie Friganza, Lily Langtry, Richard Mansfield, Alla Nazimova, Eva Tanquay, Lenore Ulrich, Ruth Chatterton, Anna Pavlowa, Josef Hofmann, Paderewski, and Schumann-Heink. Lon Chaney began his career there as a stage hand.

CHAPTER SEVEN

SOARING RAILS

1. The woodwork and carpentry of the mansion's interior was done by Winfield Scott Stratton who made such a whopping profit in '74 on a lot sale and who built the cottage which Helen Hunt Jackson went to as a bride.

2. Conflicting views of the roles of their respective fathers in the Midland affair were presented in *Denver Westerners Brand Book* for 1945 by William S. Jackson, Jr. and by Percy Hagerman. Judge Jackson's article is "The Record vs Reminiscence." The Percy Hagerman piece is titled "The Colorado Midland." The ranking Hagerman authority was the late John J. Lipsey of Colorado Springs, author of a fine Hagerman biography and also of "J. J. Hagerman, Building of the Colorado Midland" (*Denver Westerners Brand Book*, 1954) and "How Hagerman Sold the Midland" (*Denver Westerners Brand Book*, 1956). Much of the Hagerman material in this chapter was borrowed gratefully from Mr. Lipsey.

Hagerman realized early that the Midland cost too much to operate to make a profit and he sold the railroad to the Santa Fe in 1890 without loss to his stockholders. Thereafter the Midland ran between Colorado Springs and Grand Junction by virtue of trackage arrangements with the Denver and Rio Grande on the stretch west of New Castle. In February, 1917, the Midland, which had cost $7,000,000—and then some—was bought for $1,425,000 by A. E. Carlton, Spencer Penrose, and others. But World War I began and the last train ran on August 14, 1918, by order of William G. McAdoo, Secretary of Treasury. Most of the rails went for scrap and the roadbed became, in many places, present U.S. 24 between Divide and Leadville. The Ute Pass part (visible up the cliff above the highway) was sold to the Midland Terminal Railroad (Cripple Creek) but that became scrap too when the Midland Terminal shut down in 1949.

A last word on James J. Hagerman. After unloading his Colorado Midland, he became a heavy invester in the gold mines of Cripple Creek and then retired from the Pikes Peak region, leaving what remained of his properties in charge of his son, Percy Hagerman. The elder Hagerman became involved in unsuccessful irrigation and railroad projects in the Pecos Valley of New Mexico. He died at Milan, Italy, in 1909, a relatively poor man.

3. This grade can still be seen from a point about six miles up the present Crystal Park road.

4. Grant G. Simmons, Jr., great grandson of Zalmon G. Simmons and president of the Simmons (Beautyrest) Company, supplied much of the material on which this family story of the Cog Railroad is based.

5. Those pioneer passengers showed courage for they could not know

how safe their train was. To this date no traffic fatality has occurred on the Cog Road though daredevils have killed themselves now and then sliding down the rails on homemade contraptions. Three engines have got loose from the rack rail through the years, one of which lies buried up Ruxton Creek. In August of 1911, a man and his wife hiking up the track froze to death in a very few minutes during a hurricane near Windy Point. This freezing to death in sudden summer hurricanes has happened several times on the Mount Washington track in New Hampshire where winds reach much greater velocity than Pikes Peak winds even though Mount Washington is less than half as high as Pikes Peak.

6. Jerome B. Wheeler, born in Troy, New York, made $5,000,000 in the silver mines of Aspen and Leadville in the late 1880s and lost most of it in the crash of '93 which broke the Wheeler banks in Aspen, Manitou, and Colorado City. Aspen's Wheeler Opera House and celebrated Jerome Hotel were named for him. His summer home, Windermere, where the Manitou Post Office stands, was the show place of Manitou for many years. Wheeler made many large cash gifts to the community, including the $3,600 four-sided clock and statue from Italy in the center of town. He died in the Springs in 1918, aged seventy-seven, and his ashes were placed in Woodlawn Cemetery, New York City.

7. General Sherman visited Pikes Peak about July 11, 1889. Vanderbilt and Depew were Antlers guests on May 3, 1891, and President Harrison stopped there on May 12, 1891.

CHAPTER EIGHT

A SUNNY PLACE FOR SHADY PEOPLE

1. In his *Memories of a Lifetime in the Pikes Peak Region*, Irving Howbert related how he was in Myers' wheat field on a September afternoon in 1868 when "I saw a horseman coming from the east, riding furiously in our direction. He excitedly told us that the Indians were raiding the entire region, killing people in every direction; that Everhart, Baldwin, the Robbins boys, and probably many others, had been killed, and that the savages had driven off a large number of horses." Everhart and the Robbins boys actually were killed, although those three were the only white people of record ever to be murdered by

Indians in El Paso County.

2. This Broadmoor Dairy Farm was centered on Spring Creek and extended for a mile or so as the Creek ran eastward to join Monument Creek. Spring Creek today starts in the Broadmoor Golf Course near the club house, runs eastward through the beautiful older Broadmoor estates which lie between Pourtales Road and Broadmoor Avenue, forms the little lake just below the late Charles Baldwin's Claremont —also called "Trianon Place"—and continues to Stratton Reservoir and beyond where the dairy farm buildings used to be, just west of today's Stratton Home.

Much of the old Broadmoor Dairy Farm lies today within the limits of the large Cheyenne Mountain Ranch residential area, east of Broadmoor, which was planned during the 1970s by David K. Sunderland and financed by Charles L. Gates, Jr., president of the Gates Rubber Company in Denver. Sunderland's complex of streets, homes, shopping centers, and golf course occupy some two thousand acres of land that remained of the Stratton Estate property in Broadmoor after Spencer Penrose bought some 450 acres of it in 1915 for his Broadmoor Hotel project.

3. Count Pourtales was not listed in Almanach de Gotha during the 1880s but the story of the Pourtales family and its titles is told in Volume Thirteen of Larousse's *Grand Dictionnaire Universel du XIX Siecle*. Springs residents always pronounced the name Por-talice, with accent on the tal.

4. Ernest A. Colburn is known to posterity as the judge who granted a divorce in 1879 to Winfield Scott Stratton, the future Cripple Creek gold king. Colburn also made a fortune at Cripple Creek and built a big mausoleum for himself at Evergreen Cemetery in Colorado Springs. But he changed his mind later for he was buried in Denver. The Colburn Hotel in Denver and the Colburn automobile were named for him.

5. One dynamic human being like Pourtales can cause all sorts of things to happen. Because the Count refused to let Colorado Springs steal his Broadmoor water, Irving Howbert and others had to develop a municipal water supply high on Pikes Peak, enlarging Lake Moraine and bringing water to it from Seven Lakes. Pourtales' pressure on the street car company to build to Broadmoor resulted in the development of real estate along the way—today's Ivywild.

6. Count Pourtales told the whole story of his Broadmoor career in his book, *Lessons Learned From Experience* (translated from the German by Margaret Woodbridge Jackson, Ph.D.) which was published in 1955 by Colorado College at the behest of El Pomar Foundation. Mrs. Jackson, the expert translator, is the wife of Judge William S. Jackson, son of William S. Jackson and his second wife, Helen Fiske Banfield Jackson.

7. Thomas C. Parrish, another of Colorado Springs' pioneer Philadelphians, was one of Pourtales best friends and his business partner in the Count's Cripple Creek mining ventures of '91 and '92. Parrish was a good portrait painter and so was his wife, Anne Parrish, who painted the fine portrait of her husband which hangs in the El Paso Club and also the Godfrey Kissel portrait in the Cheyenne Mountain Country Club. Before his death in 1899, Parrish was publisher (1896-98) of the *Colorado Springs Gazette*.

8. According to Pourtales, the partners were W. F. Fisher, E. C. G. Robinson, Walter Scott, William H. Sanford, and "the Doubleday brothers."

9. Pourtales' Broadmoor Dairy Farm limped along, too, though it had a brief prosperity around the turn of the century when a puckish copywriter was titillating the Springs public with half-page *Gazette* ads containing acrostic jingles like this:

> B aby cries for it,
> R elatives Sigh for it,
> O ld Folks Demand it,
> A ll the wise ones get it,
> D addy pays for it,
> M other prays for it,
> O thers Crave it,
> O nly a few don't get it . . .
> R emember, it pays to buy
> BROADMOOR DAIRY MILK AND CREAM!

10. The Common Wealth and other valuable gold mines around it at Pearce, Arizona, were developed by John Brockman, and by Richard A. F. Penrose, Jr., a brilliant geologist and older brother of Spencer Penrose. Pourtales began discussions with these two at Colorado Springs in December, 1895, and received a tenth interest in the Common Wealth by agreeing to raise $23,000.

CHAPTER NINE

THE GENERAL'S SECOND CHANCE

1. A readable, exciting, and instructive account of the fire, "The Antlers Conflagration," by Dr. Lester L. Williams, is contained in the *Denver Westerners Brand Book* for 1956 (Johnson Publishing Co., Boulder, Colo., 1957). Dr. Williams' map shows how the wind-born fire moved from the freight depot on the tracks for two thousand feet northeasterly to the hotel, burning up Crissey & Fowler, El Paso and Newton Lumber Companies on the way. The fire was stopped at Dr. Solly's house at the corner of North Park Place and North Cascade Avenue.

2. Palmer's seizure of his railroad is told graphically by Dr. Robert G. Athearn, "The Captivity of the Denver and Rio Grande," in *The Colorado Magazine* of the State Historical Society of Colorado, January, 1960.

3. The ebullient Teddy Roosevelt was a very busy man on this particular Springs visit, all unknowing that he would become President in six weeks because of the assassination of William McKinley. He attended, with General Palmer, the unveiling of the Zebulon Pike statue in front of the Antlers Hotel, and he made his second trip to Cripple Creek on the Short Line, accompanied by Irving Howbert, James Burns, Spencer Penrose, Phil Stewart, Horace Devereux, and Will Jackson. On his first trip in April, 1901, Roosevelt had been quoted as saying, "This is the ride that bankrupts the English language!" He did even better on the August trip, exclaiming, "My gracious me! Gentlemen, just look at that view! Isn't it marvelous? Wonderful! Wonderful!" In the classic book *The Autobiography of William Allen White,* the author reports that Roosevelt held a political conclave after his return from Cripple Creek at Phil Stewart's house, with White representing Kansas. White added, "So the politicians gathered in Colorado Springs—as fine an assemblage of political gangsters as you would meet on a journey through a long summer day."

4. In her pamphlet, *Governor Hunt of Colorado Territory* (Colorado Springs, 1960) Julia Lipsey reports that Governor Hunt came to an unhappy end. In 1880, when he had acquired a large fortune, he lost his wife and son and thereafter, according to his granddaughter, dis-

sipated his wealth "in riotous living." In 1891, while he was in Chicago en route to Denver, he was stricken with paralysis and lay helpless and speechless until his death on May 14, 1894.

5. The disastrous Monument Creek flood in the spring of 1935 washed out ponds, bridges, gardens, and many other features of Mr. Van Diest's Monument Valley landscaping. The park today is merely serviceable and handsome.

6. The history of the Garden of the Gods is presented in *The Garden of the Gods Story*, by Bruce A. Woodard (Democrate Publishing Co., Colorado Springs, Colo., 1955). Among other things, Mr. Woodard outlines the development of the Easter Sunrise services and explains how the city bought the Balanced Rock and Steamboat Rock areas of two hundred and seventy five acres in 1932 and added them to the original Garden property.

7. All data on the composition of Glen Eyrie has been borrowed from John J. Lipsey whose two-part article, "Glen Eyrie, Home of General Palmer," appeared in *Week End* (Colorado Springs) on February 25 and March 3, 1956. Mr. Lipsey based his articles on an illustrated booklet prepared in 1915 by George A. Krause, resident executor of the Palmer estate, who had been instructed to sell the property. The Krause booklet described Glen Eyrie and its 2,225 acres in minute detail. Estimates of Palmer's total investment ran from one to two million dollars.

There is no barest hint that Palmer created the new Glen Eyrie just to out-build some other wealthy person. As it happened, Glen Eyrie did put an earlier Colorado show place, Senator E. O. Wolcott's Wolhurst, near Denver, in the shade. According to Caroline Bancroft in *The Melodrama of Wolhurst*, (Golden Press, Denver, 1952), Wolhurst had only thirty rooms, cost only $200,000, and occupied only five hundred acres. Much later, in 1919, William Randolph Hearst began the serious building of his four Spanish palaces on his vast acreage at San Simeon, California. But the scale of some things at Glen Eyrie outdid the fantastic Hearst estate. Palmer's Book Hall, for instance, seated—and still seats—three hundred people, as compared with the two hundred person capacity of San Simeon's big hall.

In 1916, several Oklahoma business men bought Glen Eyrie for a country club, ran it briefly as a tea room, and sold it around 1920 for $450,000 to Alexander Smith Cochrane, the multimillionaire polo enthusiast and philanthropist. Cochrane had just married Ganna Walska, the Polish opera singer, and Springs residents understood that Glen Eyrie was his wedding present to her. Miss Walska, however, cared even less for Glen Eyrie than had Queen Palmer. She refused to live there, left Cochrane in 1922, and married the second-generation reaper king, Harold Fowler McCormick, who had just bought a new set of glands for the occasion, according to Cleveland Amory in *Who Killed Society?* The bereft Cochrane did not care to live in Glen Eyrie castle without Miss Walska, and so he built a $100,000 home near it. After Cochrane's death in 1929, the whole huge place stayed empty until 1938 when George W. Strake, a Houston, Texas, oil man, bought it for $350,000. Strake disposed of ranching parts of it, and, in the 1950s, sold the Glen itself—1,140 acres and twenty-two buildings—for a reported $300,000 to a non-denominational religious training group, The Navigators. In recent years, The Navigators have conducted free tours of Glen Eyrie.

Whatever happened to General Palmer's private cars? In the 1960s a group of us saw his narrow-gauge Nomad on a Denver and Rio Grande siding at Durango, Colorado. It had become the property of a group headed by Alexis McKinney, the ex-*Denver Post* editor, who had refurbished it beautifully. Through McKinney's kindness, we spent a delightful day pretending we were the General and his daughters as we rode the little car up Animas Canyon to Silverton and back on the regular run of this last narrow-gauge passenger train in the United States.

CHAPTER TEN

DEATH OF A PATRIARCH

1. Of all Pikes Peak tourist attractions, this Manitou Cliff Dwellings Museum is in a class by itself for pure audacity—not to say wackiness—of conception. Archeologists have determined that the mysterious Cliff Dwellers lived some centuries before Christ and disappeared around 1200 A.D. None of them lived within three hundred and fifty miles of Colorado Springs. Their home was in Southwestern Colorado. Around 1900 there was vehement agitation all over the United States to protect the cliff dwellings of the Mesa Verde region from being damaged and carted away by souvenir hunters and tourist promoters. A leading Colorado Springs agitator was Mrs. Gilbert McClurg,

head of the Colorado Cliff Dwellings Association. While she fought
to keep the cliff dwellings in southwestern Colorado, several Springs
people—the Weimer family of Seven Falls, the hotel owner Jacob
Bischoff, and others—formed the Manitou Cliff Dwellings Ruins
Company, acting on the brainchild of a colorful Manitou promoter
named W. S. (Bill) Crosby. This group spent $100,000 and more haul-
ing to Manitou parts of cliff dwellings which Crosby set up in 1907
as the Manitou Cliff Dwellings Museum. He billed them as duplicates
of the famous Cliff Palace, Balcony House and Spruce Tree House in
Mesa Verde National Park. Mrs. McClurg and her group charged
that Crosby had stolen these bits of dwellings from the park itself.
As Bill explained to Dorothy Aldridge in a *Gazette-Telegraph* inter-
view of May 18, 1969, he had to convince the Denver Land Office
that he had found them on private ranch land thirty-five miles and
more north of the park. Crosby's museum of transplanted cliff dwellings are still drawing tourists by the thousands.

2. Dr. William A. Bell commissioned Herkomer to paint General
Palmer after a single sitting which apparently took place in London
in the winter of 1904. This gift portrait was completed from photo-
graphs. For many years it was the most distinguished feature of the
Antlers Hotel lobby. When the hotel was sold and torn down in the
1960s, the portrait was removed to the Board of Trustees room at
Armstrong Hall, Colorado College, where it hangs opposite Bernard
Arnest's portrait of the late Willis Armstrong, a Colorado College
trustee from 1903 on.

Palmer liked the Herkomer portrait so much that he ordered the
artist to make two copies, one of which is displayed today in Palmer
Hall, Colorado College, and the other in the auditorium of the Colo-
rado School for the Deaf and Blind. Edgar Britton, the Colorado
Springs painter and sculptor, borrowed the Deaf and Blind School
Herkomer and made it from the full-length copy which hangs in the
Pioneer Museum. He made a second copy (from the waist up) for
Frank Waddel, the *Gazette* editor. This copy hangs in the City Hall
Council Chamber. Britton has said that Herkomer was a very deft
portraitist and that he, Britton, learned things technically during the
copying process.

3. Medical men say that Palmer may, or may not, have been injured
still more while being picked up and transported by inexperienced
people.

4. This diagnosis, by Dr. Swan and two Denver specialists, Dr. Charles A. Powers and Dr. Howell T. Pershing, was read before the American Neurological Association in Washington in May, 1910, and published in the *Medical Record* of April 15, 1911. John J. Lipsey quotes from it in his "General Palmer—Strength in Adversity" (*Colorado Springs Free Press,* March 14 and 21, 1954).

5. According to Mr. Lipsey's Palmer articles, Glen Martin reminisced at the Colorado Springs Ghost Town Club on October 27, 1944, the thirty-eighth anniversary of the General's accident.

6. The little "grand-nieces" were the daughters of Maude S. van Oestveen, a daughter of Ellen Mellen.

7. No public explanation has ever been made about this late transfer of Queen's ashes on November 22, 1910. Dr. Bell, who was a guest at the Antlers Hotel on November 26, 1910, did not mention the transfer to reporters. In 1960, the Palmer lot at Evergreen contained, besides the reunited ashes of Will and Queen Palmer, the remains of Henry Chorley Watt who married Marjory Palmer on September 14, 1909, and who died in 1917; Marjory Palmer Watt, who died in 1925; and William Fisher, a Palmer employee who died in 1919. Palmer's will, which he signed in London on November 8, 1908, left property valued for tax purposes at $3,171,025, mostly to his three daughters. The will was challenged by Clark Mellen, one of William P. Mellen's sons, who had borrowed $50,000 from Palmer and had pledged properties on and near Wood Avenue as security. After Palmer's death, Mellen could not repay the loan and he sued the girls for the Wood Avenue properties on the grounds that the General's will waived the debt. The courts ruled otherwise in 1911 and the girls kept the properties.

All three daughters drifted back to England, though Marjory returned to Colorado Springs after Dr. Watt's death and was the main supporter of Sunny Rest Sanitorium. Dorothy Palmer, who never married, became a well-known welfare worker in London where she was joined by Dr. Solly's daughter, Lillian. Elsie Palmer's husband, Leopold Myers, was an ardent spiritualist and wrote several books on the subject. One of Elsie's two daughters, Mrs. Elsie Queen Nicholson of London, visited Colorado Springs in 1959, with her two daughters, Jane and Louisa. They stayed at the Antlers Hotel and were relieved there by a sneak thief of all their money, passports, and air-line tickets.

The General's memory has been kept green through the years. In 1910, a Havana cigar was named for him and a plaque in his honor

was placed in Palmer Hall signed by four hundred and eighty survivors of the Fifteenth Pennsylvania. The General William J. Palmer
Memorial Association was formed in the summer of 1909 and, during
the next twenty years, $33,000 was collected for the bronze equestrian
statue of the General at Platte and Nevada Avenues which was unveiled on September 2, 1929. Nathan D. Potter, a New York sculptor,
began work on the design in 1922 and the final version was approved
in June 1925. It was cast in bronze by the Gorham Company, Provi-
denee, Rhode Island. Anne Hyatt of Cleveland made a small plaster
model of Palmer as she imagined him when he first saw Pikes Peak
in 1869, but it was turned down by the Memorial Association. Edmond
C. Van Diest acquired it and gave it to the Museum in Palmer Hall,
Colorado College. George Foster Peabody, Palmer's old railroad
associate and one of the country's great cultural philanthropists, had
four bronze memorial tablets made, featuring a bas relief by Evelyn
Beatrice Longman showing the General seated with Yorick looking
up at him adoringly. During 1929, one was unveiled in Union Station, Denver, another in Salt Lake City, and a third in Palmer Hall.
The fourth was placed in Colonia Railway Station, Mexico City.

In October, 1943, the Liberty ship *General William J. Palmer* was
launched at Richmond, California.

CHAPTER ELEVEN

ON GOLD AND MR. STRATTON

1. Cripple Creek, the stream, is one of those small trickling western
affairs. It starts officially at a spring in the southern part of Cripple
Creek town (altitude 9,500 feet) and runs due south for seven miles
before joining Oil Creek, which meets the Arkansas seventeen miles
farther on near Canon City. Cripple Creek's banks are high and the
name came partly from the fact that cattle lamed themselves trying to
cross it. Members of the Alonzo Welty family, who homesteaded
the Cripple Creek area in 1871, have stated that the name derived
from injuries received by various Weltys while building a house over
the spring. Before 1871, Cripple Creek valley was called Pisgah Park.
2. Cripple Creek's full history is told in *Money Mountain* by Marshall
Sprague (Little, Brown & Co., Boston, 1953); in *Cripple Creek Days*,
by Mabel Barbee Lee (Doubleday & Co., Garden City, New York,

1958); and in *Midas of the Rockies* by Frank Waters (Sage Books, Denver, 1958, reprinting the original 1937 Covici-Friede edition). Personal reminiscences are contained in *Forgotten Men of Cripple Creek* by Leslie Doyle Spell and Hazel M. Spell (Big Mountain Press, Denver, 1959).

3. "Millionaires' Row" was what tour guides called Wood Avenue because so many Cripple Creek millionaires lived there. It began at Colorado College and ran north parallel to and just west of North Cascade Avenue. It was named for D. Russ Wood, a realtor, and its lower portion contained Mayfair Addition which Charles L. Tutt promoted in the early 1890s. Its show place was 1315 Wood Avenue built by James Ferguson Burns, the Springs plumber and Stratton associate who developed the great Portland Mine, a $60,000,000 producer. Burns built the beautiful Burns Theater (today's Chief) and the Burns Building on Pikes Peak Avenue in 1912.

CHAPTER TWELVE

A TROLLEY SONG

1. The Short Line (officially the Colorado Springs and Cripple Creek District Railway) and the Portland Mill were pushed through by Irving Howbert and James F. Burns of the Portland Mine. The Short Line cost $3,500,000. Construction began on January 4, 1900, and trains were running by the spring of 1901. The upstart carrier did cause lower freight rates for a time, and it fought a passenger rate war in 1902 with the Midland Terminal-Colorado Midland during which people rode for fifty cents to Cripple Creek and back—three hours each way. This low fare caused Colorado Springs hotel men to complain that they were losing trade because tourists slept on the railroads. But within four years the Short Line failed and was leased by the same group of monopolists under A. E. Carlton and Harry Blackmer whose powers it had been built to curb.

2. The Stratton trolley system did very well until 1911 when decline set in, caused by the coming of automobiles. Thereafter, fares were raised gradually, car crews were reduced to one man, and routes were shortened. In 1931, the system was replaced by buses and most of the rails had been removed by 1932. The demise of Stratton Park was swifter still. In 1925 most of it was sold to Pierce Kampe, a real estate

man, for development as a residential area.

3. In a letter to the author, dated July 13, 1953, at Miss Parrish's home on Peaceable Street, Georgetown, Connecticut. Miss Parrish, the wife of Josiah Titzell, died some years later.

4. These city properties were valued at about $4,745,000. The Denver assets included the Toltec building at 17th and Stout; the Tabor property at 17th and Broadway; the Cathedral building at 15th and Stout; a number of lots on Welton Street and a mortgage of $650,000 on the Brown Palace Hotel. Among Colorado Springs assets were the Mining Exchange Building, the Independence Building, Stratton Park, extensive car barns on South Tejon and Cascade Avenue, a building at Nevada and Pikes Peak, and another at South Tejon and Colorado Avenue.

5. The three trustees were Stratton's physician, Dr. Daniel H. Rice; William Lennox, Springs pioneer coal dealer who made a fortune at Cripple Creek; and Tyson Dines, a lawyer who handled Stratton's investments in Denver.

6. Affairs at the Home for forty years and more were directed mainly by David P. Strickler, the lawyer who did much of the work of disentangling the Stratton Estate after 1906. Strickler did not arrive on the scene until after Stratton's death and he never met Stratton.

7. Like General Palmer, Stratton has been memorialized by statuary and by having a Liberty ship named for him during World War II. At the time of his death, a sculptress from the Chicago Art Institute, Miss Nellie V. Walker, happened by chance to be visiting in Colorado Springs and was asked by Stratton's physician, Dr. Rice, to make a mask of his face as a preliminary to creating a full-length statue. Miss Walker completed the statue in 1906 and also an elaborate marker which stands at Stratton's grave in Evergreen Cemetery. The statue was placed on a bluff in Stratton Park but was moved to a site in town at Nevada and Pueblo Avenues near the El Paso County Courthouse. Later still it was placed on the grounds of Myron Stratton Home. Miss Nellie V. Walker, the sculptress, came to Colorado Springs to live in 1948 and was admitted to Stratton Home in the spring of 1960.

On August 14, 1943, the 10,500-ton Liberty ship *Winfield S. Stratton* was launched in San Francisco Bay. It was christened with champagne by Mary Bruening, a seven-year-old resident of Myron Stratton Home. By coincidence, Stratton's name was painted on the new ship by Clarence Teats, a Springs man who had graduated from the Home in 1936.

CHAPTER THIRTEEN

THE RED-BLOODED BLUE BLOOD

1. But he never did.

2. Francis Penrose came down with brain fever in 1885 and was an invalid thereafter. Philip Penrose died in Texas on June 8, 1901. The family data in this chapter is taken from *Life and Letters of R. A. F. Penrose, Jr.*, by Helen R. Fairbanks and Charles P. Berkey (The Geological Society of America, New York, 1952). "Speck" was the family's way of spelling Spencer's nickname.

3. Boies Penrose became United States Senator from Pennsylvania in 1897 and continued in that office until he died in Washington in 1921. Through this long period he was head of the machine which controlled Republican politics in Pennsylvania.

4. In 1921, President Eliot wrote to Senator Boies Penrose: "The little house in Gerry Street had a bad reputation among the neighbors so long as you and your brother Charles B. lived there. Your younger brothers, Alexander and Spencer, did not seem to need so much restraint." By "Alexander," Dr. Eliot meant Dick.

5. Company K went to war with a Parrott gun which Penrose picked up later as a souvenir. For many years it has been displayed in front of the El Pomar Carriage House near the Broadmoor Hotel.

6. But there was nothing legendary about Sally's court trial in Colorado Springs which was reported in the *Gazette* on July 15, 1897.

7. This mill trust ran the Colorado-Philadelphia and Standard mills in Colorado City, other mills in Florence and Canon City, and the original sampler at Cripple Creek. It paid out $2,190,014 in dividends up to 1907, when the partners sold it to the Guggenheims.

CHAPTER FOURTEEN

TAKE ME OUT TO THE BALL GAME

1. The story of Ma (Nora) Gaines who was born in Michigan in the early 1860s is presented by Inez Hunt and Wanetta Draper in their lively book *To Colorado's Restless Ghosts* (Sage Books, Denver, 1960). When autos replaced horse-drawn surreys, Ma stayed in the hack business as owner of several tour cars until her death in 1933. The Hunt-Draper book deals also with the strange little English lady-recluse, Captain Ellen E. Jack, who appeared at the turn of the century and set up a few rental cabins for tourists on the High Drive above Bear Creek Canyon. After Captain Jack's death in 1921, Ma Gaines owned her property for a time. Today, it is the point on the High Drive from which Sunday hikers take off for Jones Park on Bear Creek four miles west.

2. According to Elma Jane Reilley's paper, Dr. Bell and his family lived first in Kent, Lebourne Grange, after their return to England in 1890 (with frequent visits to Manitou). Then he bought Pendell Court, Bletchingly, Surrey, where he served a term as master of the old Surrey foxhounds. The Bells were in the United States during World War I and then returned to Pendell Court where Dr. Bell died of angina pectoris on June 6, 1921, at the age of 81, and the Briarhurst property in Manitou was sold. Mrs. Bell died in 1938. Bell's eldest daughter, Cara Rowena, married Harold Pearce, son of the British vice consul in Denver, in 1895. Four years later, Margaret Bell became Lady Montagu Pollock, whose son is the Denver architect, John G. M. Pollock. Hyacinthe married Lord Kelburn (later titled Lord Glasgow) in 1906. Archie Bell married May Ottley in 1916.

3. The incredible era of Alderman Coughlin is well described by Lloyd Wendt and Herman Kogan in their book *Lords of the Levee: The Story of Bathhouse John and Hinky Dink* (The Bobbs-Merrill Company, Indianapolis, 1943).

4. This Johnson ranch was homesteaded by John Wolfe (Wolfe Street connects Cheyenne Boulevard and Cheyenne Road). The ranch lay along and south of Cheyenne Road westerly from where the Eighth Street Cut-off (Mesita Road) meets Cheyenne Road.

5. This listing of Zoo Park's main features is from a detailed description in a volume titled "Book of General Information," written and "published" in 1907 by a precocious ten-year-old boy, Landell Bartlett, who appears to have practically lived at Zoo Park during all that summer.

6. Zoo Park's last days were recalled by Walter Colburn in an article by C. S. Dudley which appeared on March 25, 1951, in the Colorado Springs *Gazette Telegraph*. More data was contained in a paper, "Bathhouse John Coughlin," given by Landell Bartlett before the Historical Society of the Pikes Peak Region, June 17, 1958. The Bath's political career was summarized by John Kay Adams in *Harper's Magazine*, June, 1958.

CHAPTER FIFTEEN

IT'S A MAN'S WORLD

1. Most of the material on the history of the El Paso Club was taken from a paper which was read at the club's annual dinner meeting on February 21, 1948, by the late George H. Webster, who joined the club in 1891. More details were compiled and issued in a pamphlet during the 1960s by Walter R. Grissel and the late John J. Lipsey. Our contention that Springs residents cherish their past was bolstered in June, 1969, when L. C. Slothower Jr., president of the El Paso Club, revealed that the club's 370-odd members were assessing themselves one dollar each month for a grand party to take place on October 23, 1977, the hundredth anniversary of the club's founding. It ought to be quite a party, as close to $36,000 of party money will have been collected by that time.

2. The author spent countless hours listening to the memories of the late Percy Hagerman pertaining to the Cheyenne Mountain Country Club and many other Springs matters which he had observed since coming to Pikes Peak with his father, James J. Hagerman, in 1884. Percy Hagerman joined Cheyenne Mountain Country Club in November, 1891. He died in October, 1950, while a resident of the El Paso Club.

3. The Francis Hill-Charley Tutt feud had odd ramifications, partic-

ularly in connection with "The First Grand National Spanish Bull
Fight Ever Held in the United States" which was staged at Cripple
Creek (district) in August of 1895 by Joe Wolfe, an ingenious promoter. Hill enlisted the support of the entire United States Government in a futile effort to stop the spectacle. At the end he must have
suspected that somebody—Charley Tutt, for instance—was having
fun with him. For one thing, the scene of the bull fight was at
the new gold camp town of Gillett, owned and operated by Charley
Tutt and Spec Penrose. Furthermore, Promotor Joe Wolfe's adviser
in bull fight management was Sam Vidler, who just happened to be
also the manager of the Cheyenne Mountain Country Club and
official custodian of Charley Tutt's pigeon traps. Finally, when Hill
succeeded in having the Mexican matadors and banderillos of the
bull fight thrown into jail, a Bull Fighters' Defense Committee of
the Cheyenne Mountain Country Club gave a benefit to raise money
for their bail. It was not an ordinary benefit. Two cowboy picadors in
the bull fight, Arizona Charlie Meadows and his brother, Kid, had
been released from jail and Sam Vidler hired them to stage the benefit
show on the Club's race track. The Meadows boys were fine horsemen. Though they could not put on another bull fight, they did present a new kind of exciting Wild West Show which featured the bull-
dogging of steers and roping of calves—high on Francis Hill's list of
mortal sins. Some authorities maintain that the modern cowboy rodeo
traces back directly to this pioneer performance of the Meadows boys
at the Cheyenne Mountain Country Club.

4. Charles Baldwin was an aesthete as well as a playboy and he filled
Claremont with rare books and works of art including a dining room
chandelier with 108 candle brackets which he bought in 1907 from
Czar Nicholas II of Russia. Baldwin died in 1934. His widow, Virginia, married Prince Zourab Tchkotua of an alleged Russian lineage,
and she returned to her native San Francisco until her death in the
1950s.

Much decorating at Claremont was done for the Baldwins by
Ralph Giddings, grandson of the Springs pioneer, Ed Giddings, who
decorated the first Antlers Hotel. Ralph Giddings has called Claremont a good adaptation of the Grand Trianon at Versailles on a
smaller scale. However, in the Versailles original an open colonnade
fills the space corresponding to Claremont's living room. In her last

years, Princess Tchkotua gave the impression that Claremont had been designed by the great New York architect, Stanford White, rather than the local Thomas McLaren. The fact seems to be that in 1905 she asked White at a party in New York for advice on what style of building to put up in Broadmoor, and White recommended a French style. The Denver architect, Alan Fisher, has said that McLaren's design plans, now filed at Penrose Public Library in Colorado Springs, were dated 1907. Poor Stanford White had the bad luck to be shot to death on the roof of Madison Square Garden on June 25, 1906, by the eccentric millionaire Harry K. Thaw, who thought White was carrying on with Thaw's wife, Evelyn Nesbit, the ex-*Floradora* chorus girl.

If Claremont's career under the Baldwins seemed odd, it approached the fantastic after Princess Tchkotua-Baldwin sold the place in 1949 for $250,000 to Blevins Davis, a cultural angel and a friend of President Truman. Davis had long known the Trumans while living in Independence, Missouri, where he had been a high school principal. Later he took up radio work in New York and married (in 1946) the widow of James N. Hill, son of James J. Hill, the railroad magnate. Davis' wealthy wife died in 1948, naming Davis as an executor of her $9,000,000 estate, some $2,750,000 of which was assigned to charity. Davis was backing Ballet Theatre at the time and was its president when the company gave its famous presentation of "Porgy and Bess" in Moscow. His support of Ballet Theatre was said to have amounted to as much as $350,000 a year when he bought Claremont, renaming it Trianon Place and planning to use it as a summer ballet center. The closest it got to that was as a setting for a huge cocktail party which Davis gave on October 14, 1950, for the International Chiefs of Police during their convention.

In 1952 Davis, to meet charitable clauses in his wife's will, disposed of the Trianon to the Poor Sisters of St. Seraph, a Catholic order. Its value was put at around $450,000, as Davis had had it redecorated (Ralph Giddings again) and had brought in "art treasures" from his late wife's Big Tree Farm on Long Island. The lawyer in the transfer was John W. Metzger, a brash, engaging and imaginative ex-attorney general of Colorado who had smashed the State's illegal gambling business in 1950. The Poor Sisters found themselves much too poor to maintain the Trianon's twenty-three statue-pocked acres, so they turned it over to Metzger in exchange for a mortgage which he said got as high as $470,000 at one point. The Sisters sold the mortgage later to Empire Savings in Denver.

Meanwhile, Metzger set up the non-profit Trianon Foundation, with himself as president, and applied for a zone change in that exclusive Broadmoor residential-and-hotel district so that the Trianon could be run as an admission-charging museum. A long and bitter zone battle ensued, with meetings and counter-meetings by the dozen, including a giant rally in the Colorado Springs City Auditorium on January 23, 1964, attended by 3,000 people, mostly pro-Metzger. But the anti-Trianon Broadmoor crowd won out and the zone change was denied. "The Broadmoor Hotel can charge for booze in Broadmoor," Metzger wailed, "but I can't charge for art."

In late 1964, the stymied Metzger began a state-wide "Save the Trianon" drive. The idea was that Colorado was pretty much of a cultural desert and desperately needed to put this replica of the greatest French architecture with its priceless art treasures where it could be appreciated by culture-lovers, in contrast to the attitude of the boorish Broadmoor people. Specifically, Metzger planned to move the 40-room terra cotta building in four 140-ton sections on dollies over hill and dale some ninety miles or so to his ranch off the Valley Highway near Broomfield just north of Denver.

The drive caught on like wildfire. Soon Metzger's fiscal agent, the First National Bank of Denver, had collected cash and pledges for the estimated $175,000 moving cost from 27,000 passionate art lovers, including countless school children. Metzger's movers then discovered that the moving would have to be done on back country roads and on no roads at all and the cost would be $675,000 instead of $175,000. Meanwhile, Metzger was managing to show the Trianon to sightseers for a fee, more or less on the sly. Metzger's guides pointed out Trianon "treasures" including "a Ming bowl" and "authentic Louis XIV service plates made at the fames Sevres porcelain works in France"—claims which were challenged by the Rocky Mountain poet, Thomas Hornsby Ferril, in his Rocky Mountain Herald column. Ferril's point was that the Trianon's "million-dollars'-worth of original art treasures" might not be all they were thought to be by the school children who were robbing their piggy banks to save the Trianon. It was all pretty discouraging to Metzger and so, on April 28, 1965, he gave up the

moving idea and directed the embarrassed First National Bank of
Denver to return the thousands of Save the Trianon contributions.
The bank's officers were still trying to locate hundreds of donors
when Zeke Scher summarized the situation, "Whatever Became of
the Trianon?" in the October 6, 1968, Empire Magazine of *The
Denver Post*.

Metzger turned to more prosaic schemes for unloading his very
white elephant, including an "art treasure" sale in 1966. It happened
that the five-year-old Colorado Springs School in Broadmoor was
growing fast just then and needed a larger building—such as the
Trianon. Its Broadmoor trustees knew that Metzger would have
apoplexy at the mere thought of talking business to anybody from
Broadmoor, so they put a non-Broadmoor man on the school board,
a tactful Springs lumber tycoon and soccer expert named William W.
Boddington. For nearly a year, Boddington and Metzger negotiated,
and even got to like one another. The upshot was that the storied
Claremont-Trianon became the Colorado Springs School in 1967. The
price was not announced but presumably it made Metzger, the mort-
gager, and Empire Savings of Denver, the mortgagee, very happy.

5. In his last years, the President's son averred with steadfast honesty
that he had never done, or wanted to do, anything in his life except
for his own amusement. In 1925, he sold Edgeplain and later bought
the structure at 19 West Boulder, "Hobgoblin Hall," which a Bostonian,
"Catty" Clark, had designed apparently for the comfort of several
dozen felines. Alan Arthur was divorced from Myra in 1929 and he
married Mrs. Rowena Dashwood Graves some years later. He died on
July 18, 1937. As for Arthur's (and General Palmer's) Trinchera
Ranch, the last we heard of it was in 1969 when it was bought from
the Albert G. Simms estate by Forbes, Inc., publisher of Forbes
Magazine, for something like three and a half million dollars.

CHAPTER SIXTEEN

A REAL NICE CLAMBAKE

1. Charley Tutt announced his retirement in the *Gazette* on December
9, 1905, and confined his business interests mainly thereafter to Springs
real estate such as the Hagerman Building on Tejon Street and Irving

Howbert's Opera House which he purchased in 1906. He had been an ardent yachtsman for years, buying an island in Puget Sound and maintaining a summer home there. At about the time of his retirement he bought the five-stateroom yacht *Anemone* from an Englishman, J. Murry Mitchell, for a reported $60,000 and sailed it to the West Coast from New York by way of Cape Horn and the Hawaiian Islands. In June of 1906, Charley entered the *Anemone* in the first Pacific Yacht Race from San Francisco to Honolulu and almost won it, being barely nosed out by the *Lurline*. With the wealth and leisure to enjoy his favorite diversion, Charley seemed to have everything. But tragedy struck on January 21, 1909, when he died quite unexpectedly of a heart attack in New York City after an illness of a week—aged forty-five. The elder of his two sons, Charles L. Tutt, Jr., had just turned twenty-one, and for a year or two thereafter managed the Tutt real estate and other interests. Then Spencer Penrose hired him, first as all-around apprentice in the big Penrose suite of offices on the third floor of the Mining Exchange Building, and later as business aide. As we shall see, the Tutt family still manages the Penrose estate.

2. Information on the creation of Utah Copper derives from a letter on the subject written by Daniel C. Jackling, dated September 3, 1942, to Harry Leonard, Spencer Penrose's old Cripple Creek cabin-mate. The letter jibes in most respects with Dick Penrose's comments in *Life and Letters of R. A. F. Penrose, Jr.*, by Helen R. Fairbanks and Charles P. Berkey. The Guggenheims' role in Utah Copper has been described in *The Guggenheims* by Harvey O'Connor (Covici-Friede, New York, 1937). D. C. Jackling died in San Francisco on March 13, 1956. By that time, because of his pioneering at Bingham Canyon in the mass production of copper, he was a Utah hero practically as revered as the Mormon leader Brigham Young. He put his methods to work also in Arizona, causing that State to lead the nation as a copper producer.

3. Family data on the Alexander Lewis family was contained in a paper prepared in 1900 by Mayor Lewis' sister, Mrs. Henry P. Bridge. In May, 1952, Mrs. Spencer Penrose recalled for the author her life with James McMillan and subsequent marriage to Penrose. Dick Penrose's long letter of March 3, 1906, was published in the Fairbanks-Berkey book cited above in November, 1952, and is presented by permission of The Geological Society of America.

CHAPTER SEVENTEEN

BUILDER'S ITCH

1. The decline did not stop. In 1960, Cripple Creek gold production stood at $1,077,060, mostly from a single mine, the Ajax. Four other mines were still producing a little. Employment of miners stood at 150. Ten years later not a single mine was being worked regularly.

2. One of the Crystal Park Road steel turntables is still on view a mile or so from the top fifty feet along the abandoned switchback at a very sharp turn. Earnest sightseers who ferret out this turntable can see, when they stand on it, why it was installed. Directly underneath it, a thousand feet or so down, is the Manitou depot of the Cog Train. If the turn in the road had been widened for autos in 1913, dynamite would have been necessary which might have caused a large hunk of Iron Mountain to fall down on the depot. By turning autos on the turntable, this possible catastrophe was avoided.

3. The modern Pikes Peak Hill Climb has been taking place on July 4 each summer. The course is practically the same in location and in length as in 1916—a little over twelve miles, according to Al Rogers, a Cog Train official who has been one of the greatest of Hill Climb drivers. Today's daredevils make the run in around thirteen minutes as compared with Rea Lentz's record of almost twenty-one minutes in his 125 horsepower Romano. Lentz did very well at that, considering the conditions of his day. Modern drivers have the advantage of a far better road, greatly improved gasoline, more powerful engines, and better racing technique.

4. El Pomar was situated on 7.4 acres of land. Ashton Potter died in his early forties on August 6, 1914, and his wife, born Grace Goodyear, died a few months later.

5. On June 29, 1968, the fiftieth anniversary of the public opening of the Broadmoor, the Tutt brothers and other hotel and El Pomar officers gave a gala dinner in the ballroom duplicating the menu of half a century earlier and directed by Louis Stratta, Penrose's original chef, and John Altrichter, his original maitre d'hotel. Each dinner guest received a handsome brochure, "The Broadmoor Story," by Helen M. Geiger, who found much new material in private Penrose and Tutt papers. Mrs. Geiger wrote that Penrose closed the deal to buy the Broadmoor property from the Stratton estate in May 1916

and that Fred Sterner, the first architect, lasted just six months on the job and received $20,000 for his trouble. The old Casino was moved to its present site to serve as the golf club by none other than Thomas McLaren, creator of the Baldwin's Claremont-Trianon. Construction on the hotel began in May, 1917. Its first orchestra leader was Gyula Boxhorn, on loan from New York's Vanderbilt Hotel. In 1921, Penrose paid $2,100 for the famous Maxfield Parrish painting of the hotel (with the lake in front) which hangs in the mezzanine. Mrs. Geiger's brochure discloses that the hotel's outdoor fountain of mythical horses, at least two hundred years old and probably Venetian, was imported from Italy and set in place in May, 1923. Penrose sustained staggering losses through the depression years but he closed the place up for only one winter—September 9, 1935, to June 1, 1936. Charles L. Tutt, Jr., was his right hand man in the hotel's management from 1916 to the day of Spec's death in 1939, except for a few depression years. One of Spec's last acts was to make Tutt head of the hotel company. Charley was already on the board of El Pomar Foundation, which was headed thereafter by Julie Penrose until her death in 1956. Charley Tutt succeeded Mrs. Penrose as head of El Pomar.

CHAPTER EIGHTEEN

PENROSE ORCHARD

1. Two of the most colorful of the Broadmoor polo crowd during the Twenties were Robert Hassler and Ernest Marland, both high-spending customers at the hotel. Robert Hassler, a rugged athlete in his fifties, was an Indianapolis inventor who made flywheels, shock absorbers and generators for Henry Ford's Model T. Hassler bought an 800-acre ranch on Fountain Creek below the Myron Stratton Home for the comfort of his ponies. He built two polo fields near the edge of the Broadmoor mesa in a new Penrose addition served by a winding lane called Marland Road.

Penrose had named the road in honor of a man as remarkable and as vital as himself. Ernest Marland, a Pittsburgh native, attended England's Rugby, got a law degree at Michigan University and made a fortune in West Virginia coal. He moved to Oklahoma in 1908 to drill for oil on Ponca Indian lands. After striking oil fifty-four times in succession, he was said to control ten per cent of the world's oil, and he commenced a spectacular program of upgrading Ponca City, Oklahoma, and endowing it and his thousands of Marland Oil employees with everything under the Oklahoma sun from bird refuges to free golf courses. In summer, it was his pleasure to bring his two Ponca City polo teams to Cheyenne Mountain, rent the whole South Lake wing of the Broadmoor to house his players, and match them against Cheyenne Mountain Country Club stars—fellows like Reginald Sinclaire, Arthur Perkins, Raymond Lewis, Colonel W. H. Neil, Freddie Prince, a ringer from New York, and Randall Davey, the Santa Fe artist.

In 1927, Penrose persuaded Marland to carry his polo enthusiasm a bit further. He sold to him a hundred-acre strip along Marland Road extending from the Cooking Club reservoir down to Robert Hassler's polo fields. A number of homes were to be built on the strip for Marland's players and for executives of the Marland Oil Company. But sad fate stepped in and spoiled the Marland colony before it got started. Early in 1928, Marland found himself in very serious financial straits, lost his oil firm and saw it transformed into the Continental Oil Company.

Perhaps it was for the best, as far as Cheyenne Mountain and Penrose were concerned. By family ties and inclination, Penrose was a staunch Republican. Marland became an ardent Democrat. Worse yet, in 1932 he was elected to Congress as a Roosevelt New Deal Democrat, and then, in 1935, he became the New Deal Governor of Oklahoma. Penrose's opinion of President Franklin D. Roosevelt involved the use of quite a few words rarely heard in polite society and he would not have been pleased if one of those New Deal radicals held a conspicuous acreage in his Broadmoor. Even today, Marland Road is not exactly overpopulated with Democrats.

2. But there is another version, probably a fable, of how Prince Albert met his end. Some years ago, Herman Ewers, the Wichita oil man, bought for his summer home at Cascade a vast stag head. The Springs taxidermist who sold it to him called it "the largest elk ever shot in Wyoming." Soon after, Ewers showed the antlered head to the late Charles E. Thomas, who had been Penrose's architect on Cheyenne Mountain. This colloquy ensued:

> THOMAS: As I live and breathe! There's Prince Albert!
> EWERS: How's that again?

THOMAS: That's Spec Penrose's pet elk. I know by the points. I always wondered what happened to him after the hunt.

EWERS: What hunt?

THOMAS: Why, the time the Maharajah of Indore visited the Penroses! Spec had hunted tigers with him in India and had promised to take him elk hunting in Wyoming. They were all set to leave next morning. While they were having a snort or two at El Pomar before dinner, the Maharajah mentioned that the Wyoming trek might be too strenuous for him. Spec thought a minute. Then he said that they didn't really have to go all the way to Wyoming. If the Maharajah wanted to, he could shoot the biggest elk in the world right now, in ten minutes, and right here in Broadmoor—it was that wonderful a place. The Maharajah wanted to. Spec phoned Milt Strong to turn Prince Albert loose on the Cheyenne Mountain Highway at once. Spec and his potentate had another quick snort, loaded their guns, donned pith helmets and headed by car for the toll gate below the Zoo. It was a beautiful moonlight night, and I guess that's all there is to tell. The Maharajah got his elk—and there he is above your fireplace.

3. Mrs. Geiger's "The Broadmoor Story" disclosed that Penrose became sole owner of the Broadmoor on December 5, 1932, by bidding in the hotel and forming a new company. Her brochure adds that Spec wrote the next day: "We had the sale of the Broadmoor yesterday ... We broke two whole bottles of champagne, one to bury the old hotel, as it had never had much luck, and the other to christen the new hotel ... I'm glad the old one is gone and perhaps the new one will be more fortunate and bring in some income."

4. The fifth trustee was Penrose's private secretary, Merton W. Bogart.

CHAPTER NINETEEN

PORTRAIT OF A SMALL COLLEGE

1. According to the late Charlie Brown Hershey in his *Colorado College, 1874-1949* (Denton Printing Co., Colorado Springs, 1952), Colorado College was the first degree-giving institution in the mountain West. It held first classes for its preparatory department on May 6, 1874. The first classes of the Colorado School of Mines at Golden were held on September 15, 1874. The University of Denver, founded

in 1864 under the name Colorado Seminary did not give degrees until 1880. The University of Colorado was incorporated in 1861 but it was not opened until 1877.

2. The quoted phrase is the property of Robert M. Ormes, professor of English at Colorado College, and son of Manly D. Ormes, the College librarian from 1904 to 1929. Robert Ormes sat coaching at the author's elbow through the preparation of this chapter and contributed much of the writing.

3. Another thing a number of them liked was the exclusive little summer colony of intellectuals which they established and named "College Gulch" up Ute Pass near Crystola.

4. As former President Charles Mierow has recalled it, Stratton gave $70,000 in all to Colorado College, including sums for the stuffed animals and birds in the Museum. The story prevails that the gold king made a cash bequest of $250,000 to the college in his will but cancelled it when President Slocum refused to permit him to run his street car line uninterruptedly along North Tejon Street through the college campus.

5. Colorado College football and track meets take place at Washburn Field, named in 1899 for the Reverend Philip Washburn who was a city member of the Athletic Association. The first Washburn Field grandstand, seating 800, was given in 1900 by the Cripple Creek millionaire, Jimmie Burns. The present Van Diest Stadium was the gift in 1926 of E. C. Van Diest, who designed the city park system for General Palmer.

6. The handsome 70-foot tapering steel flag pole near Rastall Center was presented to the college on June 9, 1931, by Mrs. Augusta D. Swart-Earle, whose son William Earle was a faculty member. It was designed by Stephen Beames of Evanston, Illinois, and cast by the Chicago Art Bronze Company. Beames' bronze base consists of four tigers, a border of Colorado columbines, the college shield and seal, an open book, and the motto Scienta et Disciplina. If an undergraduate kisses a co-ed at this base it is supposed to be pretty serious.

CHAPTER TWENTY

C STANDS FOR CULTURE

1. On October 5, 1919, the first board of trustees of the Broadmoor Art Academy, Inc., was composed of D. V. Donaldson (president), F. Drexel Smith, Mrs. Spencer Penrose, Anne G. Ritter, and Charles L. Tutt. The first director was R. L. Boutwell. Within a few months, Mrs. Penrose replaced Donaldson as president.

2. When Alice Bemis Taylor died in 1942, Colorado College was in such financial difficulties that her $400,000 bequest had to be spent to keep the place afloat rather than to build a new library.

3. Mrs. Meredith Hare resigned in late 1936 as the Fine Arts Center's first president and returned East where she died in 1948. Boardman Robinson headed the Fine Arts Center school until a few years before his death in 1952.

4. Though the solid-stone Shrine was "built to last as long as the mountain itself," wind-driven rain has a way of seeping through to the murals which Davey has restored twice since 1937. Soon after the dedication, members of Will Rogers' family complained that the Shrine murals were all about Penrose and Pikes Peak and told nothing about Rogers. Penrose instructed Davey to make some Rogers sketches for upstairs in the tower, but then Spec lost interest and the murals were never completed.

CHAPTER TWENTY-ONE

HARVEST TIME

1. This anecdote is taken from Helen Clapesettle's biography, "Dr. Webb of Colorado Springs," which is a full account of this Englishman's 50-years at Pikes Peak as a nationally renowned T. B. specialist and as a pioneer in the search for a vaccine against the disease.

Innumerable stories have kept the memory of Spencer Penrose burning bright—some of them true. One of the true stories has to do with his liquor supply. With the approach of National Prohibition in 1919 Penrose had nightmares for fear he might not be able to get a drink. Accordingly he bought and stored away 2,400 cases of assorted liquors in New York and another thousand cases in the cellar of his El Pomar home—some $250,000 worth. He bought fine ryes like Hannisville and Monogram, Scotches like Clyne Lisk and Talisker; fifty cases of real absinthe, a hundred cases of vintage champagne, and the best in French Bordeaux, Burgundy, and Spanish sherry. When the Eighteenth (Prohibition) Amendment was repealed in 1933, Spec had the 2,400 cases freighted from New York to Colorado Springs under heavy guard in two box cars. A third car load arrived from Philadelphia, Spec having inherited the large stock of his brother Dick. Penrose stored all of it in his El Pomar cellar and protected it with a full-time detective.

Most of this priceless liquid treasure after Penrose's death in 1939 was moved to the liquor vaults of the Broadmoor Hotel. In the year 1940 it so happened that the hotel was overflowing with military brass from Washington in search of a site for Camp Carson. The generals were cut off from their usual liquor supply by the German submarine blockade. When they ordered refreshment in the Broadmoor Tavern after the day's work they expected to endure the wartime poison—green rum or third-rate Scotch. Instead they found listed on Broadmoor menus all the historic vintages of the Golden Age before World War I, the rarest liquors of Europe and America, matured to perfection in the cool cellar at El Pomar.

It is not surprising that these generals returned to Washington deeply impressed by the military advantages of the climate and clean air at Pikes Peak, and also by the high quality of the environment in the Broadmoor Tavern. Or so old timers say when they tell you why Camp Carson was built near Colorado Springs in 1941.

2. Howard J. Arnsberg in his "Informal History" of the C. S. Department of Public Utilities tells how in 1923 the voters obligated the city to take over ownership and operation of its gas, electric and water systems. Today the Utilities Department pays many millions of dollars annually into the city's general fund and provides municipal services free. Utility rates in Colorado Springs are among the lowest in the U.S.

3. For more than a century the Tutt family has spread its activities through the history of Colorado Springs. Charles Leaming Tutt (the first) was born in Philadelphia in 1864. He settled in Colorado Springs in 1884 (he died in 1909). His son, Charles L. Tutt, Jr. (born 1889, died 1961) his sons, Charles Leaming Tutt III (born 1911); William Thayer Tutt (born 1912); Russell T. Tutt (born 1913); John Wood Tutt (born 1940); Charles Leaming Tutt IV (born 1938, son of C. L. T. III); William Bullard Tutt (born 1941), son of C. L. T. III); Russell Thayer Tutt, Jr., born 1955, son of R. T. Tutt; Charles Robert Tutt (born 1966) son of C. L. T. IV; William Benjamin Tutt (born 1970), son of W. B. Tutt.

After the death in 1939 of Spencer Penrose (he had no children), some member of the Tutt family has served on the board of Penrose's charitable

estate, El Pomar Foundation, the many gifts of which have been of incalcu-
lable benefit to the residents of Colorado Springs.

In 1987, El Pomar Foundation was directed by a seven-man board. The
board members were (listed in order of seniority): William Thayer Tutt,
Russell T. Tutt, Ben S. Wendelken, Joel H. Webb (Dr. Gerald Webb's son),
Karl E. Eitel, William J. Hybl, and R. Thayer Tutt, Jr., (son of Russell T.
Tutt).

4. Sister Myra James Bradley was born in Cincinnati, Ohio, of Irish parents.
After high school, she completed her novitiate in Cincinnati with the Sisters
of Charity. Since then she has had experience in all phases of hospital busi-
ness and personnel administration—in Dayton, Ohio, Trinidad, Colo., San
Antonio, Texas, Pueblo, Colo., and Mt. Clemens, Michigan. In Colorado
Springs she directs the Healthcare Institution. She serves on the board of the
American Hospital Association, the Catholic Hospital Association and the
Colorado Hospital Association.

5. The 21,000 acre Banning-Lewis Ranch ten miles east of Colorado Springs
which Frank Aries bought for $96 million dollars in 1985 was for fifty years
one of the most famous Hereford ranches in the United States. In 1895, the
Banning Ranch belonged to William Banning owner of the Union Ice and
Coal Company in Colorado Springs. Banning died in 1914, leaving his ranch
and coal company to his daughter, Ruth Banning, a 1915 Phi Beta Kappa
graduate of Wellesley College. She raised Percheron draft horses on Banning Ranch to haul her coal wagons, until 1921 when she married a Hereford
rancher from Fowler, Colorado, Raymond W. (Pinky) Lewis, a Colorado
College (1914) football star and polo player. In 1927, the Banning Ranch
evolved into the greatly enlarged Banning-Lewis Ranch for registered Here-
fords. In the 1940s Ruth Banning Lewis became the second woman to become elected to the Colorado Springs City Council. Both Lewises were ardent conservationists. For many years "Pinky" Lewis gave a large barbecue
party at Jimmy Camp Bluff on the ranch attended by most of Colorado's
leading politicians, Hereford breeders and educators. An old Colorado Midland private railroad car served as the bar for the barbecue and tents were
provided for the crap shooters.

Bibliography

Colorado Springs History in General

Fisher, John S. *A Builder of the West*. Caxton Printers, Caldwell, Idaho, 1939.

Howbert, Irving. *Memories of a Lifetime in the Pikes Peak Region*. G. P. Putnam's Sons, New York, 1925.

Ormes, Manly D. and Eleanor R. *The Book of Colorado Springs*. Dentan Printing Co., Colorado Springs, 1933.

Ormes, Robert M. *Pikes Peak Atlas*. Privately printed, 1959.

Waters, Frank. *Midas of the Rockies*. Sage Books, Denver, 1959. Enlarging and reprinting the original, Covici-Friede, New York, 1937.

Wilcox, Rhoda Davis. *The Man on the Iron Horse*. Dentan Printing Co., Colorado Springs, 1959.

Early Days

Bell, William A. *New Tracks in North America*. Chapman and Hall, London, 1869.

Brayer, Herbert Oliver. *William Blackmore*. 2 vols. Bradford-Robinson, Denver, 1949.

Palmer, Mrs. William J. *Journal* (honeymoon diary starting November 9, 1870). Handwritten. Pioneer Museum, Colorado Springs.

Reid, J. Juan. *Colorado College*: The First Century. Colorado Springs, 1980.

Reilly, Elma Jane. "William A. Bell." A paper prepared 1952, filed with the Historical Society of the Pikes Peak Region, Colorado Springs.

West, Paul V. "English Influence in the Early Life of Colorado Springs." Paper, prepared 1952, filed with the Historical Society of the Pikes Peak Region.

Wolcott, Frances M. *Heritage of Years*. Minton, Balch & Co., New York, 1932.

Woodard, Bruce A. *The Garden of the Gods Story*. Pamphlet. Democrat Publishing Co., Colorado Springs, 1955.

Eighties and Nineties

Cather, Willa. *A Lost Lady*. Alfred A. Knopf, New York, 1923.

Hagerman, Percy. "The Colorado Midland." *The Westerners Brand Book*, 1945. Bradford-Robinson, Denver, 1946.

Jackson, William S. "The Record vs Reminiscence." *The Westerners Brand Book*, 1945. Bradford-Robinson, Denver, 1946.

Lipsey, John J. "How Hagerman Sold the Midland." *The Westerners Brand Book*, 1956. Johnson Publishing Co., Boulder, Colorado, 1957.

Lipsey, John J. "J. J. Hagerman." *The Westerners Brand Book*, 1954. Johnson Publishing Co., 1955.

Lipsey, John. "The Lives of James John Hagerman." *Golden Bell Press*, Denver, 1968.

Odell, Ruth. *Helen Hunt Jackson*. D. Appleton-Century Co., New York, 1939.

Pourtales, Count James. *Lessons Learned from Experience*. Translated from the German by Margaret Woodbridge Jackson, Ph.D., W. H. Kistler, Denver, 1955.

Williams, Dr. Lester L. "The Antlers Conflagration." *The Westerners Brand Book*, 1956. Johnson Publishing Co., Boulder, Colorado, 1957.

After 1900

Fairbanks, Helen R., and Berkey, Charles P. *Life and Letters of R. A. F. Penrose, Jr.* The Geological Society of America, New York, 1952.

Hunt, Inez, and Draper, Wanetta W. *To Colorado's Restless Ghosts*. Sage Books, Denver, 1960.

Lee, Mabel Barbee. *Cripple Creek Days*. Doubleday & Co., Garden City, New York, 1958.

Lipsey, John J. "Glen Eyrie, Home of General Palmer." Colorado Springs *Week End*, February 25, 1956.

Lipsey, John J. "The Last Days of General William Jackson Palmer." Colorado Springs *Free Press*, March 14, 21, 1954.

Sprague, Marshall. "Good bye, Little London." *Colorado Magazine*, Summer, 1965.

Sprague, Marshall. *Money Mountain: The Story of Cripple Creek Gold*. Little Brown & Co., Boston, 1953.

Sprague, Marshall. "Mr. Broadmoor: The Life of Spencer Penrose," *Empire Magazine*, The Denver Post, February 15, 22 and March 1, 1953.

Note: All factual data and chronology used in this book have been taken from the complete daily or weekly files of *Out West*, Colorado Springs *Gazette* and Colorado Springs *Gazette-Telegraph* at Coburn Library, Colorado College.

Later Books

Abele, Deborah Edge. "The Westside" (Colorado City), published by the City of Colorado Springs, 1986.

Breckenridge, Juanita L. "El Paso County Heritage," Curtis Media Corp., 1985. A massive compendium of county history and local biographer.

Budd, Barbara T. & Harriette R. Small: "Colorado Springs Today", Great Western Press, Colorado Springs, 1985. An indispensable guide for visitors to the city.

Conover, Everett: "The Pikes Peak Range Riders" (1982), a fine illustrated history of the group.

Sprague, Marshall: "Colorado Springs Fine Arts Center" A History and Selections from the Permanant Collections: (1986), Intro. only, with essays by Christopher Wilson, Jonathan Batkin, Charles A. Guerin.

Sprague, Marshall: "The Grizzlies", a history of the Cheyenne Mountain Country Club, privately printed (1983).

Index